Copan-Building, São Paulo.

Costa/Niemeyer, and others, Ministry of Education and Health, Rio de Janeiro.

Oscar Niemeyer
Eine Legende der Moderne I A Legend of Modernism

herausgegeben von I edited by
Paul Andreas und Ingeborg Flagge

mit Beiträgen von I with contributions by
Paul Andreas, Max Bill, Lauro Cavalcanti, Elmar Kossel,
Carsten Krohn, Niklas Maak, Oscar Niemeyer,
José Carlos Süssekind

Deutsches Architektur Museum
Frankfurt am Main

Birkhäuser – Publishers for Architecture
Basel · Boston · Berlin

Dieses Buch erscheint anlässlich der Ausstellung /
This book is published at the occasion of the exhibition:

Oscar Niemeyer.
Eine Legende der Moderne / A Legend of Modernism
1. März / March – 11. Mai / May 2003 im / at
Deutsches Architektur Museum, Frankfurt am Main

kuratiert von / curators: Cecília Scharlach, Haron Cohen

DAM und / and Ernst & Young
in Kooperation mit / in co-operation with Fundação O. Niemeyer,
Instituto Moreira Salles, BrasilConnects Cultura & Ecologia,
Ministério das Relações Exteriores do Brasil

Herausgeber / Editors: Paul Andreas, Ingeborg Flagge
Redaktion / Copy-editing: Paul Andreas
Übersetzung / Translation: Chantal und Jacob Bill,
Lea Viveiros de Castro, Jeremy Gaines, Dorothee Meyer,
Peter Schau
Layout / Design: Muriel Comby, Basel

A CIP catalogue record for this book is available from
the Library of Congress, Washington D.C., USA.

Bibliographic information published by Die Deutsche Bibliothek
Die Deutsche Bibliothek lists this publication in the
Deutsche Nationalbibliografie; detailed bibliographic data is
available in the Internet at < http://dnb.ddb.de >.

Ministério das
Relações Exteriores
do Brasil

Korrigierter Nachdruck, 2003
Corrected Reprint, 2003

FUNDAÇÃO OSCAR NIEMEYER

IMS
INSTITUTO MOREIRA SALLES

BrasilConnects
Cultura & Ecologia

9 8 7 6 5 4 3 2 1

Oscar Niemeyer. Eine Legende der Moderne
Oscar Niemeyer. A Legend of Modernism

Er ist 95 Jahre alt und ein Mythos. Er hat so viel gebaut wie kaum ein anderer Architekt der Moderne, und er baut weiter. Kaum jemand polarisiert wie Oscar Niemeyers Persönlichkeit und sein Oeuvre. Er dürfte weltweit einer der politisch engagiertesten und kritisiertesten Architekten sein. Dennoch ist er häufig ausgezeichnet worden und hat zahlreiche Anerkennungen und Preise für Architektur erhalten.

Oscar Niemeyer war Mitarbeiter Le Corbusiers, aber er geht in der skulpturalen Gestaltung seiner Bauten weiter als dieser. Ein reiner Funktionalismus war für ihn immer zweifelhaft; selbst dort, wo er ein rationales Raster verwirklichte, hat er nie geleugnet, dass Architektur für ihn zuerst und vor allem eine expressive und plastische Kunst ist. Obwohl er Kommunist ist, sieht Niemeyer den Architekten nicht als Sozialreformer. Architektur kann seiner Meinung nach die Gesellschaft nicht grundsätzlich verändern. Es sei vielmehr die Aufgabe des Architekten, Werke von ebenso großer Schönheit wie Ausdruckskraft zu bauen – Niemeyer fand sie vor allem in dem Baustoff Beton.

In Brasília gelang es Niemeyer, bis heute einprägsame Formen für die Repräsentation des Staates in der neuen Hauptstadt zu finden. In dieser Architektur verbindet sich plastische Monumentalität mit klassischer Ordnung.

Die Ausstellung im DAM gibt einen Einblick in das reiche Werk des kontrovers gesehenen Architekten. Diese Ausstellung, die von Cecília Scharlach und Haron Cohen in São Paulo im Jahre 1997 konzipiert wurde, übernimmt das DAM nach Rio de Janeiro, Buenos Aires, Lissabon, Paris und Brüssel als einzige deutsche Station. Kuratorin im DAM ist Cecília Scharlach, die Ausstellungsarchitektur wurde auch hier von Haron Cohen verantwortet. Das DAM bedankt sich bei dem brasilianischen Generalkonsul in Frankfurt, Herrn Renato Prado Guimarães, für die Vermittlung.

Für die Ausstellung in São Paulo wurde ein Katalog in portugiesischer Sprache erstellt. Diesen zu übersetzen, fehlte bei den Stationen in Europa das Geld. Das DAM hat sich deshalb entschlossen, keinen Katalog, aber ein Buch zur Ausstellung herauszubringen, das Oscar Niemeyer vor allem aus europäischer Sicht kommentiert und ein Verzeichnis seiner vielen Projekte und Bauten enthält. Die Verantwortung für das Buch, wie auch für die Anpassung der sehr viel größeren Ausstellung an die Gegebenheiten des DAM trägt Paul Andreas, dem ich für diese Leistung danke.

Diese Ausstellung wird gemeinsam von DAM und Ernst & Young veranstaltet, ohne deren finanzielles Engagement weder die Ausstellung noch das Buch möglich gewesen wären.

Ingeborg Flagge

He is 95 years old and a living legend. He has constructed more buildings than almost any other modern architect and he has still not stopped. Hardly anyone has prompted people to so clearly take sides as has Oscar Niemeyer with his particular approach and oeuvre. He is probably one of the most criticized and politically committed architects in the world today. That said, numerous are the distinctions he has received, as are the architectural awards and prizes bestowed upon him.

Oscar Niemeyer was a colleague of Le Corbusier, but Niemeyer has always gone one step further when it came to the sculptural feel of his buildings. He has always been wary of thoroughbred functionalism and even where basing his work on a rationalist gridding plan, he has forever insisted that for him architecture was first and foremost an expressive and sculptural form of art. Although he is a communist, Niemeyer does not consider the architect to be a social reformer. In his opinion, architecture cannot fundamentally change society. Instead, it is the task of the architect to build objects that are as beautiful as they are expressive – it was specifically in concrete that Niemeyer found these qualities.

In Brasília, Niemeyer succeeded in devising forms for buildings destined to represent the state that remain equally poignant today. His architecture combines sculptural monumentality with classic order.

The exhibition at the DAM provides an insight into the multi-faceted work of this controversial architect. The exhibit was conceived by Cecília Scharlach and Haron Cohen in São Paulo in 1997. After going on display in Rio de Janeiro, Buenos Aires, Lisbon, Paris and Brussels, the show has now arrived at the DAM, which will be its only exhibition stop in Germany. The curator in the DAM is Cecília Scharlach, and Haron Cohen is once again responsible for the exhibition design. The DAM would also like to thank the Brazilian Consul General in Frankfurt, Mr. Renato Prado Guimarães, for his efforts as an intermediary bringing the exhibition to Frankfurt.

A catalogue in Portuguese was produced for the exhibition in São Paulo. A shortage of funds made it impossible to translate this catalogue for the exhibition's European tour. Instead of a catalogue, the DAM has therefore decided to publish a book which Oscar Niemeyer has himself annotated for a European audience. It also contains a list of his many projects and works. I would like to offer my cordial thanks to Paul Andreas for his work on the book as well as for his efforts in adapting this exhibit which originally was much larger, to the conditions on hand at the DAM.

This exhibit is jointly sponsored by the DAM and Ernst & Young without whose financial support neither the exhibit nor the book would have been possible.

Ingeborg Flagge

Casa do Baile, Tanzrestaurant,
Pampulha. Ansicht der
geschwungenen Kolonnade.

Casa do Baile, Dancehall and
restaurant, Pampulha.
View of the swung colonnade.

Kasino, Pampulha.
Eingangssituation.

Casino, Pampulha.
Entrance situation.

Kirche des Heiligen
Franziskus, Pampulha.
Ansicht zur Straße.

Saint Francis' Church,
Pampulha. View of
the façade to the road.

Haus in Canoas, Rio de Janeiro.
Ansicht vom Zugangsweg.

House at Canoas,
Rio de Janeiro. View from
the entrance.

→
Haus in Canoas, Rio de Janeiro.
Aussicht auf das Sera-do-Mar-
Gebirge.

House at Canoas, Rio de Janeiro.
View of the Sera do Mar
Mountains.

→
Haus in Canoas, Rio de Janeiro.
Innenansicht mit dem Felsen.

House at Canoas, Rio de Janeiro.
Interior with the rock.

←
Sul-América Hospital,
Rio de Janeiro.

Sul-América Hospital,
Rio de Janeiro.

←
Hospital da Sul, Rio de Janeiro.
Ansicht der Pilotis.

Hospital da Sul, Rio de Janeiro.
View of the pilotis.

Ibirapuera Park, São Paulo.
Biennale-Pavillon. Innenansicht.

Ibirapuera Park, São Paulo.
Biennial Pavilion. Interior.

Die Kurven des Lebens – ein Interview mit Oscar Niemeyer
The curves of life – an interview with Oscar Niemeyer

*Niklas Maak im Gespräch mit dem Architekten über Amerika, Jean-Paul Sartre,
Frauen, Häuser und die Notwendigkeit einer Revolution*
*Niklas Maak in conversation with the architect about America, Jean-Paul Sartre,
women, houses, and the need for a revolution*

Ein Büro im sechsten Stock eines türkisfarbenen Art-Déco-Hauses in Rio de Janeiro. Es ist 10 Uhr morgens, und es sind 28 Grad im Schatten. Die Fotografin zieht ihren Lippenstift nach. Durch die verglasten Erker sieht man auf die Copacabana. Seit 60 Jahren arbeitet Oscar Niemeyer an diesem Zeichentisch. Weltbekannt wurde er 1960 mit seinen Bauten für die künstliche Hauptstadt Brasília. Heute ist er 92 Jahre alt. Wenn man in den Erker tritt, sieht man den breiten Strand, Palmen, ein wenig Dunst und ein paar geschwungene Apartmenthäuser aus den sechziger Jahren. Dann kommt er aus seinem Arbeitszimmer: Oscar Niemeyer, Kurvenstar, Kistenbauer, Revolutionär, Kommunist. Der vielleicht größte lebende Architekt der Moderne. Niemeyer erscheint an diesem Morgen im T-Shirt, darüber Hosenträger, die Hose ist bis unter die Brust gezurrt. Er trägt elegante, sehr spitze Schuhe. Ein Mann aus einer anderen Zeit. Er spricht ein rollendes, perfektes Französisch. Mit Oscar Niemeyer traf sich im April 2000 Niklas Maak.

An office on the sixth floor of a turquoise-colored Art Deco house in Rio de Janeiro. It is 10 a.m., and 28 degrees in the shade. The photographer touches up her lipstick. The glazed oriel offers a view out over the Copacabana. Oscar Niemeyer has worked at this drawing board for the last 60 years. He achieved world fame in 1960 with his buildings for the artificial new capital, Brasília. Today, he is 92 years old. When you walk up to the bay window you see a broad beach, palm trees, a little haze and a couple of curving apartment blocks from the 1960s. Then he walks in from his study: Oscar Niemeyer, champion of curves, box builder, revolutionary, communist. Arguably the greatest living Modernist architect. Niemeyer is dressed this morning in T-shirt and trousers held by braces. The trousers are hoisted right up to beneath his armpits. He wears elegant, very pointed shoes. A man from a different age. He speaks rolling, perfect French. Niklas Maak interviewed Oscar Niemeyer in April 2000.

Maak: Eine schöne Le-Corbusier-Liege haben Sie da.
Niemeyer: Oui, très belle. Schon sehr alt. Ein sehr schönes Möbelstück, vielleicht das schönste.

Le Corbusier hat ja auch ein sehr schönes eckiges Sofa entworfen.
Ja, aber ich mag die kurvige Form. Es ist die Form des Menschen. Eines Tages hat Le Corbusier zu mir gesagt: „Wenn du entwirfst, hast du die Berge von Rio in deinen Augen." Mir gefällt aber besser, was Malraux mal über Le Corbusier gesagt hat: „Er hat in sich sein ganz spezielles Privatmuseum, in dem sich alles befindet, was er liebt und was ihm wichtig ist." Das gilt auch für mich.

Und was befindet sich in Ihrem inneren Museum?
(Niemeyer sagt nichts, schaut müde. Plötzlich steht er auf.)
Kommen Sie mit. Ich kann es Ihnen besser erklären, wenn ich zeichne. *(Niemeyer sucht in seinem Büro nach einem Stück Papier und beginnt zu zeichnen. Die Fotografin läuft in dem kleinen, stickigen Raum herum und macht Aufnahmen. Niemeyer schaut ihr zu, lächelt, zeigt mit dem Finger auf sie.)*

Maak: *That's a fine Le Corbusier chaise longue you have there.*
Niemeyer: Oui, très belle. And very old, too. A very beautiful piece of furniture, his most beautiful perhaps.

Le Corbusier also designed a very beautiful angular sofa, didn't he?
Indeed, but I prefer the curved shape. It is the human form. One day Le Corbusier said to me: When you design you have the mountains of Rio in your eyes. But I prefer what Malraux once said about Le Corbusier: He has within himself his own special private museum, containing everything he loves and holds dear. It is the same for me.

And what does your interior museum contain?
(Niemeyer says nothing, looks tired. Suddenly, he stands up.)
Come with me. I can explain it better when I'm drawing. *(Niemeyer searches around his office for paper and starts to draw. The photographer runs around in the small, stuffy room and takes pictures. Niemeyer looks at her, smiles, points his finger at her.)*

Oscar Niemeyer
in seinem Büro.

Oscar Niemeyer
in his office.

Wie heißen Sie?
Anna.

Gut. Kommen Sie mal mit.
Ich?

Ja. Ich zeichne Ihnen etwas. *(Niemeyer beginnt eine wackelige schwarze Linie zu zeichnen. Man erkennt die Umrisse einer nackten Frau vor dem neuen Museum von Niterói, einem von Niemeyers letzten Entwürfen.)*
Ich weiß nicht, wie Sie aussehen, wenn Sie am Strand liegen. Aber so stelle ich Sie mir vor. *(Die Fotografin errötet. Niemeyer kehrt in sein Arbeitszimmer zurück, einen fensterlosen kleinen Raum voller Bücher. An den freien Wänden hängen Zeichnungen und Fotos von nackten Frauen. Daneben steht die Geschichte der französischen Kommune, ein paar Bücher von Nerval und Sartre, viele Gedichtbände.)*

What's your name?
Anna.

Fine. Come with me.
Me?

Yes. I'll draw something for you. *(Niemeyer begins to trace a wobbly, black line. You recognize the outlines of a naked woman in front of the new museum in Niteroi, one of Niemeyer's latest designs.)*
I don't know what you look like when you lie on the beach, but this is how I imagine you to be. *(The photographer blushes. Niemeyer returns to his study, a small room without windows crammed full of books. On the available wall space hang drawings and photos of naked women. Near at hand stands the history of the French commune, a few books by Nerval and Sartre, countless volumes of poetry.)*

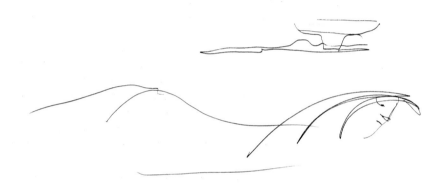

Die Fotografin am Strand.

The photographer
on the beach.

Kommunismus und Körper – ist das Büro hier eine Art Manifest?
Sie wollen sagen, es sei eine Inszenierung, kein Arbeitszimmer. Interessant, was die Leute immer gleich denken. Nein. Ich arbeite seit 60 Jahren. In meinem Leben gibt es nichts Besonderes, und dies hier ist das Büro eines ganz normalen Menschen.

Und was bedeutet die nackte Frau da, die Sie an die Wand gezeichnet haben?
Hmm! Ein Scherz. Ein gebauter Scherz, eine große Skulptur in Frauenform.

Haben gute Baukörper etwas mit der Kenntnis vom Körperbau zu tun?
Was? Ja natürlich! Die Kurve ist die Natur: Berge, Körper, Wasser. Alles fließt. Und man darf die Natur nicht immer überall gegen rechte Winkel rennen lassen. In meinem Haus, das ich mir 1953 über den Hügeln von Rio entwarf, habe ich den Pool um den Felsen herumgebaut, das Haus schwingt sich in den dichten Wald hinein. Die Natur kommt ins Haus, das Haus umfasst die Natur.

Communism and female forms – is this office a kind of manifesto?
You are implying it is orchestrated, not a study. Interesting the ideas people come up with. No. I have worked for 60 years now. There is nothing special in my life, and this is the office of a totally normal person.

And the picture of the naked woman you drew there on the wall. What meaning does that have?
Hmm! A joke. A built joke, a large sculpture of the female form.

Is there a connection between well constructed buildings and a knowledge of the human body?
Sorry? Yes, of course! Curves are nature: mountains, bodies, water. All flowing lines. And you cannot always allow nature to collide with right angles. For my house that I designed in 1953 above the hills of Rio, I constructed the pool around the rocks, the house curves into the dense forest. Nature enters the house, the house embraces nature.

Some modern architects have criticized you strongly for the many curves in your buildings. Max Bill referred to your architecture as an "orgy of anti-social extravagance" that is only "photogenic and spectacular". Heinrich Klotz called Brasília "kitsch".
I don't know this man. Well, if he thinks so.

You recently visited Brasília again for the 40th anniversary celebrations. Would you build it like that again?
Yes. The cathedral and the Plaza of the Three Powers I would. But the city has become ugly, it has no uniformity, there is no beauty in the new satellite towns. The people that live there are poor but

Für die vielen Kurven in Ihren Bauten haben einige moderne Architekten Sie heftig kritisiert. Max Bill hat Ihre Architektur eine „Orgie der antisozialen Verschwendung" genannt, die allein „fotogen und spektakulär" sei. Heinrich Klotz nannte Brasília „Kitsch".

Ich kenne diesen Mann nicht. Na ja. Wenn er meint.

Vor kurzem waren Sie zur Vierzig-Jahr-Feier mal wieder in Brasília. Würden Sie es noch einmal so bauen?

Ja. Die Kathedrale, den Platz der Drei Gewalten, ja. Aber die Stadt ist hässlich geworden, es gibt keine Einheit, keine Schönheit in den neuen Außenbezirken. Die Menschen dort sind zu arm, aber das ist keine Frage guter oder schlechter Architektur. Das ist eine Frage der Politik.

Wenn die Politik das Eigentliche ist – warum sind Sie Architekt geworden?

Seit 60 Jahren immer die gleiche Frage. Ich antworte immer dasselbe: Als ich ein kleiner Junge war, habe ich immer Zeichnungen in die Luft gemacht. Sie haben mich immer gefragt: Was machst du da mit deinem Finger für komische Sachen – und ich habe gesagt: Zeichnungen. So bin ich Architekt geworden. Sie müssen verstehen, wie meine Architektur entsteht. *(Niemeyer beginnt, Kreise auf den Tisch zu malen.)*
Ich arbeite nicht gerne in Gruppen. Ich sitze seit 60 Jahren an meinem Schreibtisch, ich führe seit 60 Jahren am Zeichentisch Selbstgespräche. Bauen ist etwas Spontanes. Ich gebe meine Zeichnungen meinen Mitarbeitern. Was dann passiert, interessiert mich nicht mehr. Ich sehe mir nur noch das fertige Gebäude an.

Erzählen Sie ruhig noch ein bisschen.

Nach und nach merken die Leute, wenn sie mit mir über Architektur reden, worum es wirklich geht: um den Menschen. Architektur ist mir nicht so wichtig wie das Leben, die Familie. Ich habe auch viel lieber Romane gelesen als irgendwelche Architekturbücher, wissen Sie? Literatur, Poesie, Philosophie! *(Wir stehen vor Oscar Niemeyers Zeichentafel. Auf die Wände hat er hagere Gestalten gezeichnet, Bettler und Arme vielleicht. Daneben stehen handgeschriebene Slogans. Einer lautet: Wenn das Leben schlecht wird und die Menschen keine Hoffnung mehr haben, dann kommt die Revolution. Daneben weitere Zeichnungen, Menschen, das Meer, der Horizont.)*

So. Schauen Sie hier. Ich sehe immer auf diese Zeichnungen, bevor ich zu entwerfen beginne. Ich habe eine sehr spezielle Art und Weise zu arbeiten. Ich suche eine Lösung und denke nach, und plötzlich fange ich an zu zeichnen. Schauen Sie, so

that is not a question of good or bad architecture. That is a question of politics.

If it's all a matter of politics why did you become an architect?

People have asked me the same question for the last sixty years. I always give the same answer: When I was a small boy I used to make drawings in the air. They always asked me: What in heaven's name are you doing with your finger – and I replied: drawings. That's how I became an architect.
You must understand how my architecture is born. *(Niemeyer starts to draw circles on the table.)*
I don't like working in groups. For 60 years I've sat at my desk, for 60 years I have talked to myself at the drawing board. Architecture is something spontaneous. I give my drawings to my staff, but what then happens does not interest me any more. I only look at the finished building.

Please feel free to continue.

After a while the people who talk to me about architecture notice what I really consider important: people. Architecture is not as important to me as life, the family. And you know something? I much prefer to read novels than architecture books. Literature, poetry, philosophy! *(We stand in front of Oscar Niemeyer's drawing board. On the walls hang his drawings of gaunt figures, beggars and poor people perhaps. Next to them are hand-written slogans. One reads: When life becomes bad, and people no longer have any hope, then the revolution comes. And next to that more drawings of people, the sea, the horizon.)*

Now. Look at this. I always look at these drawings before I start work. I have a very special way of working. I search for a solution, start to ponder, and suddenly I begin to draw. You see this is how the idea for the cathedral in Brasília came about. *(Niemeyer draws a couple of curved columns.)* The building curves skywards. That had not been done before. And now *(Niemeyer draws an underground ramp that leads to the light)*: Now comes man, and his gaze rises up towards the light. I once read a poem by Baudelaire in which he says the prime objective is to produce a surprise. For my work as an architect I always found it a great help what Le Corbusier once said to me: "Oscar, architecture is primarily about invention." Brasília – you may love it or leave it, but it is something that never existed before. Take the cathedral in Brasília: There are far more attractive buildings but none that look exactly like it. That is what it is about. The happiness that the surprise evokes in you. That is architecture.

entstand die Idee zur Kathedrale von Brasília. *(Niemeyer zeichnet ein paar geschwungene Säulen.)* Das Gebäude biegt sich zum Himmel. Das hat es noch nie gegeben. Und jetzt *(Niemeyer zeichnet eine unterirdische Rampe, die zum Licht führt)*: Jetzt kommt der Mensch, und sein Blick steigt zum Licht auf. Ich habe mal ein Gedicht von Baudelaire gelesen, in dem es hieß, es käme vor allem auf die Überraschung an. Für meine Arbeit als Architekt hat es mir sehr geholfen, als Le Corbusier einmal zu mir sagte: „Oscar, Architektur ist in erster Linie Erfindung." Brasília kann man lieben oder nicht, aber es ist etwas, das es noch nie gegeben hat. Zum Beispiel die Kathedrale von Brasília: Es gibt viel schönere Bauten, aber keine, die genau so aussehen. Darauf kommt es an. Auf das Glück, das die Über-raschung in dir hervorruft. Das ist Architektur.

Wie war das, als Sie Le Corbusier zum ersten Mal begegneten?
Das war vor genau 64 Jahren, wirklich großartig! Ich war ziemlich jung damals. Wir waren völlig außer uns, wir haben ihn ja vergöttert. Aber heute muss ich sagen, dass seine Arbeit ganz anders ist als meine. Ich will eine leichtere und freiere Architektur machen. Transparenter, luftiger, wie das in unserem Klima eben möglich ist. Le Corbusier sprach immer vom rechten Winkel, ich spreche immer von den Kurven. Aber ich war immer sehr begeistert von seinen Winkeln.

Und was sagte er zu Ihren Kurven?
Seine letzten Arbeiten, die geschwungene Kapelle von Ronchamp vor allem, zeigten genau, was er von meinen Kurven hielt.

Sie haben auch einmal in Deutschland gebaut.
Ja, in Berlin, im Hansaviertel. Ich habe es gesehen, wie es mittlerweile aussieht. Es hat nichts mehr mit meinem Entwurf zu tun. Alles Großzügige fehlt, sie haben es kaputtgemacht. Eine Katastrophe. Aber ich war auch seit Jahrzehnten nicht mehr da, ich weiß nicht, wie es heute in Berlin aussieht. Hof-fentlich besser. Ich war, wenn ich nach Europa kam, öfter in Paris.

Wo Sie Ende der Sechziger den Sitz der Kommunis-tischen Partei Frankreichs gebaut haben.
Es war sehr spannend damals. Ich habe Jean-Paul Sartre getroffen. Ich fand ihn großartig. Der Mensch, ins Universum geworfen. Das Sinnlose und die Verantwortung, die der Mensch trotzdem vor dem Menschen hat. Das ist sehr gut. *(Niemeyer wirkt etwas zerstreut, friemelt an einem Paket Cigarillos herum.)* Sartre. Ich lebte damals beim La Coupole, am Boulevard Raspail. Man konnte ihn dort treffen. Er war ein mürrischer Typ. Er sah ziemlich komisch aus. *(Niemeyer zeichnet mit zitteriger Hand einen*

What was it like when you met Le Corbusier for the first time?
That was exactly 64 years ago, it was amazing! I was quite young at the time. We were quite beside ourselves, after all, we idolized him. But today I have to say that his work is quite different to mine. I want to create a lighter, more liberal architecture. More transparent, more airy, precisely as is possible in our climate. Le Corbusier always spoke about the right angle, whereas I always speak about curves. But I was always highly enthusiastic about his angles.

And what did he say to your curves?
The last plans he devised, in particular the curved chapel at Ronchamp, show what he thought of my curves.

You once designed a building in Germany.
Yes, for the Hansa district in Berlin. And I have seen what it looks like today. There is no longer any simi-larity to my design. It is totally devoid of any sense of spaciousness, they have destroyed it. A catas-trophe. But I have not been there for decades, I don't know what Berlin looks like today. Better, I hope. When I went to Europe, I made frequent visits to Paris.

Where you built the headquarters for the French Communist Party at the end of the 1960s.
Those were heady days. I met Jean-Paul Sartre. I thought him extraordinary. Man, cast out into the universe. Meaninglessness, and yet the respon-sibility that people nevertheless have for each other. An excellent idea. *(Niemeyer appears somewhat distracted, fiddles around with a packet of cigarillos.)* Sartre. I lived at La Coupole, on the Boulevard Raspail. You could meet him there. He was a sullen man. And he looked pretty strange, too. *(With a shaking hand Niemeyer draws a wobbly circle, then another. It is impossible to tell what it is.)* That is Sartre's face. You wouldn't have recognized it, would you? *(Niemeyer smiles gently.)* But he was very, very intelligent. I had great respect for him.

You love Sartre's existentialism, and you like building cathedrals?
A church is something very beautiful. It is nice when people feel happy in it. But I am not a religious man. Look at us, and then at the infinity of space. We are rather small insignificant creatures wouldn't you say?

Though you have always referred to yourself as a communist, you built the barracks and army HQ for the dictatorial regime under Medici. (Niemeyer ignores the question. A packet of white Davidoffs lies on the desk. Niemeyer takes a cigarillo.)

wackeligen Kreis, dann noch einen. Es ist unmöglich,
zu erkennen, was es darstellen soll.) Das ist Sartres
Gesicht. Sie hätten es nicht erkannt, nicht wahr?
(Niemeyer lächelt fein.) Aber er war sehr, sehr intelligent. Ich verehre ihn sehr.

Sie lieben Sartres Existentialismus, und Sie bauen
gerne Kathedralen?
Eine Kirche ist etwas sehr Schönes. Schön,
wenn sich Menschen dort glücklich fühlen. Aber ich
bin kein religiöser Mensch. Schauen Sie uns an,
und dann den endlosen Weltraum. Ziemlich kleine
Häufchen sind wir da, nicht wahr?

Sie haben sich immer als Kommunist bezeichnet,
dann aber die Kasernen und das Heeres-Haupt-
quartier für das diktatorische Regime unter
der Regierung Medici gebaut. (Niemeyer überhört
die Frage. Auf dem Tisch liegt eine Packung weißer
Davidoffs. Niemeyer nimmt sich einen Cigarillo.)
Für wen haben Sie am liebsten gebaut?
Bitte? Für alle, die anders waren. Ich habe sehr
gern die Arbeit für das Stadtzentrum in Le Havre
gemacht, aber auch den Sitz des Mondadori-
Verlags in Mailand. Arbeiten, die etwas Neues versuchen. Die Säulen von dem Mondadori-Gebäude
sind alle unterschiedlich groß, von 15 bis 3 Meter.
Ein Wagnis. Die fünf Stockwerke hängen an
der Decke. Eine statische Revolution. Wir machen
immer das modernst Mögliche, auch im schwebenden Museum von Niterói.

Was haben Sie als nächstes vor?
Ach, dies und das. Aber das Wichtigste für uns
ist nicht Architektur. In Brasilien ist das Wichtigste
die Bewegung der Landlosen. Sie waren bei mir und
haben mit mir geredet. Ich habe ihnen ein Denkmal
entworfen, ein Symbol für ihren Kampf. Sie haben
es aufgestellt, aber die Rechten haben es verbrannt,
vor ein paar Tagen. *(Niemeyer wird plötzlich lebhaft).*
Ich sage immer: Wenn das Leben schlecht wird
und die Menschen keine Hoffnung mehr haben, dann
kommt die Revolution. Genug jetzt mal mit der Architektur, wir müssen hier über etwas sprechen, das viel
wichtiger ist. Wir müssen es beim Namen nennen:
Es ist die neue agressive Kolonisation von Lateinamerika.

Wie bitte?
Ja. Wir haben nie viel über den Imperialismus
gesprochen. Wir brauchen ein neues Bewusstsein.
Überall sind die Leute so entpolitisiert, sie sitzen
herum und gucken in die Gegend, suchen was
Schönes und finden nichts. Wir haben nie über Patrio-
tismus gesprochen. Wir wollten eine Welt ohne
Grenzen; eine offene Welt, offen für den Austausch
der Gedanken und der Waren.

Who did you most like building for?
What? For everyone who was different. I really
enjoyed my project for the city center in Le Havre,
but equally the head office of the Mondadori
publishers in Milan. Projects that attempt something different. The columns in the Mondadori
building are of differing heights, ranging from 3 to
15 meters. Really daring. The five floors are suspended from the ceilings. A structural revolution.
We always build the most modern structure possible, as was the case in the modern art museum
in Niterói that seems suspended in space.

What do you plan to do next?
Oh, this and that. But the most important thing
for us is not architecture. In Brazil the most important thing is the movement of those without land.
They came here and spoke to me. I designed
a monument for them, a symbol for their struggle.
They erected it but the right wing burnt it down
a few days ago. *(Niemeyer suddenly becomes ani-*
mated.) I always say: When life becomes bad and
people have no hope, revolution comes. But enough
of architecture, we have to talk about something
that is much more important. We have to give it a
name: It is the new aggressive colonization of
Latin America.

Pardon me?
Yes. We have never talked much about imperialism.
We need a new awareness. There is so little political conscience these days, people sit around and
look about, search for something beautiful, and find
nothing. We have never talked about patriotism.
We wanted a world without borders; an open world,
open for the exchange of thoughts and products.
The UN building and Brasília stood for this world.
Today, this world believes in neo-Liberalism. But
what is this neo-Liberalism? It only means for the
first time people want to have whatever they need
to attain personal happiness. Before becoming
enthusiastic about globalization you should first of
all look at the damage this invention has done in
Africa. North American imperialism pursues a single
aim: to incorporate our economy and our firms.
Latin America needs to demonstrate solidarity and
fight against America. I am not talking about making
war, we have no objection to the Americans, only
to their politics. *(Niemeyer smiles contentedly.*
He has held a cigarillo in one hand for the last two
minutes. The photographer offers him a light.)
No thanks.

Das Uno-Gebäude und Brasília waren Ausdruck dieser Welt. Diese Welt glaubt heute an den Neoliberalismus. Aber was ist dieser Neoliberalismus? Er bedeutet nur, dass man vor allem erstmal das haben will, was einem noch zu seinem persönlichen Glück fehlt. Wenn Sie von der Globalisierung schwärmen, dann sollten Sie erst mal schauen, was diese tolle neue Erfindung in Afrika anrichtet. Der nordamerikanische Imperialismus hat nur eins im Sinn: sich unsere Wirtschaft, unsere Firmen einzuverleiben. Lateinamerika sollte sich solidarisieren und gegen Amerika kämpfen. Ich meine damit keinen Krieg, wir haben ja nichts gegen die Amerikaner, nur gegen ihre Politik. *(Niemeyer lächelt zufrieden. Er hält seit zwei Minuten einen Cigarillo in der Hand. Die Fotografin gibt ihm Feuer.)* Nein, danke.

Ich dachte, Sie wollten rauchen. Nein, danke. Oder ja, doch. *(Niemeyer raucht. Ob er noch einen Traum habe, will die Fotografin wissen. Niemeyer schüttelt den Kopf.)* Ich muss arbeiten. Ich habe nur noch wenig Zeit. Ich werde weiter arbeiten – bis ich umfalle.

I thought you wanted to smoke. No thank you. Or maybe I will. *(Niemeyer smokes. Does he still have a dream asks the photographer. Niemeyer shakes his head).* I have to keep working. I don't have much time left. I shall work until I drop.

Oscar Niemeyer und die brasilianische Tradition der Moderne
Oscar Niemeyer and Brazilian Modernism

Lauro Cavalcanti

Der Weg Oscar Niemeyers ist eng mit der Geschichte der modernen Architektur Brasiliens verwoben, und er steht in engem Zusammenhang mit dem Bruch zweier bis dahin festgefügter Traditionen, der der brasilianischen Moderne und des Beitrags peripherer Länder zur universellen Sprache der Architektur. Der erste Bruch betrifft die Ausbreitung der Moderne, die sich bis dato auf Europa und insbesondere den Bau von Büro- und Verwaltungsgebäuden in Deutschland oder Zweitwohnungen für intellektuelle Eliten in Frankreich beschränkte. Mit dem Bau des Erziehungs- und Gesundheitsministeriums (1936–1943), von einer brasilianischen Arbeitsgemeinschaft unter der Leitung von Le Corbusier konzipiert, wurde die Moderne erstmals in großem Maßstab an einem Regierungsbau versucht. Damit wurde ihre Übertragbarkeit auf tropische Klimate und die Weiterentwicklung über die bisherigen „weniger anspruchsvollen" Objekte wie Lagerhallen, sozialer Wohnungsbau, Fabriken oder Bahnstationen hinaus nachgewiesen. In dieser Hinsicht trug der Bau des brasilianischen Ministeriums, dessen endgültige Fassung von Oscar Niemeyer maßgeblich bestimmt wurde, zur Behauptung der Moderne als breite Bewegung mit weltweiter Ausdehnung und weitgefächerter Anwendungspalette bei. Die zweite Tradition, mit der gebrochen wurde, war die der eigenen Geschichte der brasilianischen Architektur. Bis dahin hatte das Land noch niemals einen originären Beitrag zur Entwicklung der weltweiten Baugeschichte geleistet. Mit dem Bau des Pampulha-Projekts (1942–1943) brach Oscar Niemeyer mit den einvernehmlich herrschenden Auffassungen der rationalistischen Architektur und wies neue Möglichkeiten im Umgang mit der Moderne auf, die aus der engen Beziehung zwischen Architektur und Struktur entstanden ist.

Die Moderne erreichte Brasilien in den zwanziger Jahren durch die Einwanderung oder den Kontakt mit europäischen Architekten, durch die Rückkehr von Brasilianern, die in Europa studiert hatten, und hauptsächlich durch die Begeisterung seitens der jüngeren Architektengeneration dem neuem Stil gegenüber. Bis Mitte der dreißiger Jahre zeigte die brasilianische Architektur keine Überraschungen, sie war zweckorientiert und berücksichtigte die herr-

Oscar Niemeyer's career is intimately bound up with the history of modern architecture in Brazil. He is also closely connected to the rupture between two traditions that had until then gone hand in hand, namely, Brazilian Modernism and the contribution of peripheral countries to the universal language of architecture. The first is concerned with the dissemination of Modernism which, until that time, was limited to Europe and particularly to the construction of office and administration buildings in Germany as well to the building of second homes for the intellectual elite in France. The plans for the Ministry of Education and Health (1936–1943) devised by a Brazilian team headed by Le Corbusier marked the first attempt in the history of Modernist architecture to construct a large-scale government building. This proved that the Modernist style could be adapted and applied to a tropical climate and showed that it could be taken forward to include what had until then been considered to be "less serious" objects such as warehouses, council housing, factories and railway stations. In this respect, the construction of the Brazilian ministry – the final version of which was largely the brainchild of Oscar Niemeyer – contributed to Modernist architecture gaining sway as a broad movement with a global reach and a wide range of applications. The second tradition with which he broke was the history of Brazilian architecture itself. Until that time, the country had never made an original contribution to the annals of world architectural history. With his Pampulha project (1942/1943), Oscar Niemeyer exploded the prevailing consental view on rationalistic architecture while demonstrating new ways of bringing Modernist architecture to bear by closely linking architecture and structural considerations.

In the 1920s, Modernism reached Brazil through immigration, through contact with European architects, and especially through the young generation of Brazilians who had studied in Europe and then returned home, full of enthusiasm for the new style. There were no surprises in Brazilian architecture until the middle of the 1930s. It was purpose-oriented and took the prevailing tropical climate into consideration. It was similar to all the styles imported in

schenden tropischen Klimaverhältnisse. Sie ähnelte all den schon in den vorherigen Jahrhunderten importierten Stilrichtungen, abweichend in der Form, aber vom selben Geiste geprägt. Dieses Erscheinungsbild wurde 1936 mit dem Bau des Erziehungs- und Gesundheitsministeriums radikal geändert. Ab dann tauchte eine aussagekräftige Architektur auf, die die „Avantgarde" und die Tradition zu vereinigen vermochte. Zahlreiche Beispiele, darunter insbesondere die Bauten Oscar Niemeyers, dokumentieren in ihrer Vielfalt und Originalität die Loslösung vom Kanon der europäischen Moderne. Zwanzig Jahre später schließt Brasília (1956–1960), weltweit die einzige Stadt, die ausschließlich nach den Regeln des modernen Städtebaus errichtet wurde, jene Periode ab, die man als die brasilianische Hochmoderne bezeichnen könnte.

Welche Voraussetzungen machten diesen Wechsel aber überhaupt möglich? Wie konnte ein Land, das sich in einer Randlage befand und bestenfalls durch seine Exotik bekannt war, einen solchen Beitrag zur internationalen Architektur, vor allem in den Bereichen Technologie, Finanzierung und Benutzerkomfort, leisten?

Die Geschichte der modernen Architektur Brasiliens ist mit einer Gruppe junger Architekten und Intellektueller, wie Carlos Drummond, Mário de Andrade und Gilberto Freyre, verbunden. Sie waren in den dreißiger Jahren entschlossen, die kulturellen Lücken des „Estado Novo"[1] auszufüllen und ihr Land durch die Durchsetzung fortschrittlicher Gedanken zu verändern. Brasilien erlebte eine Phase prosperierender Wirtschaft, und die Regierung bemühte sich um eine „Modernisierung" des Landes. Die Regierung Getúlio Vargas beabsichtigte ihre Spuren in der Hauptstadt Rio de Janeiro durch die Errichtung großer Repräsentationsbauten zur Unterbringung der Ministerien und neuen Verwaltungen zu hinterlassen. Es entzündete sich dabei eine hitzige Diskussion unter den Verfechtern der Moderne, den Neokolonialisten und den Akademikern, in welchem Baustil die neuen öffentlichen Bauten Rio de Janeiros errichtet werden sollten. Akademiker und Neokolonialisten vertraten historistische Positionen, sie bevorzugten eine stark ornamentierte Architektur, wobei erstere die europäische Vergangenheit evozierten und letztere in den Formen der Kolonialarchitektur eine eigene Identität suchten. Der Stil öffentlicher Bauten war in einem Land, in dem sich die gesellschaftlichen Eliten und Privatunternehmen an der öffentlichen Architektur orientierten, von eminenter Wichtigkeit.

Die Geschichte der modernen Architektur Brasiliens ist jedoch nur in Relation zum internationalen Baugeschehen zu verstehen. Die vorherrschend konservativ orientierte und hierarchisch strukturierte

previous centuries – deviating in form yet imbued with the same spirit. All this changed radically in 1936 with the construction of the Ministry for Education and Health. From that point onward, an expressive style of architecture appeared which attempted to unite the "avant-garde" with the traditional. Numerous examples, especially works by Oscar Niemeyer, document the diversity and originality of this liberation from the canons of European Modernist architecture. Twenty years later, this period drew to a close with Brasília (1956–1960). It is the only city in the world which was built exclusively according to the rules of modern urban planning and it can be described as the paramount example of Brazilian High Modernism.

What conditions made this change possible? How could a marginal country which was known at best for its exoticism, make such a contribution to international architecture, specifically in the fields of technology, finance and user-friendliness?

The history of modern architecture in Brazil is associated with a group of young architects and intellectuals such as Carlos Drummond, Mário de Andrade and Gilberto Freyre. In the 1930s, they were determined to fill the cultural gaps of the "Estado Novo"[1] and to change their country by bringing progressive ideas to bear. The economy in Brazil was prospering and the government was seeking to "modernize" the country. The government under Getúlio Vargas intended to leave its mark on the capital, Rio de Janeiro, by constructing large representative buildings for the ministries and administration. A heated discussion was sparked among the advocates of Modernist architecture, neo-colonialists and academics on the style of architecture to be used for the new public buildings in Rio de Janeiro. Academics and neo-colonialists took an historicist position. They preferred a strongly ornamental style of architecture with the academics evoking the European past and the neo-colonialists endeavouring to establish an identity for the country through colonial architecture. The style of architecture was of utmost importance in a country in which the social elites and private corporations modelled their own buildings on the official architecture.

That said, the history of modern architecture in Brazil can only be understood in relation to the international architectural currents of the day. The prevailing conservative orientation and hierarchical structured mind-set taken by architecture in Europe left little room for the champions of the new style – a condition which worsened with the Depression and the outbreak of World War II. Architects such as Donat Agache, Le Corbusier and the Italian

Denkweise der Architektur in Europa gab den Verfechtern des neuen Bauens wenig Gelegenheit, zum Zuge zu kommen, was sich durch die Wirtschaftskrise und den Ausbruch des Zweiten Weltkriegs noch verschlimmerte. Architekten wie Donat Agache, Le Corbusier und der Italiener Marcello Piacentini sahen deshalb in den aufkommenden öffentlichen Bauvorhaben der brasilianischen Regierung eine Möglichkeit, ihre Ideen zu verwirklichen, Kontakte zu knüpfen und Verbündete zu finden. Im Gegensatz zu den Vereinigten Staaten haben sich keine renommierten Architekten wie Mies van der Rohe, Walter Gropius oder Marcel Breuer in Brasilien niedergelassen. Die Verbindung mit Le Corbusier war allerdings maßgebend für die Durchsetzung der modernen Architekten Brasiliens beim Projekt des Erziehungsministeriums. Er verhalf ihnen zum Durchbruch innerhalb der brasilianischen Architektur, zeigte aber auch, dass diese Architektur für die Errichtung öffentlicher Repräsentationsbauten geeigneter war als die historistischen Stile.

Die Planung und der Bau des Erziehungs- und Gesundheitsministeriums dauerten sieben Jahre, die reich an Zwistigkeiten und Kehrtwendungen waren. Die Ausschreibung des Wettbewerbes, von Professoren der Kunsthochschule formuliert, sah Festlegungen bei der Standortwahl vor, die jede erneuernde Idee von vornherein zunichte machte. Archimedes Memória gewann den Wettbewerb mit einem „Marajoara-Palast-Entwurf" – so genannt nach einer imaginären griechischen Zivilisation, die sich auf der Amazonasinsel Marajó befunden haben soll. Er war ein Kompromiss zwischen der akademischen und der neokolonialen Strömung, die sich vereint hatten gegen die Moderne, den gemeinsamen Feind. Der Minister Gustavo Capanema, durch Intellektuelle in seinem Stab und insbesondere durch seinen Büroleiter, den Dichter Carlos Drummond, gewarnt, bemerkte die Gefahr, ein Ministeriumsgebäude, welches das künftige Brasilien darstellen sollte, mit einer „Vergangenheitsfantasie" in Verbindung zu setzen. Er beschloss, Memória den Preis auszuzahlen, seinen Entwurf aber nicht umzusetzen. Zugleich beauftragte er Lúcio Costa, einen neuen Entwurf auszuarbeiten. Der künftige Stadtplaner Brasílias stellte ein brasilianisches Entwurfsteam zusammen, an dem Oscar Niemeyer, Affonso Reidy, Jorge Moreira und Ernani Vasconcelos beteiligt waren. Auch nach Genehmigung des neuen Entwurfes war Costa mit dem Ergebnis nicht zufrieden. Er engagierte Le Corbusier als Obergutachter der Gruppe. Dieser, in Frankreich bisher eher als Autor avantgardistischer Literatur über Architektur und Städtebau bekannt und auf die Realisierung von Einfamilienhausprojekten beschränkt, witterte die Chance, seine neuen Bauprinzipien in großem Stil umsetzen zu können. Er verbrachte drei Monate

Marcello Piacentini therefore believed the Brazilian government's nascent building plans were an opportunity to realize their ideas, to find useful contacts, and to join forces with allies. Unlike the United States, no well-known architects such as Mies van der Rohe, Walter Gropius or Marcel Breuer settled in Brazil. However, the connection to Le Corbusier, through the project for the Ministry of Education, was the key to Modernist architecture gaining sway in Brazil. It enabled the necessary breakthrough within Brazilian architecture and demonstrated that Modernism was more appropriate than the historical as a style of architecture for the construction of public representative buildings.

The Ministry for Education and Health was planned and built over a period of seven years, a time during which there were many disputes and shifts in direction. The invitation to tender was compiled by professors of the art academy and was so specific as to the location that virtually every new idea amounted to nothing. The competition was won by Archimedes Memória with his design for "Marjoara Palace" – named after an imaginary Greek civilisation which was supposed to have existed on the Amazon island of Marajó. It was a compromise between the academic and neo-colonial movements which had united in order to form a front against the common enemy: modernism. The Minister, Gustavo Capanema, had been warned by the intellectuals on his staff and in particular by his office head, the poet Carlos Drummond, of the dangers of a ministry building destined to represent the future of Brazil with a "fantasy from the past". He decided to pay out the prize money to Memória but not to execute his plan. At the same time, he commissioned Lúcio Costa to make a new plan. The future designer of Brasília assembled a team for the job, which included Oscar Niemeyer, Affonso Reidy, Jorge Moreira and Ernani Vasconcelos. But even after approval of the design, Costa himself was not satisfied. He engaged Le Corbusier as chief consultant for the group. Until this time, Le Corbusier was better known as an author of avant-garde literature about architecture and city planning in France and his experience was limited to the construction of single-family dwellings. Yet he sensed the opportunity to realize his new building principles on a large scale. He spent three months in Brazil and developed two proposals for the ministry at two different locations: one on the coast and the other at its location today. The design team was headed by the talented Oscar Niemeyer and altered the European master's plan and adapted it to the conditions of the actual site. The ensuing design by the Brazilian architect was much more than a simple adaptation: it changed the position of the main building by placing it in the middle of the building site and located

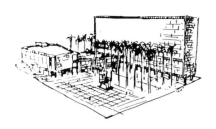

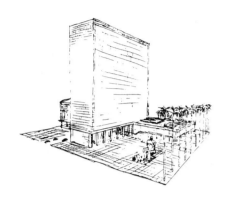

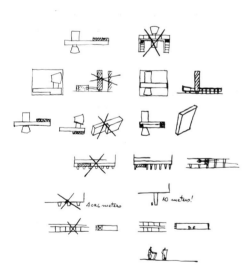

Projekte für das Ministerium
für Erziehung und Gesundheit.
Links der Vorschlag
von Le Corbusier, rechts von
Costa / Niemeyer u. a.

The projects for the Ministry
of Education and Health.
Left: Le Corbusier; Right:
Costa / Niemeyer, and others.

in Brasilien und entwickelte zwei Vorschläge für
das Ministerium an zwei unterschiedlichen Stand-
orten, eines am Meer und das andere an seinem
heutigen Standort. Das Entwurfsteam, bereits damals
unter der Leitung des talentierten Oscar Niemeyer,
veränderte den Entwurf des europäischen Meisters
und passte ihn an die Gegebenheiten seines endgültigen Standortes an. Der abschließende Entwurf
des brasilianischen Architekten war weit mehr als
eine schlichte Transferierung: Er veränderte die Position des Hauptgebäudes, indem er es in die Mitte
des Grundstücks versetzte, und verlegte das Auditorium und die Ausstellungshalle so, dass sie sich
zum Hauptplatz öffneten. So wurde diese Fläche
unter dem auf Stützen stehenden Gebäude erweitert
und bildete einen überdachten öffentlichen Raum.
Mit diesen Änderungen boten die Stützen, die mit
8 Metern doppelt so hoch ausfielen wie der Corbusier'sche Entwurf, eine losgelöste und imposante
Ansicht. Beim Hauptgebäude hat er die seitlich
angelegten Flure mittig angeordnet und löste damit
das Problem einer Hierarchie von Haupt- und Rück-
fassade. Außerdem wurden die aus der Fassade
herauskragenden Sanitärblöcke in das Innere des
Gebäudes verlegt, wodurch das Prisma des Baus
an Reinheit und Eleganz gewann. Der Sonnenschutz,
der ursprünglich von Le Corbusier in Form starrer
Elemente vorgesehen war, wurde in Form von be-
weglichen Lamellen ausgebildet. Eine der größten
Herausforderungen für das junge Team war die
Schaffung eines Regierungsbaus in einem Stil, der
auf jedes dekorative Element verzichtet, was bis
dahin überwiegend bei Industrie- und sozialen Woh-
nungsbauten angewendet wurde. So wurden Spar-
samkeit und Luxus, Einfachheit und Erhabenheit
miteinander verbunden, um ein Gebäude zu schaffen, das sich als Sitz eines Ministeriums eignete.
Damit verbunden war aber auch die Idee des Monumentalen, die Verwendung von Luxusmaterialien
und die Einbindung von Kunstwerken. Beim Erzie-
hungsministerium wurde erstmals der „curtain wall"
realisiert, der in den USA erst viel später beim Bau
des Lever House Building 1954 bekannt wurde.
In den Worten von Lúcio Costa: „Diese Glasfassaden, die im Allgemeinen den Stil der amerikanischen
Architektur charakterisieren, sind gar nicht amerika-
nisch, sondern etwas Europäisches, das erstmals
in Brasilien, in Südamerika, in einem monumentalen
Maßstab angewandt wurde."[2]

Der Siegeszug der Verfechter der Moderne setzte
sich gleichermaßen beim Erhalt des Kulturerbes fort.
Für die Generation Niemeyer bedeutete der Erhalt
der Tradition die Konzeption eines Baus, der auf
dem Studium und dem Wiederauflebenlassen ver-
gessener lokaler Traditionen basierte. Die brasilianische Moderne ersetzte gleichsam die historistischen
Strömungen bei gleichzeitiger Wahrung des natio-

the auditorium and exhibition hall so that they
opened to the main square. In this way, the area
under the building, which stood on pilotis, was
enlarged and converted into covered public space.
Through these changes, the pilotis (which were
now 8 meters high and therefore double the height
foreseen in the original plan by Le Corbusier) also
seemed detached and imposing. Niemeyer also
moved the corridors at the sides of the main building, thereby solving the problem of the hierarchy
of the main and back facades. Also, the sanitary
blocks which protruded from the façade, were
moved to the interior lending the prism of the building greater purity and elegance. The sun shades,
which Le Corbusier had designed with fixed
elements, were changed to feature adjustable slats.
One of the biggest challenges for the young team
was the creation of a government building in a style
that deliberately avoided any decorative elements.
Until then, this style had only been used for industrial buildings and council housing. Through the lack
of ornamentation, economy and luxury as well
as simplicity and the sublime were combined into
a building suitable for a ministry. However, the building also had to be monumental and use luxurious
materials. It also had to be a place appropriate for
the integration of art. For the first time, a "curtain
wall" was used in the Ministry of Education. Such a
wall was to be used much later in the United States,
namely in 1954 in the construction of the Lever
House Building. Lúcio Costa himself stated: "These
glass facades, which in general characterize the
American style in architecture, are not American at
all. They are somewhat European, used for the first
time in monumental proportions in Brazil, in South
America."[2]

This triumphal march by the champions of Modernism is also to be seen in their preservation of
the cultural heritage. For Niemeyer's generation,
the preservation of tradition meant designing buildings based on the study and the rehabilitation of
forgotten local customs. Brazilian Modernism both
replaced historicist trends and preserved the
national building heritage. Unlike international Modernism, in Brazil a dialectic bridge was built between
the past and the future whereby the structural ana-
logy between the simple structures of the 18th
century and the new were emphasized. Increasingly,
historical and artistic interpretations became accepted and a governmental agency for the protection
of monuments was established, which was to be
responsible for the formation of the "symbolic
national capital". It oversaw the listing and preservation of buildings which were considered national
monuments. In this way, proponents of Modernism
came to decide whether Brazilian edifices and
cultural entities were to be classified as monuments

nalen Bauerbes. Anders als bei der internationalen Moderne entstand hier eine dialektische Brücke zwischen Vergangenheit und Zukunft, wobei die strukturelle Analogie zwischen den schlichten Bauten des 18. Jahrhunderts und dem Neuen eine besondere Beachtung fand. Zunehmend setzte sich ihre historische und künstlerische Interpretation durch. Ferner wurde eine Denkmalbehörde eingerichtet, die für die Bildung eines „symbolischen nationalen Kapitals" verantwortlich zeichnete. Ihr oblag die Auswahl und Erhaltung von Gebäuden, welche als nationale Denkmäler angesehen wurden. Die Vertreter der Moderne wurden so zu Entscheidungsrichtern über die Einstufung brasilianischer Bau- und Kulturgüter in die Kategorie eines Denkmals, sie entschieden über Abriss und Erhalt. So gelangten sie zu einer enormen symbolischen und faktischen Macht, indem sie bestimmten, was ein Denkmal war, und darüber entschieden, was in seinem Umfeld zu geschehen hatte. Sie wurden indirekt zu Stadtplanern, die über das Erscheinungsbild historischer Städte und Stadtkerne bestimmten.

Oscar Niemeyer arbeitete zwei Jahre im nationalen Denkmalamt. Bei seiner Architektur allerdings ist die Tradition eher der Ausgangspunkt und nie das Ziel. Seine Verpflichtung sah er immer im Aufbau einer brasilianischen Weltbürgerschaft. Niemeyer gründete die Tradition neu mit der Feststellung, dass die Baugeschichte Brasiliens nicht viel zu bieten habe, im Gegensatz etwa zu den historischen Bauwerken Mexikos oder Perus. Er zog es vor, die Geschichte als Kontext der Entwicklungsprozesse zu sehen, und nicht als hemmende Verpflichtung. Seine Architektur sucht heute die Vergangenheit von morgen. Getreu seiner dialektisch-materialistischen Prinzipien galt seine Hauptaufmerksamkeit der Technik als Element der Wissenschaft, die zum Fortschritt führt. Er versuchte sie gleichwohl mit einer poetischen und nicht-mechanistischen Vision des Menschen zu verbinden. In dieser Hinsicht ist seine Architektur das Ergebnis eines poetischen Moments, welches überrascht, erregt und das Tagein-tagaus der Massen unterbricht. Die Architektur eröffnet in jedermanns Empfindung die Tragweite des Augenblicks. Es ist ein Phänomen, welches uns mit poetischen Möglichkeiten konfrontiert und die Menschheit in der Wahrnehmung jedes Einzelnen wiederherstellt. Es fällt Niemeyer die Aufgabe zu, die brasilianische Tradition zu erfinden, getreu dem Aphorismus des größten brasilianischen Kunstkritikers Mario Pedroso, wonach Brasilien zur Modernität „verurteilt" ist.

and thus saved for posterity, or torn down. By deciding what was classed as a monument and what should happen to it and its surroundings, they achieved tremendous symbolic as well as de facto power. They indirectly became urban planners who made decisions about the appearance of historical cities and the cores of the most important cities.

Oscar Niemeyer worked for two years at the National Monuments Agency. However, in his architecture, the traditional is usually the starting point and not the goal. He considered it his obligation to help establish a cosmopolitan Brazil. Niemeyer founded tradition anew when he concluded that, contrary to Mexico or Peru, the history of architecture in Brazil had little to offer. He preferred to see history as the context in which processes of development unravelled and not as a hampering debt to the past. His architecture searches today for tomorrow's past. True to his principles with their roots in dialectical materialism, he prioritized technology as an element of science which leads to progress. Yet he tried to wed it to a poetic and non-mechanistic vision of man. In this respect, his architecture is the result of a poetic moment which surprises, agitates and interrupts the daily routine of the masses. His is an architecture that kindles the human sensitivity to the scope of the moment. It is a phenomenon which confronts us with poetic opportunities and re-establishes humanity through the realization of the individual. It is Niemeyer's task to invent the Brazilian tradition in line with the aphorism by the greatest Brazilian art critic, Mario Pedroso, who said that Brazil is "condemned" to modernity.

A good example of this outlook was one of his first works, the Grand Hotel in Ouro Preto, made in 1938. Built on a site in the center of the most important colonial city in Brazil, Niemeyer refused to produce a pasticcio and built an extraordinarily modern structure. By maintaining the scale and colors of the town, Niemeyer retained the present with this building, which is absorbed by its surroundings. At the time of its construction, this building caused a veritable controversy. Traditionalists accused Niemeyer of debauching the historic city. Lúcio Costa, architect at the National Monument Agency, defended the design with the argument that it reflected the contemporary truth and that reproduction of a copy would be just as ridiculous as many American citizens who decorate their telephones with cornucopia and Rococo ornaments. In addition, good quality architecture of one period could always be combined with that of the past. This does not mean just defending Niemeyer's work, it was elevated to the level of art and placed in

Grand Hotel.
Ouro Preto.

Grand Hotel.
Ouro Preto.

Ein gutes Beispiel für diese Einstellung war eine seiner ersten Arbeiten, der Bau des Grande Hotel in Ouro Preto (1938). Auf einem Grundstück im Zentrum der wichtigsten Kolonialstadt Brasiliens gebaut, weigerte sich Niemeyer, ein Pasticcio herzustellen, und errichtete einen äußerst modernen Bau. Indem er Maßstab und Farbpalette der Stadt beibehielt, behauptete Niemeyer mit seinem Bau die Gegenwart, die sich letztendlich in der Umgebung auflöst. Sein Bau verursachte eine ungeheure Polemik, die Traditionalisten beschuldigten ihn, die historische Stadt entweiht zu haben. Lúcio Costa, Architekt am Denkmalamt, verteidigte den Entwurf mit dem Argument, dass er die Wahrheit seiner Zeit wiedergebe und dass die Erstellung einer Kopie des Bestehenden genauso lächerlich sei wie manche amerikanische Bürger, die ihre Telefone mit goldenen Füllhörnern und Rokokoschnörkeln verzierten. Überdies ließe sich die gute Architektur einer Epoche immer mit derjenigen der Vergangenheit vereinbaren. Die Arbeit Niemeyers wurde so nicht nur verteidigt, sondern auch als Kunstwerk unter die besten der brasilianischen Baugeschichte eingestuft. Genauso wichtig war jedoch die Feststellung, dass historisierende Pasticcios vermieden und zeitgenössische Bauten innerhalb historischer Zentren bevorzugt werden sollten.

Die internationale Geschichte der Anfänge der modernen Architektur Brasiliens beschränkte sich nicht nur auf die Kontakte mit den europäischen Erneuerern. Ende der dreißiger und Anfang der vierziger Jahre trugen zwei Ereignisse, die von zentraler Bedeutung zur Konsolidierung unseres modernen Stils waren, zur Behauptung und Unabhängigkeit gegenüber den ursprünglichen europäischen Vorbildern bei.

Die brasilianische Regierung Vargas' schwankte im Zweiten Weltkrieg zwischen Neutralität und Kriegseintritt an der Seite der Achsenmächte oder der Alliierten. In den Vereinigten Staaten verfolgte man unter Nelson Rockefeller die Politik der „Guten Nachbarschaft" in der Absicht, Nordamerikas politischen, ökonomischen und kulturellen Einfluss in Lateinamerika zu vergrößern. Insbesondere galt das für Länder wie Argentinien und Brasilien, die starke wirtschaftliche Bande mit Deutschland und Italien hatten.

Im Rahmen des Programms der „Guten Nachbarschaft" wurde im New Yorker Museum of Modern Art im Januar 1943 die Wanderausstellung „Brazil Builds" eingeweiht. Es handelte sich dabei um ein umfassendes Panorama der neuen brasilianischen Architektur und es war die erste Ausstellung, die einmalige Verbindung zwischen den revolutionären Formen und der Entdeckung und Erhaltung histori-

the same category as some of Brazil's best historical architecture. Equally important was the conclusion that historical pasticcios were to be avoided and that contemporary structures were to be preferred in historic centers.

The international history of the beginning of Modernist architecture in Brazil is not limited to contact with European copies. At the end of the 1930s and beginning of the 1940s, two events occurred which were of central importance to the consolidation of our modern style and to its self-assertion and liberation from the original European models.

In World War II, the Brazilian government – under Vargas – vacillated between neutrality and entering the war on the side of the Axis or the Allies. Influenced by Nelson Rockefeller, the United States followed a "good neighbor" policy with the aim of increasing North America's political, economic and cultural influence in Latin America. This was especially true for countries such as Argentina and Brazil, which had strong economic ties with Germany and Italy.

Within the framework of the "good neighbor" program, the touring exhibition "Brazil Builds" was inaugurated in the New York Museum of Modern Art in January, 1943. It portrayed a comprehensive panorama of new Brazilian architecture and was the first exhibit to show the unique connection between revolutionary forms and the discovery and preservation of historical buildings. Even though North America's architecture was still relatively traditional, the architecture department of the MoMA developed a discussion forum centered on the dissemination of architectural innovations under the leadership of Philip Johnson. The exhibit "Brazil Builds" toured 48 cities on the North American continent in three years and the catalogue with texts by Philip Goodwin and photos by G.E. Kidder-Smith reached the most important building centers of the world. Critics and architects turned their attention to the ambitious buildings of a country which up until that moment had been associated with tropical folklore.

The World Fair of 1939–1940 in New York was another event which led to increased activity in the movement for modern architecture in Brazil. The theme was "Construct Tomorrow's World" and it was stipulated that only North American states could present historical buildings while the exhibition pavilions of foreign countries had to be in a modern style. The government of Brazil was therefore forced to rescind a decree from 1922 stating that buildings which represent Brazil in other countries had to be built in neo-colonial style. In the ensuing competition, the design of Lúcio Costa and

scher Gebäude aufzeigte. Auch wenn die Architektur Nordamerikas noch ziemlich traditionell war, entwickelte sich die Architekturabteilung des MoMA unter der Leitung Philip Johnsons zum Diskussionsforum und zum Mittelpunkt der Verbreitung architektonischer Innovation. Die Ausstellung „Brazil Builds" wanderte drei Jahre lang durch 48 Städte des nordamerikanischen Kontinents, und der Katalog, mit Texten von Philip Goodwin und Fotos von G.E. Kidder-Smith, erreichte die wichtigsten Bauzentren der Welt. Kritiker und Architekten wandten damit ihre Aufmerksamkeit den anspruchsvollen Bauten eines Landes zu, dessen Namen bisher mit tropischer Folklore verbunden war.

Die Weltausstellung 1939–1940 in New York war ein weiteres Ereignis, das zu neuem Antrieb in der Bewegung der Moderne Brasiliens führte. Das Thema lautete: „Die Welt von morgen aufbauen" – mit der Festlegung, dass sich lediglich die nordamerikanischen Staaten mit historistischen Gebäuden präsentierten, während die ausländischen Ausstellungspavillons in einem modernen Stil errichtet werden sollten. Die Regierung Brasiliens sah sich daher gezwungen, ein Dekret aus dem Jahre 1922 aufzuheben, wonach Gebäude, die Brasilien im Ausland repräsentieren, zwingend im neokolonialen Stil zu errichten seien. Im darauf folgenden Wettbewerb siegte der Entwurf von Lúcio Costa und Oscar Niemeyer. Obwohl das Grundvokabular Le Corbusiers benutzt wurde, wurden bereits künftige Formen vorweggenommen, wie die freie Form der Rampe, die flexible Raumgestaltung, die festen Sonnenschutzelemente, die Kurve als Ausdrucksform und der fließende Übergang zwischen Innen und Außen. Hiermit begann eine eigene brasilianische Architektursprache, losgelöst von den europäischen Vorbildern. In den Worten Henry-Russel Hitchcock Jr.'s „ist es unbestreitbar, dass die letzten Jahre die Entstehung eines neuen nationalen Idioms innerhalb der internationalen modernen Architektur erlebt haben".[3]

Brasiliens Pavillon war ein wichtiger Beitrag zur Stilkonsolidierung und zu den internationalen Erfahrungen, die das Team Costa/Niemeyer, unabhängig von den Kontakten mit Le Corbusier, machte. Sie verbrachten etwa ein Jahr in New York und gewannen einen umfassenden Einblick in die Ästhetik der Moderne. In dem Wissen, dass der benachbarte französische Pavillon ein überdimensionales, in klassizierendem Stil konzipiertes Gebäude sein würde, entschieden sie sich für einen kleinen und radikal modernen Bau, der durch seine poetische Zerbrechlichkeit einen Kontrast setzte und dadurch seine zeitlich begrenzte Existenz unterstrich. Sie konnten ein offenes Gebäude bauen, unabhängig von

Oscar Niemeyer triumphed. Although they used Le Corbusier's basic vocabulary, futuristic ideas like the free form of ramps, flexible space design, unmovable elements for sun protection, the use of the curve as an expressive form and flowing transitions between interiors and exteriors were part of the design. This marked the beginning of a unique Brazilian architectural idiom liberated from its European models. In the words of Henry-Russel Hitchcock Jr., "it is indisputable that the last years have experienced the formation of a new national idiom within international modern architecture".[3]

Brazil's pavilion was an important contribution to the consolidation of style and to the international experiences of the Costa/Niemeyer team, independent of Le Corbusier. They spent about one year in New York and gained comprehensive insights into the aesthetics of Modernist architecture. Knowing that the neighboring French pavilion would be an oversized building in classicist style, they decided on a small and radically modern structure that would stand out through its poetic fragility and thereby emphasize its limited lifespan. They were able to build an open building, disregarding New York's climactic fluctuations. Brazil's pavilion was also the beginning of an important theme in Niemeyer's work – the architectural pathway. Any visitor to the edifice in Flushing Meadows began by ascending a ramp which afforded him a view of the fair and the different levels of the building. When he reached the partially covered terrace on the upper floor, he could look down to the courtyard and pond. With this structure, Oscar Niemeyer achieved international standing within Modernist architecture. With Alvar Aalto, he is considered to be the creator of an alternative to the "mainstream" rationalism of Modernism. Like Finland's pavilion, the Brazilian edifice filled architectural critics like Siegfried Giedion with enthusiasm. "It is extraordinarily important that our civilization not develop from a single center outwards and that creative work emerge from countries like Finland and Brazil that had previously been considered provincial."[4]

The construction of Pampulha (1942–1943) is one of Oscar Niemeyer's most important works. Upon invitation by the then governor and future president and builder of Brasilia, Juscelino Kubitschek, he designed the nucleus of a new quarter in modern style on the banks of an artificial lake. Belo Horizonte, the capital of the state of Minas Gerais was to expand from here. The Church of St. Francis, the Casino and the Casa do Baile (a restaurant with dance floor) symbolize the beginning of an independent Brazilian language of architecture and the end of the adaptation of international principles to

Costa/Niemeyer, Brasilianischer Pavillon auf der Weltausstellung New York, 1939. Zeichnung.

Costa/Niemeyer, Brazilian Pavilion at New York's World's Fair of 1939. Sketch.

den klimatischen Schwankungen New Yorks. Der Pavillon Brasiliens ist zugleich der Beginn einer wichtigen Thematik im Werk Niemeyers, die des architektonischen Weges. Der Besucher des Baues in Flushing Meadow beginnt mit dem Aufstieg der Rampe, gewinnt einen Überblick der Ausstellung und der verschiedenen Gebäudeebenen, und wenn er die teilüberdachte Terrasse im oberen Geschoss erreicht, erblickt er den darunter liegenden Hof ← p. 10 mit Teich. Oscar Niemeyer gewann mit diesem Bau internationales Ansehen innerhalb der Moderne. Zusammen mit Alvar Aalto wird er als Schöpfer einer Alternative zum Rationalismus des „Mainstreams" ← p. 11 der Moderne gesehen. Ebenso wie der Pavillon Finnlands hat der brasilianische Bau Kritiker wie Siegfried Giedion begeistert. „Es ist von außerordentlicher Wichtigkeit, dass unsere Zivilisation sich nicht aus einem einzigen Zentrum entwickelt und dass ← p. 9 kreative Werke in bis dahin provinziellen Ländern entstehen, wie Finnland und Brasilien".[4]

Eine der zentralen Arbeiten innerhalb des Werkes Oscar Niemeyers ist die Bebauung von Pampulha (1942–1943). Vom damaligen Präfekten Juscelino Kubitschek – dem künftigen Präsidenten und Erbauer Brasílias – eingeladen, entwirft Niemeyer ← pp. 13–15 an den Ufern eines künstlichen Sees die Keimzelle eines neuen Stadtteils im modernen Stil. Von hier aus sollte sich Belo Horizonte, die Hauptstadt des Bundesstaates Minas Gerais, ausdehnen. Die Kirche des Heiligen Franziskus, das Kasino und die Casa do Baile (ein Restaurant mit Tanzlokal) stehen für den Beginn einer selbständigen brasilianischen Architektursprache und nicht mehr für die Anpassung der internationalen Prinzipien an die tropischen Verhältnisse. Lange vor den Architekten anderer Länder hat Oscar Niemeyer zu Beginn der vierziger Jahre die immensen plastischen Möglichkeiten der Stahlbetonbauweise ausgelotet, indem er mit dem falschen Gegensatz zwischen der Schöpfungsfreiheit gegenüber der technisch bedingten Disziplin brach. Pampulha war dem Ende des rationalen Funktionalismus um dreißig Jahre voraus und deutete bereits auf Alternativen gegenüber dem ästhetischen Bürokratismus, der die Moderne der vierziger Jahre bedrohte. Das Kasino, als erster Entwurf ← S. 10 neben dem See errichtet, war gewissermaßen Schauplatz des Dramas der Anwendung und Abkehr von ← S. 11 den Corbusier'schen Prinzipien. Die Kirche des Heiligen Franziskus, die mit ihren selbsttragenden Gewölben unterschiedlicher Spannweite durch die Nutzung des strukturellen und plastischen Potentials des Betons ein „wellenförmiges Dach auf einer fast immateriellen, mit Azulejos gekachelten Wand"[5] ausbildet, ist dagegen die Geburtstunde einer eigenen brasilianischen Architektur. Die Loggia der Casa ← S. 9 do Baile vermittelt einen architektonischen Weg, indem sie die Krümmungen des Seeufers nachvoll-

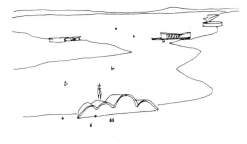

Zeichnung mit den vorgeschlagenen Gebäuden für Pampulha.

Sketch of the proposed buildings for Pampulha.

tropical circumstances. In the 1940s and long before architects in other countries, Oscar Niemeyer began to examine the immense sculptural potential of reinforced concrete. He broke with the erroneous contrast between creative freedom and discipline as determined by technology. Pampulha was 30 years ahead of the end of rational functionalism and it pointed the way for alternatives to aesthetic bureaucracy which threatened the modern architecture of the 1940s. The casino was the first structure to be built next to the lake and it was in many ways the showplace for the drama of acceptance and denial of Le Corbusier's principles. The Church of St. Francis is the birthplace of proper Brazilian architecture. With its self-supporting vaulting of varying dimensions, it makes use of the structural and sculptural potential of concrete which is used to form a "waved roof on an almost non-existent wall tiled with azulejos".[5] The loggia of the Casa do Baile is an architectural conduit. It follows the curves in the bank of the lake, isolating the sky and suggesting a meandering pathway into nature.

A good way to tap into Oscar Niemeyer's world of ideas is to observe how he approaches "classic" themes in international architecture. The house that he built for himself in the Floresta de Tijuca in 1953 is an original contribution on the subject of glass houses. The core of the concept is a large rock around which he devised the entire house and swimming pool. The flat roof, which is surrounded and accentuated by the free form of space, mediates between the interior and the exterior by entering into a dialog with the luxuriant mountain.

With this project Niemeyer resolves two of the biggest disadvantages of glass structures: the way the sunlight enters and the uncomfortable feeling of being observed at night from outside when the lights are on. The glass living room is protected by the vaulting of the arched roof; the private rooms are on the lower floor and are reached by a stairway that has been sculpted into the rock. Niemeyer put an end to the belief that integration with nature can only be achieved through the replication or actual use of natural materials. In this house there is a dialog between concrete, glass, steel and the abstraction of surrounding forms. It becomes part of the rock, the mountains and the sea.

Oscar Niemeyer reported that after a visit, Walter Gropius inquired about the possibility of duplicating this house. He answered that not every example of architecture can be reproduced and that many factors had determined this structure. What can be reproduced, however, is the intellectual freedom to reinterpret the theme, which seemingly met its demise in modern architecture.

zieht, den Himmel ausschneidet und die Windungen eines Weges in die Natur suggeriert.

Eine gute Möglichkeit, sich die Ideenwelt Oscar Niemeyers zu erschließen, liegt in der Beobachtung seiner Herangehensweise an sogenannte „klassische" Themen der internationalen Architektur.

← S. 13–15

Das Haus, das er für sich 1953 in der Floresta da Tijuca entwarf, ist ein originärer Beitrag zur Thematik der Glashäuser. Kern des Entwurfes ist ein großer Felsen, um den herum der Architekt das ganze Haus mit Schwimmbad entwickelt. Das flache Dach umringt und unterstreicht in seiner freien Form die Räume, vermittelt zwischen Innen und Außen, indem es einen Dialog mit der üppigen Berglandschaft eingeht.

In diesem Projekt löst Niemeyer zwei der größten Nachteile gläserner Bauten, den Sonneneinfall, die Einsichtmöglichkeit und das unangenehme Empfinden, nachts bei Beleuchtung der Betrachtung von Außen ausgesetzt zu sein. Das verglaste Wohnzimmer wird durch die Auskragung des gebogenen Flachdaches geschützt, die Einzelzimmer befinden sich im Untergeschoss und werden über eine in den Felsen gehauene Treppe erschlossen. Niemeyer räumte mit dem Glauben auf, dass Integration mit der Natur nur durch Mimetismus oder Verwendung natürlicher Materialien möglich sei. In diesem Haus findet ein Dialog zwischen Beton, Glas, Stahl und der Abstraktion der Formen mit der Umgebung statt; es löst sich in den Felsen, den Bergen und dem Meer auf.

Oscar Niemeyer berichtete, dass Walter Gropius bei einem Besuch nach einer Vervielfältigung dieses Hauses gefragt hätte. Er antwortete, dass nicht jede Architektur vervielfältigt werden könne, da eine Unmenge an Faktoren diesen Bau bedingt hätten. Vervielfältigt werden könne allerdings die geistige Freiheit der Reinterpretation der Thematik, die scheinbar in der modernen Architektur abgeschlossen sei.

Die Frage der Reproduzierbarkeit ist jedoch intim mit dem Bau sozialer Wohnungen verbunden. Es war eines der Hauptziele der Moderne, nicht nur aus ästhetischen Gründen auf Ornamente zu verzichten, sondern im großem Maßstab die Problematik des sozialen Wohnungsbaus zu lösen. Nach Le Corbusier waren alle Bauprogramme im 20. Jahrhundert in den Händen von Ingenieuren, mit Ausnahme des sozialen Wohnungsbaus. Er forderte, dass dieser zum Schwerpunkt der Berufsethik der Architekten werden sollte.[6] Als Kommunist hat Oscar Niemeyer sich immer geweigert, das Wohnungsbauproblem als Hauptbegründung der Moderne anzusehen. Er argumentierte, dass die Wohnungen für Reich und Arm gleich sein sollten und soziale Wohnungsbau-

The question of reproducibility is intimately associated with the construction of council housing. It was one of the main goals of modern architecture to do without ornamentation not only for aesthetic reasons but in particular to solve the problem of low income housing. According to Le Corbusier, all building projects in the 20th century were in the hands of engineers which the exception of low income housing. He insisted that such projects should be emphasized in the professional ethics of architects.[6] As a communist, Oscar Niemeyer refused to recognize the construction of housing as the main impetus for modern architecture. He argued that housing should be the same for the poor and the rich and that council housing should not be a separate building program. He also argued that justice should be achieved through class warfare and never through the "simplification" of form in order to enable inexpensive building. The structural problems of a capitalist society could not be eliminated in this way and only new hindrances and constrictions to creative activity would result.

Oscar Niemeyer's oeuvre consists of the celebration of the technological know-how of man, which is applied poetically and overcomes everyday life. For him, it was not enough to create accurate and rational solutions because these would not touch the sensibilities of the user. It was the creation of visual emotions which characterize Niemeyer's architecture for future traditions.

1 Estado Novo = New State [Note by the translator]
2 Lúcio Costa: Registo de uma Vivência, São Paulo, 1995.
3 Henry-Russel Hitchcock Jr.: Latin American Architecture since 1945, Museum of Modern Art, New York, 1955.
4 Siegfried Giedion: "Brazil and the Contemporary Architecture"; in: Henrique Mindlin (ed.): Modern Architecture in Brazil, Rio de Janeiro, 1956.
5 Italo Campofiorito and Lauro Cavalcanti: When Brazil was Modern. Guide to Architecture 1928–1960, New York, 2002.
6 Le Corbusier: La Maison des Hommes, Paris, 1942.

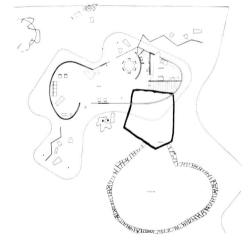

Haus in Canoas, Rio de Janeiro. Grundriss des Hauptgeschosses.

House at Canoas. Ground plan of the main floor.

programme keine spezifischen Programme bilden
sollten. Er argumentierte weiter, dass Gerechtigkeit
durch Klassenkampf zu erreichen sei und niemals
durch „Vereinfachung" der Form, um billiges Bauen
zu ermöglichen. Auch würden auf diesem Weg
die strukturellen Probleme der kapitalistischen Gesellschaft nicht ausgeräumt, sondern erneut Hindernisse
und Einengungen für die schöpferische Tätigkeit
erzeugt.

Oscar Niemeyers Werk feiert das technologische
Können der Menschen, das zu poetischen Gesten
ansetzt und das Alltägliche überwindet. Ihm reichte
es nicht, richtige und rationale Lösungen zu schaffen,
denn sie würden das Empfinden der Nutzer nicht
berühren. Die Schaffung visueller Emotionen war es,
die Niemeyers Architektur für künftige Traditionen
auszeichnet.

1 Estado Novo = Neuer Staat (A.d.Ü.).
2 Lúcio Costa: Registo de uma Vivência, São Paulo 1995.
3 Henry-Russel Hitchcock Jr.: Latin American Architecture
   since 1945, Museum of Modern Art, New York 1955.
4 Siegfried Giedion: „Brazil and the Contemporary
   Architecture"; in: Henrique Mindlin (Hrsg.):
   Modern Architecture in Brazil, Rio de Janeiro 1956.
5 Italo Campofiorito und Lauro Cavalcanti: When Brazil
   was modern. Guide to architecture 1928–1960.
   New York 2002.
6 Le Corbusier: La Maison des Hommes, Paris 1942.

Ordnung und Fortschritt. Der Stadtplaner Oscar Niemeyer
Order and progress. Oscar Niemeyer, urbanist

Carsten Krohn

„Aber wir können immer ein wenig träumen und unseren bescheidenen Vorschlag für eine Stadt der Zukunft präsentieren." [1]
Oscar Niemeyer

"But we can always dream a little and present our modest proposal for the city of the future." [1]
Oscar Niemeyer

Als Juscelino Kubitschek 1955 Präsident von Brasilien wurde, hatte auch die Stunde Oscar Niemeyers geschlagen. Die beiden waren befreundet, und seit langem hatte der Politiker den Architekten mit privaten und öffentlichen Aufträgen versehen. Für Niemeyer war dies der Zeitpunkt, sich mit dem Entwerfen von Städten zu beschäftigen. Er fing an, sich zu diesem Thema zu äußern und eigene Pläne zu entwickeln. Wie aber stellte er sich eine Stadt der Zukunft vor?

In einer Zeit des beginnenden Wirtschaftswunders in Europa galt Brasilien nach wie vor als Entwicklungsland. Über den Weg einer effektiven Industrialisierung herrschten unterschiedliche Auffassungen. Seit der Unabhängigkeit war die Geschichte des Landes von einem permanenten Konflikt der politischen Ideologien geprägt. Während sich demokratische und totalitäre Regierungsformen ablösten, vollzog sich der erhoffte Fortschritt nur sehr zögerlich. Mit dem Amtsantritt von Kubitschek bahnte sich schließlich eine verstärkte wirtschaftliche Anlehnung an den „Westen" an, die mit Fortschritt verbunden wurde und einen formalen Ausdruck suchte.

Die brasilianischen Städte glichen damals in ihren Einzelformen Vorbildern aus Europa und den Vereinigten Staaten, waren jedoch durch ein extremes Wachstum gekennzeichnet. 1934 überschritt São Paulo die Millionengrenze, als sich in nur einem Jahrzehnt die Einwohnerzahl verdoppelte. Vor dem Hintergrund dieser dramatischen und bis heute anhaltenden Entwicklung sind die urbanistischen Konzepte des Landes entstanden. Die schnelle Ausdehnung der Metropolen vollzog sich weitgehend ohne regulierende Planung. Zudem wurden permanent alte Gebäude durch neue ersetzt, so dass im Laufe des 20. Jahrhunderts die Einheit und Ordnung des kolonialen Stadtbildes verloren ging.

When Juscelino Kubitschek was appointed president of Brazil in 1955, the bell tolled for Oscar Niemeyer. They had been friends for a long time and the politician had always made sure that the architect received many private and public commissions. For Niemeyer, the time had come to concern himself with urbanism. He began by expressing his opinions on the topic and devising plans of his own. But what did he imagine the city of the future to look like?

In the post-war period with the European economy starting to boom, Brazil was still considered to be a developing world country. Opinions differed as to the most effective means of industrialization. Since independence, the history of Brazil had been characterized by permanent conflicts on political ideology. As democratic and totalitarian governments alternated, only slowly could hopes for progress be realized. When Kubitschek came to power, economic dependence on the "West" increased in relation to with progress and there was a need to find a means of formally expressing this.

At this time, the component parts of Brazil's cities took their cue from European and North American models while being characterized by truly rampant growth. In 1934, São Paulo surpassed the one million mark, with its population having more than doubled in the space of only one decade. Brazil's urban planning concepts arose in the light of these dramatic events – and they persist to this day. The swift sprawl of the cities occurred by and large without any regulatory planning. Simultaneously, old buildings were constantly being replaced by new ones, so that in the course of the 20th century, the unity and order that had shaped the face of the colonial towns disappeared.

Le Corbusiers Vision

1929 besuchte Le Corbusier Brasilien. In einem Vortrag vor dem Architektenverband in Rio de Janeiro bekundete er eine leidenschaftliche Begeisterung für diese Stadt. Er schwärmte für das Meer, die Schiffe und die Landschaft, aber nicht für die Häuser und die Straßen.

„Ich war ganz neu nach São Paulo gekommen und hatte die Wandkarte im Arbeitszimmer des Präfekten und auf ihr dieses Straßengewirr – diese über- und untereinander herlaufenden Straßen – entdeckt und den ungeheuren Durchmesser der Stadt festgestellt; so konnte es geschehen, dass ich ausrief: ‚Sie befinden sich in einer Verkehrskrise – Sie können unmöglich 45 Kilometer quer durch die Stadt rasch bewältigen, wenn Sie solch ein Straßenlabyrinth haben!' Den Piloten bat ich: ‚Fliegen Sie in Richtung Stadtmitte São Paulo; zuerst dicht über dem Boden; ich möchte sehen, wie die Stadt sich im Profil darstellt, wo sie ansteigt, wo sie infolge des unwiderstehlichen Drucks der Geschäfte übereinander gebaut ist.' Im eigentlichen Zentrum des ganzen Gebietes sahen wir die Stadt ansteigen – sanft zuerst und dann, inmitten, ganz gewaltig. Beginn des Wachstums. Deutliche Anzeichen; klare Diagnose: Stadtmittelpunkt-Krankheit. Dann haben wir mit dem Auto Experimente gemacht."[2]

Seine Lösung sah zwei geradlinige Autobahnen vor, die sich im Zentrum der Stadt im rechten Winkel kreuzen sollten. Diese Straßen, so stellte er sich vor, bildeten die Dächer von zwei gigantisch langen Gebäuden. Für Rio schwebte ihm der gleiche Typus eines langen monumentalen Baublocks vor, der sich als geschwungenes Band parallel zu den Stränden erstreckte.

Als Le Corbusier einige Jahre später beauftragt wurde, ein modernes Hochhaus in Rio zu bauen, arbeiteten in seinem Team unter anderem der damals 28-jährige Oscar Niemeyer sowie sein Lehrer Lúcio Costa. Obwohl Corbusiers Botschaft an Südamerika eine städtebauliche war, nahm Niemeyer diesen Aspekt nicht ernst. „Ich muss gestehen, dass uns damals diese Lösung als pure Fantasie erschien […]."[3] Diese Auffassung änderte sich jedoch, nachdem Le Corbusier Anfang der fünfziger Jahre in Indien eine neue Stadt entwarf und auch realisierte. Als Niemeyer erkannte, dass die städtebaulichen Entwürfe seines ansonsten bewunderten Vorbilds keine Utopie mehr blieben, begann er, dessen brasilianische Vision zu würdigen: „[…] aber sollte heute die Stadtplanung Rios in großem Stil wieder aktuell werden, würde sie sicher den einzuschlagenden Weg weisen."[4]

Le Corbusier,
Projekt für São Paulo,
Zeichnung um 1929.

Le Corbusier,
Project for São Paulo.
Sketch around 1929.

Le Corbusier's vision

Le Corbusier visited Brazil in 1929. In a lecture to the Association of Architects in Rio de Janeiro, he declared his passionate enthusiasm for that city, mentioning his enthusiasm for the sea, the ships and the physical setting, but not praising the buildings and the streets.

"I was new to São Paulo and was looking at the wall map in the prefect's office when I discovered the chaos of its streets – crossing above and below each other – and the quite unbelievable diameter of the city; and so it happened that I said aloud: 'You have a real traffic crisis here – it is impossible to cross 45 kilometers through the city quickly with such a maze of streets!' I asked the pilot to 'fly toward the centre of São Paulo – but keep as low as possible so I can see a cross-section of the city – where it rises and where it is built on top of itself due to the irresistible pressures of business.' In the actual centre of this area we saw the city rise – first gently and then colossally in the middle. The beginning of growth. An obvious symptom; a simple diagnosis – the downtown disease. Then we tried the car experiment."[2]

Le Corbusier's solution was two straight motorways which would cross at right angles in the center of the city. He imagined that these roads would form the roofs of two gigantically long buildings. He also imagined a monumentally long structure of the same type, which would run parallel to Rio's beaches like a flowing ribbon.

Several years later when Le Corbusier was authorized to build a modern high-rise in Rio, the 28-year-old Oscar Niemeyer as well as his teacher, Lúcio Costa, were members of his team. Although Le Corbusier's message to South America was about city planning, Niemeyer did not take this aspect seriously. "I must confess that this solution seemed like pure fantasy to us at the time […]"[3] This opinion changed at the beginning of the 1950s; however, after Le Corbusier designed a new city in India that was then actually built. When Niemeyer realized that the plans created by his otherwise so admired role model were no longer just utopia, he began to appreciate the latter's Brazilian vision: "[…] but if city planning for Rio were to become relevant again today in a big way, then it would surely indicate the route to follow."[4]

The dream of a well arranged city

After Kubitschek came to power in 1955 and started working on the project for a new capital, Oscar Niemeyer began to express himself on the question of "urbanism". As the co-publisher of a new architectural journal, he began to disseminate his ideas in

Der Traum von einer geordneten Stadt

Nachdem Kubitschek 1955 an die Macht gekommen war und das Projekt einer neuen Hauptstadt in Angriff nahm, fing Oscar Niemeyer an, sich zum Thema „Urbanistik" zu äußern. Als Mitherausgeber einer neuen Architekturzeitschrift begann er seine Ziele in englischer, französischer und deutscher Übersetzung zu verbreiten. Er war damals bereits als Architekt international bekannt, aber auch umstritten, da kritisiert wurde, dass frei geschwungene Betonkonstruktionen nicht sozial seien.[5] In einer der ersten Ausgaben seiner Zeitschrift reagierte er darauf, indem er die soziale und politische Komponente des Bauens im Bereich der Stadtplanung ansiedelte.

„Das Ärgste jedoch – weil beinahe immer unabänderlich – ist der traurige, bedauernswerte Zustand unserer Städte, die der Gleichgültigkeit der Behörden und dem verderblichen Treiben der Grundstücksspekulation ausgeliefert sind […]. Gegen diese Missstände müssen wir uns auflehnen, indem wir vor allem nach logischen, zweckentsprechenden und verantwortlichen Plänen verlangen."[6]

Niemeyer forderte den Masterplan für eine geordnete Stadt. Als Beispiel führte er die damalige Planung für Moskau an. Die symmetrische Gliederung und die weitläufige Ausdehnung betrachtete er als vorbildlich. Eine ideale Stadt konnte er sich nur im Zusammenhang mit einer klassenlosen Gesellschaft vorstellen. Um zu beklagen, dass im eigenen Land städtebauliche Entwürfe „unweigerlich auf dem Papier bleiben",[7] lobte er die monumentale, unter Stalin entstandene Planung für Moskau.

„Zum ersten Mal in der Geschichte kann der Architekt, frei von seinen bisherigen individuellen Verpflichtungen, die eigentliche Rolle spielen, die ihm in der Gesellschaft zukommt und die ihm die gewünschte Mitarbeit an der Lösung der kollektiven Probleme zusichert. Während er in anderen Ländern beinahe ausschließlich den Wünschen einer Minderheit der dominierenden Klasse nachkommen muss, steht hier im Gegensatz seine Leistungskraft im Dienste der großzügigen urbanistischen Pläne, die Zufriedenheit und Wohlergehen der Kollektivität zum Ziel haben."[8]

Schließlich wurde Niemeyer beauftragt, eine ideale Stadt für 200.000 Menschen im Landesinneren von Brasilien zu entwerfen.[9] Der Plan schrieb eine konsequente Trennung von Auto- und Fußgängerverkehr vor. Zudem sollten auch die unterschiedlichen städtischen Zonen klar voneinander abgegrenzt sein. Nach einem linearen Prinzip reihten sich identisch strukturierte Abschnitte aneinander. Dieses Band ist in der Mitte von einer quer verlaufenden monumentalen Achse durchschnitten, die auf einen

English, French and German translations. He was already known internationally as an architect but he was controversial because some critics claimed that freely curving concrete edifices were not socially relevant.[5] In one of the first editions of his magazine, he responded by stating that the social and political sides to building fell within the domain of city planning.

"What is most frustrating – because it is almost impossible to change – is the sad and regrettable condition of our cities, which are exposed to the indifference of the authorities and the corrupt ways of property speculation […]. We must oppose these abuses by insisting on logical, purposive and responsible planning."[6]

Niemeyer called for master plans according to which an orderly city could be built. As a model, he cited the plans at that time for Moscow, considering symmetrical components and an expansive site to be ideal. He could imagine an ideal city only in connection with a classless society. Complaining that in his own country city plans "inevitably remain on paper",[7] he praised the monumental plans for Moscow resolved under Stalin's aegis.

"For the first time in history, the architect is not trammeled by individual obligations and can play the genuine role which society has given him and which assures that he takes part in finding a solution to collective problems. While in other countries, he has to fulfill the wishes of a minority of the dominating class, here, in contrast, his abilities are at the service of spacious urban plans which aim to foster the satisfaction and well-being of the society as a whole."[8]

Ultimately, Niemeyer was commissioned to plan an ideal city for 200,000 inhabitants in the interior of Brazil.[9] The plan called for a strict separation of traffic and pedestrians. In addition, the various urban zones were to be kept clearly distinct. Following a linear principle, sections of identical structures were to be built in rows. This belt was to be broken in the middle by a perpendicular monumental axis which advanced to a dominant complex of buildings set in a park. Like Le Corbusier's town of Chandigarh in India, this "central" area was located on the periphery so that the architecture would be framed by the landscape rather than by other buildings. In India, Le Corbusier designed this section himself, while the buildings in the city were devised by others. To separate the unified ensemble of sculptural monuments in visual terms from the group of purpose-built structures, Le Corbusier placed artificial hills in Chandigarh; whereas Niemeyer proposed high-rise segments. These would form a line to the right and to the left of the monumental axis.

A.V. Vlasov u. a.,
Plan für Moskau.
Modell um 1950.

A.V. Vlasov and others,
Plan for Moscow.
Model around 1950.

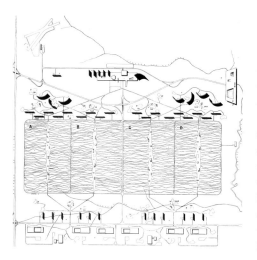

Cidade marina. Projekt
für das Urucuia-Flusstal.
Plan um 1956.

Marina City. Project for
the Valley of Urucuia River.
Plan around 1956.

dominierenden Gebäudekomplex mit einer Platz-
anlage zuläuft. Dieser „zentrale" Bereich ist, wie in
der damals von Le Corbusier in Indien gebauten
Stadt Chandigarh, an der Peripherie angeordnet,
damit sich dort die reine Architektur vor der Landschaft und nicht vor den Bauten anderer abzeichnet.
In Indien hatte Le Corbusier diesen Teil allein gestaltet, während die Häuser in der Stadt von anderen
gebaut wurden. Als optische Trennung zwischen
dem einheitlichen Ensemble der skulpturalen Mon-
umente und der Ansammlung von Zweckbauten
hatte Le Corbusier in Chandigarh künstliche Hügel
errichtet, während Niemeyer Hochhausscheiben
vorschlug. Wie in einem Spalier reihen sich diese
links und rechts der monumentalen Achse auf.

Für die einfache Wohnbebauung war in diesem
Plan ein ausgedehnter Streifen vorgesehen, dessen
unregelmäßig gewelltes Wegenetz wie eine natürliche Maserung erschien. Die Menschen sollten
in einer weitläufigen Parklandschaft leben, als deren
Entwerfer Roberto Burle Marx genannt wird. Unabhängig davon, inwieweit dieser nie realisierte Plan
auf den Landschaftsplaner, den Architekten oder
bloß auf dessen Mitarbeiter zurückzuführen ist:
Stadtplaner der neuen Hauptstadt Brasília sollte
Oscar Niemeyer werden.

Als Präsident des Landes beauftragte Kubitschek
Niemeyer direkt, da „die natürliche Wahl" auf ihn
gefallen war. Bekanntlich lehnte der Architekt ab.
Er erklärte rückblickend: „Den Flächennutzungsplan
wollte ich nicht entwerfen. Ich wollte mich auf die
Architektur konzentrieren, für die Stadtplanung gab
es andere, besser qualifizierte Leute."[10] Niemeyer
bat seinen Lehrer Lúcio Costa den Vorsitzenden
der Jury zu bestimmen, der wiederum für Costa ein-
trat. Dessen prämierter Plan von Brasília war wie
auf Niemeyer zugeschnitten, dem noch im Vorfeld
der Entwurf sämtlicher Regierungsbauten zuge-
sichert worden war.

Eine ideale Stadt als Utopie
In der 1957 begonnenen und in nur wenigen
Jahren realisierten neuen Hauptstadt des Landes,
Brasília, konnte Oscar Niemeyer einen ganzen Bezirk
bauen, ohne Kompromisse eingehen zu müssen.
Der berühmte Masterplan in Form eines Flugzeugs
war von Lúcio Costa entworfen. Auch wenn sich
Niemeyer innerhalb von Costas Schema bewegte,
begriff er seinen eigenen Beitrag ebenfalls als städte-
baulich. „Eines der wichtigsten Probleme des mo-
dernen Städtebaus ist das der architektonischen
Einheit, diesem konstanten Faktor der Schönheit und
Harmonie in den alten Städten Europas."[11] Niemeyer
schuf in Brasília einen Stadtraum wie aus einem
Guss. Er konzipierte seine Bauten in Bezug aufeinander, um eine „Einheit des Stadtbildes"[12] zu erzielen.

He envisaged an extended strip for the simple residential structures, imagining an irregular wavy net
of streets shaped like a natural wood grain. The inhabitants would live in an extensive park designed
by Roberto Burle Marx. Regardless of whether the
ideas can be attributed to the landscape planners,
the architects or simply the co-workers, these plans
were never realized. But the town planner for the
new capital, Brasília, was to be Oscar Niemeyer.

Once president, Kubitschek directly commissioned
Niemeyer, referring to him as "the natural choice".
It is a well-known fact that Niemeyer declined the
offer. He explained in retrospect: "I did not want
to design the land zoning plan. I wanted to concen-
trate on the architecture; there were other, better
qualified people for the town planning."[10] Niemeyer
asked his teacher, Lúcio Costa, to name the
chairman of the jury, who in turn supported Costa.
The latter's winning plan was almost tailor-made
for Niemeyer who had been assured in the run-up
to the drafting of the plan that he would be commissioned to plan all the governmental buildings.

Ideal city as utopia
Brasília, the new capital, was begun in 1957 and only
a few years later it was complete. Oscar Niemeyer
was able to construct an entire district without
having to compromise along the way. The famous
master plan in the shape of an airplane, was the
brainchild of Lúcio Costa. Even when working within
Costa's scheme, Niemeyer felt he was making an
equally important contribution to the town planning.
"One of the most important problems in modern
urban planning is to achieve architectural unity, that
consistent factor responsible for the beauty and
harmony of the old cities of Europe."[11] In Brasília,
Niemeyer created urban space as though it were
cast from a single mold. His structures were conceived in relation to one another with the objective
of engendering a "city with a united face".[12]

If one wanted to define urban design as distinct
from urban planning, it would be wise to differentiate
between aesthetic and social aspects. For example,
at US universities "urban design" and "urban planning" are different fields of study; one is about form
and the other is about sociological factors. In this
respect, Niemeyer, as an architect, was more interested in design than in planning.

The planning for Brasília began with the search
for the ideal location. The most important considerations were climate, availability of water, transportation links, physical beauty and also simplicity
of expropriation. Lúcio Costa's master plan then
formed an additional part of a complex process of
development; whereas Niemeyer was able to con-

Wollte man Städtebau in Abgrenzung zu Stadtplanung definieren, wäre es sinnvoll, zwischen ästhetischen und sozialen Aspekten zu unterscheiden. So werden zum Beispiel an amerikanischen Universitäten „urban design" und „urban planning" als verschiedene Fächer begriffen; beim einen geht es um Formen und beim anderen um soziologische Grundlagen. In diesem Sinne war Niemeyer als Architekt mehr an Design als an Planung interessiert.

Die Planung Brasílias begann mit der Suche nach einem idealen Ort in Bezug auf klimatische Bedingungen, Wasserversorgung, Verkehrsanbindung, landschaftliche Schönheit, aber auch in Hinblick auf eine leichte Enteignungsmöglichkeit. Der Masterplan von Lúcio Costa bildete schließlich einen weiteren Teil in dem umfangreichen Prozess der Gesamtentwicklung, während sich Niemeyer für einige Jahre auf das Gestalten konzentrieren konnte – bis zum Militärputsch im Jahre 1964, als die Diktatur ihn ins Exil trieb. Mit tiefer Enttäuschung musste er die Veränderungen Brasílias beobachten.

„Am Anfang gab es einen Plan, und nun ist die Stadt, wie sie ist. Deswegen bin ich traurig. Lúcio Costa schuf die Stadtplanung für Brasília. Er entwarf einen wichtigen Teil der Architektur im monumentalen Bereich und einige andere Gebäude in der Stadt. Dann haben Menschen das ganze Gebilde in eine große Unordnung verwandelt. In Brasílias Nebenstraßen ist die Architektur schrecklich. Die Zeiten, als der Ort eine architektonische Einheit aufwies, sind lange vorbei. Die Gebäude waren nicht so hoch. Es gab eine Architektur, die sich selbst wiederholte. In Brasília versuchen die Banken einen fürchterlichen Zustand durchzusetzen. Ich bin sehr enttäuscht gewesen. Vor Jahren war es eine gute Stadt. Es gab eine Einheit. Nun baut man mehr als schlecht, und es gibt kein Konzept."[13]

Als sich um Brasília Trabantenstädte zu bilden begannen, floh Niemeyer 1964 nach Israel ins Exil, wo er sich für mehrere Monate in einem Hotelzimmer versteckt hielt und eine Idealstadt entwarf. Er wurde gebeten, für einen konkreten Ort Gebäude zu entwickeln, einengende Vorgaben lehnte er jedoch ab. Er wählte sich die Negev-Wüste als Tabula rasa für eine symmetrische Anlage, die sich wie eine Oase um einen zentralen Platz gruppiert. Die Menschen sollten in identischen Wohntürmen leben und Autos nur für Fernfahrten benötigen. Die umfahrbare Stadt bildete eine in sich abgeschlossene Einheit, die sich reproduzieren und linear aneinander reihen lassen sollte. Ein unkontrolliertes Wachstum sollte verhindert werden.

centrate on design for a number of years – until he was exiled in 1964 after the military coup. It was with great disappointment that he was then compelled to follow the ensuing changes in Brasília.

"There was a plan in the beginning, and now the city is the way it is. I am sad for it. Lúcio Costa designed Brasília's urbanism. He designed a major part of the architecture for the monumental places and some other buildings in the city. And then people transformed the whole thing into a mess. In Brasília's secondary streets the architecture is horrible. Times when the town had an architectural unity are long gone. The buildings were not so high. There was an architecture repeating itself. […] In Brasília the banks try to establish a horrible condition. It did not work. I have been disappointed. Years ago it was a good city. There was a unity. Now what they build is even worse then very bad and there is no concept any longer."[13]

While satellite towns were beginning to develop around Brasília in 1964, Niemeyer fled to Israel where he lived in exile. He hid in a hotel room for several months and designed an ideal city. He was asked to design buildings for a specific location, yet he refused to be constrained in such a way. He chose the Negev Desert as a tabula rasa for a symmetric plan which would be grouped around a central square like an oasis. The residents were all to live in identical towers and use automobiles only for long journeys. He foresaw a bypass around the city and the town forming a self-contained unit that could be reproduced and extended lineally. Uncontrolled growth was to be avoided.

Belief in progress and disillusionment

After the Negev plan was published, journalists approached Oscar Niemeyer to ask him about the "city of the future". At a time that was influenced by the general belief in the unlimited possibilities of modern technology, the architect formulated his vision of a vertical city. In 1966, a magazine cited his descriptions of a gigantic residential tower for tens of thousands of inhabitants and a city floating on the sea.[14] The heart of this city, or so he imagined, would be covered by huge glass domes so that large areas could be air-conditioned and heated. Apparently, some of Niemeyer's concepts were inspired by the ideas pursued back then by Buckminster Fuller and many young architects.

In the 1960s, cities began to change radically because the realization of the city as tailored to the automobile was generally regarded as an achievement. Countless satellite towns sprung up around Brasília, turning it into a prototype for worldwide

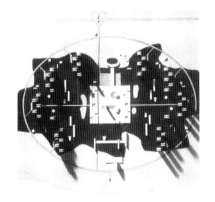

Negev-Plan.
Modell um 1964.

Urban Plan for Negev.
Model around 1964.

Entwurf für eine „Stadt
der Zukunft".
Entwurfsskizze um 1966.

Plan for a "City of the Future".
Sketch around 1966.

Fortschrittsglaube und Ernüchterung

Nach der Veröffentlichung des Negev-Plans traten
Journalisten an Oscar Niemeyer heran, um ihn über
die „Stadt der Zukunft" zu befragen. In einer Zeit,
die von einem allgemeinen Glauben an unbegrenzte
Möglichkeiten der modernen Technik geprägt war,
formulierte der Architekt die Vision einer vertikalen
Stadt. 1966 zitierte ihn eine Zeitschrift, wie er gigan-
tische Wohntürme für Zehntausende von Bewoh-
nern und schwimmende Meeresstädte beschrieb. [14]
Die Stadtzentren, so stellte er sich vor, würden von
riesigen Glaskuppeln überspannt werden, um große
Bereiche zu klimatisieren. Bei diesen Spekulationen
ließ sich Niemeyer offenbar von Konzepten inspi-
rieren, die Buckminster Fuller und viele junge Architekten damals verfolgten.

In den sechziger Jahren begannen sich Städte
radikal zu verändern, da die Umsetzung der auto-
gerechten Stadt allgemein als Errungenschaft
betrachtet wurde. Der Bau von unzähligen Satelli-
tenstädten ließ Brasília nicht nur zum Prototyp einer
weltweiten Entwicklung werden, auch die Kritik,
die sich an dieser Entwicklung entzündete, führte
dazu, dass Niemeyer zunehmend im Kontext der
Stadtplanung rezipiert wurde. Er wurde zum Reprä-
sentanten einer urbanistischen Idee, für die er ursprünglich gar nicht verantwortlich war.

Niemeyers Laufbahn verlagerte sich, als man anfing,
ihn insbesondere in städtebaulichen Belangen zu
konsultieren. Er entwarf urbanistische Pläne für die
Algarve in Portugal (1966), für Grasse in Frankreich
(1967) und für Algier in Algerien (1968). In allen
diesen Projekten folgte er Le Corbusiers Konzept von
gleichartigen Hochhausscheiben mit weiten Frei-
räumen, einem damals gängigen Modell – zu futuristischen Fantasien ließ er sich nicht mehr hinreißen.
Städtebauliches Entwerfen begriff er als Gestal-
tungsaufgabe, bei der es ihm – wie bei einem Haus –
vor allem um räumliche Beziehungen ging.

Und doch: Auch wenn Oscar Niemeyer städtebauliche Lösungen für konkrete Orte entwickelte,
distanzierte er sich nicht von seiner urbanistischen
Utopie. Das Prinzip des Negev-Plans griff er auch
viele Jahre später wieder auf, als er eine weiter-
entwickelte Variante präsentierte. Bei dieser Idealstadt schwebten ihm zwar runde Hochhaustürme
vor, die sich symmetrisch um ein quadratisches
Zentrum gruppierten, aber das verkehrsplanerische
Konzept blieb das Gleiche. Niemeyer forderte
eine Architektur auf dem Stand des technischen
Fortschritts und eine Stadt der klaren Ordnung.

Keines der urbanistischen Projekte Niemeyers wurde
je realisiert. Auch als er 1986 beauftragt wurde,
für São Paulo einen städtebaulichen Masterplan zu

development and the criticism of such a form
of development became very vociferous, with many
experts now citing Niemeyer in the context of such
urban planning. He became the representative
of an urban idea for which he had by no means originally been responsible.

The emphasis of Niemeyer's career shifted as
people began to consult him mainly on matters of
urban development. He designed urban plans for
the Algarve in Portugal (1966), for Grasse in France
(1967) and for Algiers in Algeria (1968). In all of
these projects he followed Le Corbusier's concept
of identical high-rise slabs with wide open spaces –
a common model at the time, and eschewed the
former futuristic fantasies. Urban design became
a matter primarily of conceiving of spatial relation-
ships – like in a building.

However, even though Oscar Niemeyer developed
solutions for specific places, he did not turn his back
on his urban utopia. Many years later, he returned to
his Negev plan which he presented in an advanced
variant. Although the latter ideal city included round
high-rise towers grouped around a square center,
he retained his original transportation concept.
Niemeyer insisted on architecture that took its cue
from new technology and a clearly ordered city.

None of Niemeyer's urban projects were ever realized. Even when he was asked to develop an urban
master plan for São Paulo in 1986, nothing was
brought to fruition. As a communist, he remained
true to his belief that expropriated land was the best
basis for ideal city planning. Even though his plan
seemed out of date, his proposal to improve the
inner city by laying out a park along the Tieté River
to enhance the status of the inner city is worthy of
attention. The river is used as a canal for sewage
and is located between two motorways; to this very
day it divides the city into two halves.

The architect's urban vision was not compatible
with the realities of South America and today he con-
cedes that "I am not an urbanist." In retrospect
he describes his urban planning projects as "mere
ideas, nothing more than speculation". [15] His architectural vision of unity of construction and architecture is demonstrated by a few outstanding buildings
but he has resigned himself as regards the social
side to building construction.

"With respect to urban planning, the young architect
feels extremely frustrated; especially when land
is cut up into tiny pieces for the profit of speculators.
At this point it becomes disgustingly clear that
his work is a part of the hateful system which brings

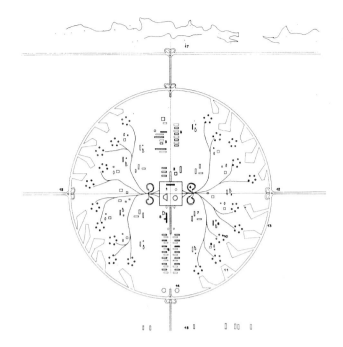

Entwurf für die „Stadt
von Morgen"
Plan um 1979.

"City of Tomorrow" project.
Plan around 1979.

Niemeyer u.a.,
Parque do Tieté.
Projekt für São Paulo.
Modell um 1986.

Niemeyer and others,
City Plan of Park Tieté.
Project for São Paulo.
Model approx. 1986.

entwerfen, kam nichts davon zur Umsetzung. Als
Kommunist blieb er seiner Überzeugung treu, dass
eine Enteignung des Bodens die Grundlage einer
idealen Stadtplanung bilde. Auch wenn sein Entwurf
wie aus einer vergangenen Zeit erscheint, ist sein
Vorschlag beachtenswert, einen großen Park entlang
des Flusses Tieté anzulegen, um diesen inner-
städtisch aufzuwerten. Der als Abwasserkanal ge-
nutzte Fluss liegt zwischen zwei Autobahnen und
zerschneidet die Stadt bis heute in zwei Hälften.

Die urbanistische Vision des Architekten hat sich
nicht mit der südamerikanischen Realität vertragen,
und so räumt er heute ein: „Ich bin kein Stadtplaner." Rückblickend bezeichnet er seine stadtpla-
nerischen Projekte als „bloße Ideen, nichts als
Spekulation".[15] Seine architektonische Vision der Einheit von Konstruktion und Architektur konnte er in
herausragenden Einzelbauten demonstrieren,
aber hinsichtlich des sozialen Bereichs beim Bauen
zeigt er sich resigniert.

„Was die Stadtplanung angeht, so wird hier der
junge Architekt ganz besonders frustriert, nämlich
besonders dann, wenn er den Boden in kleine Teil-
chen zerschnitten sieht und dieser allein für den
Profit der Immobiliengesellschaften vorgesehen ist.
Dann wird er sich mit ganzer Abscheu darüber klar,
dass seine Arbeit ein Teil des verhassten Systems
ist, welches allein der reichsten Klasse Nutzen bringt
und nicht der ausgebeuteten Klasse, welche in
Brasilien ausgestoßen ist und in tiefem Elend lebt."[16]

benefit only to the wealthiest class and not to the
exploited class, who live as outcasts in utter misery
in Brazil."[16]

Oscar Niemeyer still dreams of an ordered city.
Nevertheless, he rejects regulation by the authorities because it restricts the freedom of design.
He works like an artist and describes himself as
a realist. In the meantime, he views Le Corbusier's
urban planning with skepticism. "His proposal
for Rio is nothing, it's impossible to realize. His proposal for Paris was very bad. If Paris had been
changed according to his plans, the city would have
disappeared. Le Corbusier's urban plans for
Paris would have been an absolute disaster. It was
a fantasy, if a very beautiful one."[17]

1 Oscar Niemeyer: "A City for the Year 2000," in:
   Unesco – The Courier, no. 3, 1985, p. 19.
2 Le Corbusier: Feststellungen zu Architektur und Städtebau,
   Braunschweig & Wiesbaden, 1987, 2nd ed., pp. 220
   (Précisions sur un état présent de l'architecture et de l'urbanisme,
   Paris, 1930)
3 Oscar Niemeyer: "Über den Wettbewerb für Brasilia,"
   in: Módulo, no. 8, 1957.
4 Ibid.
5 See Max Bill: "Architect, architecture and society." Talk on
   June 9, 1953 in the Faculty of Architecture and Urban development
   of the University of São Paulo, Printed in this book pp. 115
6 Oscar Niemeyer: "Current Problems with Brazilian Architecture,"
   in: Módulo, no. 3, 1955. Printed in this book pp. 123.
7 Ibid.
8 Ibid.

Noch immer träumt Oscar Niemeyer von einer geordneten Stadt. Behördliche Regulierungen lehnt er jedoch ab, da diese gestalterische Freiheiten beschränken. Er arbeitet wie ein Künstler und bezeichnet sich als Realist. Le Corbusiers Stadtplanung betrachtet er mittlerweile wieder mit Skepsis. „Was er für Rio vorschlug, ist nichts, unmöglich zu realisieren. Was er für Paris vorschlug, wäre sehr schlimm. Wenn man Paris nach seinen Plänen verändert hätte, wäre die Stadt verschwunden. Le Corbusiers Stadtplanung für Paris wäre ein absolutes Desaster. Es war eine Phantasie, aber wunderschön." [17]

1 Oscar Niemeyer: „A City for the Year 2000";
   in: *Unesco – The Courier*, 3/1985, S. 19.
2 Le Corbusier: Feststellungen zu Architektur und Städtebau,
   Braunschweig-Wiesbaden 1987, 2. Aufl., S. 220ff.
   (Précisions sur un état présent de l'architecture et de l'urbanisme,
   Paris 1930).
3 Oscar Niemeyer: „Über den Wettbewerb für Brasília";
   in: *Módulo*, Nr. 8, 1957, o. S.
4 Ebda.
5 Vgl. Max Bill: „architekt, architektur und gesellschaft." Vortrag
   vom 9. Juni 1953 an der Fakultät für Architektur und Urbanistik
   der Universität São Paulo. Abgedruckt in diesem Buch S. 115 ff.
6 Oscar Niemeyer: „Aktuelle Probleme der brasilianischen
   Architektur"; in: *Módulo*, Nr. 3, 1955, o. S. Abgedruckt in
   diesem Buch S. 123 ff.
7 Ebda.
8 Ebda.
9 Das Projekt „Cidade marina" wurde 1955 oder 1956 von
   der Firma Colonizadora Agrícola e Urbanizadora, S. A. für einen Ort
   in der Nähe des späteren Brasília entwickelt. Als Architekt wird
   Oscar Niemeyer und als Landschaftsarchitekt Roberto Burle Marx
   genannt. Vgl. Oscar Niemeyer: „Cidade marina";
   in: *Módulo*, Nr. 18, 1960.
10 Oscar Niemeyer in einem Interview mit Alexander Fils
   im September 1984 in Rio de Janeiro; in: Alexander Fils (Hrsg.):
   Brasília – Moderne Architektur in Brasilien, Düsseldorf 1988,
   S. 138.
11 Ebda.
12 Oscar Niemeyer: „Die Einheit des Stadtbildes";
   in: *Módulo*, Nr. 12, 1959, o. S.
13 Oscar Niemeyer in einem Gespräch mit dem Verf. am 9.10.2002
   in Rio de Janeiro.
14 Über Oscar Niemeyers Vision der „Stadt der Zukunft" berichtete
   die Zeitschrift *Fatos & Fotos* in ihrer Märzausgabe von 1966.
15 Oscar Niemeyer in einem Gespräch mit dem Verf.
   am 9.10.2002 in Rio de Janeiro.
16 Oscar Niemeyer: „Omercado de trabalho"; in: *Módulo*,
   Nr. 54, 1979; deutsch in: Alexander Fils (Hrsg.): Oscar Niemeyer –
   Selbstdarstellung Kritiken Oeuvre. Münsterschwarzach 1982,
   S. 74.
17 Oscar Niemeyer in einem Gespräch mit dem Verf.
   am 9.10.2002 in Rio de Janeiro.

9 The project Marina City was developed in 1955 or 1956
   by the Colonizadora Agrícola e Urbanizadora, S. A. company
   for a location near to that where Brasília was later built.
   Oscar Niemeyer was named architect and Roberto Burle Marx
   was the landscape designer. See Oscar Niemeyer: "Cidade marina,"
   in: *Módulo*, no. 18, 1960.
10 Oscar Niemeyer in an interview with Alexander Fils in September,
   1984, in Rio de Janeiro; in: Alexander Fils (ed.): "Brasília –
   Moderne Architektur in Brasilien," Düsseldorf, 1988, p. 138.
11 Ibid.
12 Oscar Niemeyer: "Die Einheit des Stadtbildes,"
   in: *Módulo*, no. 12, 1959.
13 Oscar Niemeyer in conversation with the author on
   October 9, 2002 in Rio de Janeiro.
14 The magazine *Fatos & Fotos* reported on Oscar Niemeyer's
   vision of the "city of the future" in its edition of March, 1966.
15 Oscar Niemeyer in conversation with the author in Rio de Janeiro
   on October 9, 2002.
16 Oscar Niemeyer: "Omercado de trabalho,"
   in: *Módulo*, no. 54, 1979.
17 Oscar Niemeyer in conversation with the author in Rio de Janeiro
   on October 9, 2002.

Integration von Architektur und Ingenieurwissenschaft im Werk Oscar Niemeyers
The integration between architecture and structure in Oscar Niemeyer's work

José Carlos Süssekind

Die Kuppel des Pantheons in Rom, das vor zwei-
tausend Jahren aus Mauerwerk aus nebeneinander
gesetzten Steinblöcken errichtet wurde, und die
lichten Weiten der Hauptsäle des noch im Spätmittel-
alter gebauten Dogenpalastes, die – ungeachtet
der mangelnden mathematischen und physikalischen
Grundlagen – mit Holzfachwerk gemeistert wurden,
sind vortreffliche Beispiele für die Entwicklung der
Ingenieurwissenschaft im Sinne des Eingehens auf
architektonische Bedürfnisse. Es gibt daher keinen
Grund zu bestreiten, dass sich die Ingenieurwissenschaft, ausgehend von Impulsen der Architektur, im
Laufe der Zeit weiterentwickelt, stets auf der Suche
nach größeren freien Räumen und neuen, schöpferi-
schen Lösungen. Wenn der Architekt Wagnisse
eingeht, werden neue Baustoffe und Bausysteme
erprobt und studiert, bis sie schließlich universell
und allgemein üblich werden.

Mit dem Pampulha-Projekt bricht Oscar Niemeyer
in den vierziger Jahren mit dem diktatorischen Charakter des Funktionalismus zugunsten von Schönheit
und Harmonie der geschwungenen, asymmetrischen
Formen und verhilft so der Ingenieurwissenschaft
zu wachsender Wertschätzung, indem er darauf hin-
arbeitet, die Konstruktion vollständig sichtbar zu
machen, ihre Eigenarten und Nuancen zu nutzen und
sie mit dem Ganzen in Einklang zu bringen. Die zylin-
drischen Schalen, die die San-Franziskus-Kirche
bedecken, und die Seitendächer, die die Gelände-
form aufnehmen, heben sich vollständig ab und
stellen Grundelemente in der Schönheit und Ausge-
wogenheit des Ganzen dar. Von dieser Linie entfernt
sich der Architekt nie mehr. Wer wäre in der Lage,
wenig mehr als zehn Jahre später beim Betrachten
der Kathedrale von Brasília zu trennen, was Architektur und was Konstruktion ist, in einem Entwurf,
der die Synthese der Weltarchitektur im 20. Jahrhundert darstellt?

Der von der Architektur eingenommenen Haltung,
die Konstruktion aufzuwerten, entspricht die Haltung
der Ingenieurwissenschaft, die architektonische
Schöpfung zu ermöglichen. Die grundsätzliche Ten-
denz bei den Ingenieuren, unter dem Vorwand
der Kostenminimierung, alles, was neu und gewagt –
alles, was sich den traditionellen Regeln entzieht –

The dome of the Pantheon in Rome, erected two
thousand years ago, in rubblework, the blocks
juxtaposed one to another, and the main spans in
the Doges' Palace, built during the Middle Ages,
despite the basic lack of mathematical and physical
knowledge for static, surmounted by wooden
trusses: both are admirable examples of evolution
of the engineering that was necessary to fulfill the
demands of architecture. It is, therefore, impossible
to deny that engineering has progressed and improv-
ed over the course of times starting from impulses
generated by architecture, always in search of the
largest span and new and creative solutions. It is
when the architect knows to be bold that new materials and new constructive systems are tested and
studied, assuming universal domain and current use.

In the forties, Oscar Niemeyer – the project was
Pampulha – breaks the dictatorial character of functionalism and favors the beauty of curved and
asymmetric forms, bringing to engineering its appre-
ciation of the crescent, acting in order to totally
exhibit the structure, making the best of its proper-
ties and nuances, bringing it in harmony with the
whole. The cylindrical shells that cover the church
of Saint Francis and the marquees that accompany
the shape of the ground are entirely detached and,
no doubt, essential to the beauty and the balance
of the ensemble. The Architect will never abandon
this course of action. A little more than a decade
afterwards, when contemplating the Cathedral of
Brasília, one asks: Who is able to separate architecture from structure in this emblematic project that
synthesizes the architecture of the twentieth
century?

To the attitude adopted by architecture of valorizing
the structure, corresponds a similar one adopted
by engineering of making feasible the architectonical
creation. The engineers' tendency, under the pre-
tence of reducing costs, to condemn everything that
was new and audacious, everything that abandoned
the traditional precepts, was interrupted little by little,
when it stopped being a heresy to accept those
innovations a plastic architectonic form demanded:
columns intensely reinforced at the base (1958
façades of the Palaces of Alvorada, Planalto and

zu verurteilen, wurde durchbrochen, als es nicht länger einer „Ketzerei" gleichkam, jene Innovationen zu verwenden, derer eine plastische architektonische Form bedurfte: stark armierte Stützen (1958 Fassade des Palácio da Alvorada, des Palácio do Planalto und des Obersten Gerichtshofes, Brasília), Aufhängungen (1968 Verlagsgebäude Mondadori, Mailand) Auskragungen von 25 Metern und Spannweiten von 50 Metern (1969 Universität Constantine, Algerien).

Die Entwicklung von Niemeyers Werk war stets eng mit dem Fortschritt der Stahlbetontechnik verknüpft. Kein anderer Baustoff sollte ihm so viel Freiheit geben – eine Freiheit, die zu der wachsenden Kühnheit der Konstruktion hinzukam. Anfang der fünfziger Jahre kam der Spannbeton in Brasilien auf, ab Mitte der sechziger Jahre fand er in steigendem Maße in den Projekten Oscar Niemeyers Verwendung. Und weil wir es verstanden, das ganze Potential des Betons zu nutzen und die Grenzen zu suchen, die die Schöpfung Oscar Niemeyers oftmals auferlegt, konnten wir in den Bereichen Entwurf und Ausführung als Land international eine herausragende Stellung einnehmen. In die Geschichte eingegangen ist das Beispiel der Universität Constantine (Algerien), die Ende der sechziger Jahre unter französischen Fachleuten als konstruktiv und baulich undurchführbar galt und die ausgehend von dem Wissen und der Erfahrung der Brasilianer ohne Probleme geplant und gebaut worden ist.

Die Persönlichkeit des Künstlers Oscar Niemeyer zeigt sich bei der Zusammenarbeit mit dem Ingenieur im Prozess der Schöpfung. Niemeyer legt seine ersten Skizzen vor, erläutert, wie Form und Raum im Einzelfall für die Architektur wichtig sind. Die Unterhaltung geht plötzlich mit der Suche nach der konstruktiven Entscheidung weiter und dann folgt die vorläufige Festlegung der Grunddimensionen. Sehr beeindruckend ist, dass diese Gespräche, auch bei großen Projekten, kaum länger als eine Stunde dauern und dass sich in der überwiegenden Zahl der Fälle die in den ersten Skizzen des Architekten versuchsweise angenommenen Proportionen am Ende als diejenigen herausstellen, die technisch am ehesten zu empfehlen sind – ein instinktiver, ungewöhnlicher ästhetischer Sinn dafür, was die Konstruktion braucht.

In den wenigen Situationen, in denen eine Anpassung des ursprünglichen Konzepts notwendig wird, ist es immer spannend, den Reichtum an Alternativen zu sehen, die der Architekt dem Ingenieur in kürzester Zeit vorlegt. Selbst die komplexesten Aufgaben, mit denen ich zu tun hatte – darunter insbesondere das Museu de Brasília und das Kongresszentrum in Rio, die beide noch

Supreme Court, Brasília), suspensions (1968 Mondadori publishing head office – Milan), cantilevers of 25 meters and spans of 50 meters (1969 University of Constantine – Algeria).

The development of Niemeyer's work has always been closely related to the advances in the technology of reinforced concrete. No other material will give him so much freedom in the moment of creation – freedom that increases with the structural audacity of the crescent. In the beginning of the 1950s prestressed concrete was used in Brazil, from the middle sixties onwards it became more and more present in the projects of Oscar Niemeyer. Because we knew how to take full advantage of the potential of concrete, in search of the limits that Oscar Niemeyer's creation often imposes, we obtained international distinction, as a country, in the fields of project and construction. History is the example of the University of Constantine (Algeria), that was considered, by the end of the 1960s, structurally and constructively unfeasible by French technicians and that was projected and built, without any difficulty whatsoever, due to the knowledge and the experience of Brazilian professionals.

The personality of the artist Oscar Niemeyer becomes exposed in the course of the creative process, when he works together with the engineer. Niemeyer presents his first sketches, explains how structure and space are important in that case for architecture. The conversation proceeds, directly, towards the definition of the structural choice, followed by the first proposal of the basic dimensions. The most fascinating is that these conversations seldom last more than one hour, even when the project is very complex, and, very often, the proportions suggested in the first sketches of the architect, in the end, prove to be the more advisable, technically speaking – a rare instinctive aesthetic feeling of what the structure needs.

In the few occasions when it is necessary to make some adaptations to the original project, it is fascinating to see the variety of alternatives that the architect quickly presents to the engineer. Even in the most complex cases in which I was involved – and I point out the Museu de Brasília and the Convention Center in Rio, both yet to be built – we needed no more than 5 or 6 meetings to come to a final decision.

The Memorial da América Latina (which possesses the largest free span in the world) was completely detailed in one Saturday! The interaction with Niemeyer is a clear, agile process, without any

ausgeführt werden sollen –, haben im Lauf der Zeit nicht mehr als fünf bis sechs Gesprächssitzungen erfordert, bis wir die endgültige Definition hatten.

Das Memorial da América Latina (das die größte Spannweite der Welt hat) wurde – ganz Oscar Niemeyer – an einem einzigen Samstag definiert! Die Interaktion mit Niemeyer ist ein klarer, sehr flinker Prozess – ohne Zweifel und unbeschwert, selbst im Moment der Schöpfung.

Auf genau diese Weise entstanden die hier aufgeführten und im Einzelnen beschriebenen Beispiele klarer konstruktiver Lösungen, die alle Einfachheit des Konzepts mit Grandiosität im Maßstab verbinden. Dank der Entwürfe, dem Traum und der Kühnheit Oscar Niemeyers werden daher zukünftige Epochen – so wie im Fall der Pyramiden in Ägypten, des Pantheons und des Dogenpalasts in Italien – im Brasilien des 20. Jahrhunderts eine Zivilisation anerkennen, die in der Lage war, ausgehend von den Impulsen des wichtigsten Architekten jenes Jahrhunderts, die größten Spannweiten und freien Räume der Welt zu planen und auszuführen.

Die anfänglichen Lösungen (1937–1963)

Die erste Phase im Werk Oscar Niemeyers zeigt die Einführung der Krümmung und die Suche nach zunehmender Eleganz sowohl in den Deckenplatten als auch in den Stützen, und dies auch bei der klassischen konstruktiven Lösung Betonplatte-Träger-Stütze oder Betonplatte-Stütze aus Stahlbeton und insbesondere in den Kuppeln – Pampulha (Belo Horizonte), Ibirapuera Park (São Paulo).

Die am Vordach der Casa do Baile (1940) beobachteten Ergebnisse erreichen in seiner Casa das Canoas (1953) wahrhaft lyrische Aspekte und gelangen zum Kulminationspunkt in den Palastbauten von Brasília (1958–1960). In diesen letzten hat Niemeyer – nebst der Eleganz der Deckenplatten – für die Fassaden (Stützen der Dachplatte) Säulen geschaffen, deren Formen (Palácio do Planalto, Palácio da Alvorada und Oberster Gerichtshof) zu Wahrzeichen der neuen Hauptstadt wurden.

Die außergewöhnliche Wirkung der Säulen wird noch dadurch verstärkt, dass sie alle an den Auflagepunkten (wo sie Dach und Boden berühren) absichtlich extrem verringerte Dimensionen haben und so das Gefühl suggerieren, dass sie sich auf einen Auflagerpunkt reduzieren. In diesen extrem reduzierten Querschnitten sind die Teile so stark bewehrt, dass man die Anekdote erzählt, der Statiker habe empfohlen, so viele Stahlbewehrungen wie nur möglich einzubauen und danach den Querschnitt mit Beton auszufüllen.

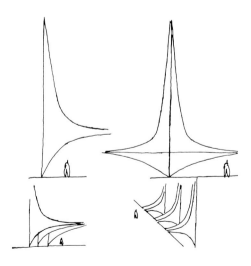

Säulen für die Regierungspaläste in Brasília. Zeichnung um 1958.

Columns for the Government Palace buildings in Brasília. Sketch, approx. 1958.

doubt or suffering even during the moment of creation.

It was exactly like this that the examples of clear structural solutions detached and detailed below sprang, always adding a moving conceptual simplicity to the magnificence of scale. Thanks to the design, the dream and the audacity of Oscar Niemeyer, the future times will recognize – as the Pyramids are to Egypt and the Pantheon and the Doges' Palace are to Italy – in Brazil, in the twentieth century, a civilization capable of conceiving and executing the largest free spans in the world, based on the creations of the most important architect of the century.

The first solutions (1937–1963)

The first phase of Oscar Niemeyer's work shows that, even upon the classical structural solution: slab-beam-column or slab-column in reinforced concrete and, especially, in the domes – Pampulha (Belo Horizonte), Ibirapuera Park (São Paulo) – he introduces the curved line and looks for the slenderness of the forms, both in slabs, beams and columns.

The results already observed in the marquee of the Casa do Baile (1940) attain a pure lyricism in Casa das Canoas (1953) and reach their culmination in the Palaces in Brasília (1958–1960). In the latter, along with the slenderness of the slabs, Niemeyer created for the façades (supports of the ceiling slab) the columns that became a trademark of the New Capital (Planalto, Alvorada, Supreme Court).

The extraordinary effect of the columns is enhanced by their extremely reduced dimensions in the sections of support (when they touch the ceiling and the ground), which all of them have in common, giving the impression that they are simply a point of support. In these limit-sections, the pieces are so intensely reinforced that there is a joke about the structural engineer that recommended the placement of as many steel bars as possible and, after that, had the section filled with concrete.

All the projects of this phase, that brought fame and recognition to Oscar Niemeyer throughout the world, arise of the structural boldness of Joaquim Cardozo. [1]

Brasília is a permanent reminder of his extraordinary talent and inventive mind, open to creation and poetry. When visiting the city, Nervi – the most important Italian engineer of that time – stood in front of the mezzanine of the Itamaraty Palace and confessed: "I designed a three-kilometer bridge, but I'm sure that to build a slab as thin as this one must be much harder."

Alle Entwürfe dieser Phase, die Oscar Niemeyer seither weltweit Bedeutung und Anerkennung gebracht haben, entspringen der konstruktiven Kühnheit Joaquim Cardozos.[1]

Brasília ist eine dauernde Ausstellung seines außerordentlichen, für Schöpfung und Poesie offenen Talents und Erfindergeists. Bei seinem Besuch der Hauptstadt hat Nervi, der bedeutendste italienische Ingenieur des 20. Jahrhunderts, vor dem Mezzanin des Palasts von Itamaraty erklärt: „Ich habe eine 3 Kilometer lange Brücke geplant, doch diese Plattenstärke hinzubekommen, erscheint mir auf jeden Fall um ein Vielfaches schwieriger."

Die Kathedrale (1959)

Die Kathedrale Brasílias ist die Synthese der Interaktion von Architektur und Konstruktion. Sie ist so überraschend einfach, dass die Frage angebracht ist, warum sie sich nicht jemand schon früher ausgedacht hat.

Konstruktiv besteht sie aus einem einzigen isostatischen Teil, der gekrümmten Rippe, die sich aus dem Boden in Richtung Himmel erhebt, was sich in einer Symmetrie der Drehung sechzehnmal wiederholt. Diese sechzehn Rippen halten sich gegenseitig im Gleichgewicht, indem sie durch den die Kathedrale bedeckenden, oberen Ring horizontal zusammengehalten werden. Es ist fast unbegreiflich, doch sechzehn sich wiederholende Teile stellen die Konstruktion und zusammen mit den Fenstern die Architektur der Kathedrale dar.

Dieses Bauwerk ist zweifelsohne ein höchster Augenblick der menschlichen Schöpfung, ein immerwährendes Monument für die Stahlbetontechnik und ein bedeutendes Vermächtnis des Gespanns Niemeyer – Cardozo.

Im Dach verankerte Lösungen (1968–1998)

Die Spannbetontechnik, bereits an sich an die Möglichkeit der Ausführung von Beton mit größerer Druckfestigkeit gekoppelt (die Möglichkeiten verbesserten sich zunehmend von 22 MPa in den sechziger Jahren bis etwa 50 MPa Ende der neunziger Jahre[2]), verringerte das Eigengewicht der Konstruktion und ermöglichte Gegendurchbiegungen, die durch die Spannung der Spannkabel sichergestellt wurden, und ebnete somit den Weg bei der Suche nach immer größeren freien Räumen und immer offeneren Pilotis.

Dies regte den Architekten an, eine Reihe von endgültigen Entwürfen hervorzubringen, angefangen bei dem Verlagsgebäude Mondadori (Mailand, 1968) bis hin zum Museu de Brasília (letzte Version im Jahr 1996), Kulmination und Höhepunkt dessen, was der

→ p. 109

Kathedrale von Brasilia.
Bauphase.

Cathedral of Brasilia.
Under construction.

The cathedral (1959)

The Cathedral of Brasília is the synthesis of the interaction between architecture and structure. It is so surprisingly simple that the obvious question is: Why had it not been thought before?

Structurally, it has only one piece that is, isostatic – the curved rib that rises from the ground towards the sky – that repeats itself 16 times in symmetry of revolution. These 16 ribs equilibrate one another when they are linked horizontally through the upper ring that covers the Cathedral. It is almost unconceivable, but 16 pieces that repeat themselves form the structure and, together with the stained glass work, the architecture of the Cathedral.

This building is, undoubtedly, a magical moment of human creation, an eternal moment for the technology of reinforced concrete and a unique legacy of the Niemeyer-Cardozo partnership.

The solutions suspended to the ceiling structure (1968–1998)

The technology of prestressed concrete already hooked up to the possibility of the execution of concrete with higher compression resistance (such was progressively feasible, from 22 MPa in the sixties to around 50 MPa by the end of the nineties),[2] reduced the weight of the structure itself and allowed to compensate for deflections through the use of prestressed cables (in opposition to the effects of gravity), opening the way for larger free spaces.

In consequence, the architect beginning to speculate, creating a number of definitive projects, starting with the Mondadori publishing head office (Milan, 1968) and concluding with the Museu de Brasília (last version in 1996), that represents the highest point reached by concrete – a building with 70-meter cantilevers without supports!

The Mondadori publishing head office has its main structure supported by 2 longitudinal façades in arches that sustain the 24-meter reinforced concrete transversal span of the ceiling level, to which the five office floors are suspended, leaving the ground floor entirely free and open.

The FATA Head Office (Turin, 1975) with a structure that has a conception similar to that of the Mondadori building – with the difference of being totally built in concrete – surmounted in transversal by an easy width of 12.5 meters, which is achieved with prefabricated parts. They are supported by both concrete longitudinal facades at the place where the load is carried by the roof supports, which is an especially successful structural and constructive

Verlagsgebäude Mondadori.
Zeichnung mit Aufriss und
Querschnitt um 1968.

Mondadori Publishing
Company building. Sketch
with elevation and cross-
section, approx. 1968.

Beton erreichen konnte – nämlich ein Gebäude mit
70 Meter langen Auskragungen ohne Stützen!

Das Verlagsgebäude Mondadori hat als Hauptkonstruktion Fassaden mit Bögen, welche die Stahl-
betonträger des Dachs tragen und in Querrichtung
eine lichte Weite von 24,3 Metern überwinden. Daran
aufgehängt sind die fünf Bürogeschosse, wobei
das Erdgeschoss völlig frei und offen gelassen wird.

→ S. 109

Das FATA-Verwaltungsgebäude (Turin, 1975) dessen
Konstruktion in der Konzeption mit dem Mondadori-
Gebäude sehr große Ähnlichkeit hat – mit dem Unterschied, dass es ganz aus Beton ist –, überwindet
in Querrichtung eine lichte Weite von 12,5 Metern,
die mit Fertigteilen erzielt wird. Sie wird von den
beiden vor Ort betonierten Längsfassaden getragen,
wo die Last an den Trägern des Dachs aufgehängt
ist, die in einem besonders glücklichen konstruktiven Entwurf des Italieners Riccardo Morandi[3] die
Auskragung von 20 Metern bewirken.

Mit wachsender Kühnheit hält Niemeyer an der Idee
der am Dach aufgehängten Gebäude fest, verändert
sie jedoch zu weiten Auskragungen, indem er vor-
schlägt, sie lediglich auf Mittelpfeilern abzustützen
(im Gegensatz zur Abstützung auf Fassaden bei den
Entwürfen Mondadori und FATA), und befreit die
Ebene der Pilotis noch radikaler. Beispiele für diese
Entwurfslinie sind unter anderem:

→ p. 54

– Das Museu da Terra (Brasília, 1971), nicht ver-
wirklicht – die Form erinnert an eine umgekehrt
aufgehängte aztekische Pyramide, deren Dach mit
quadratischem Grundriss (100 m x 100 m) sich auf
zwei zentrale Säulen (jeweils 2,5 m x 10 m) stützt
und aus einem 6 Meter hohen Gitter aus Spannbeton besteht, an dem die fünf unteren Ebenen des
Museums aufgehängt sind (ein Europäer hat damals
eine Höhe von 7 Metern vorgeschlagen, Niemeyer
jedoch „wusste, dass er bei seiner Rückkehr nach
Brasilien von den brasilianischen Technikern eine
Lösung mit 6 Metern bekommen würde").

– Das ursprünglich von Nervi als Metallkonstruktion
vorgeschlagene Centro Musical do Rio (1972),
dessen radikale Veränderung im Lauf der Zeit zu dem
komplett in Beton gehaltenen Entwurf des Museu
de Brasília (1996) mit frei schwingenden Baukörpern
von 70 Metern führte. Jahre später sagte der große
italienische Meister, als er einmal auf die Kühnheit des Entwurfs angesprochen wurde, im Scherz
zu Niemeyer: „Sie hätten zehn Jahre früher
kommen müssen…".

conception of the Italian architect Ricardo Morandi,[3]
resulting in 20-meter cantilevers.

Acting even more boldly, Niemeyer maintains
the idea of the buildings suspended to the ceiling,
but converts them into large cantilevers by pro-
posing that they rest only on central pillars (instead
of the façades as in the Mondadori and the FATA),
liberating even more radically the floor level. Some
examples of this line of creation are listed below.

– The Museu da Terra (Brasília, 1971), not built –
its form is reminiscent of a suspended and inverted
Aztec pyramid – with a square plan ceiling (100 m x
100 m) resting on two central columns (2,5 m x
10 m each) consisting of a 6 meter high grill of prestressed concrete, from which hang the five lower
levels of the museum (a European proposed, at
the time, a height of 7 meters, but Niemeyer "knew
that, when he returned to Brazil, he would obtain
a solution for 6 meters from Brazilian technicians").

– The Music Center of Rio (1972) was initially
proposed by Nervi in steel structure, but its radical
evolution in the course of time led to the project
of the Museu de Brasília (1996), with 70-meter free-
swinging cantilevers. The great Italian master, already
advanced in years, when consulted about the
project, grasping its boldness, declared playfully to
Niemeyer: "You should have come ten years ago…".

– The Parlamento Latino Americano (São Paulo,
1992), with a diameter of 42 meters, where the four
lower mezzanines and the dome of the auditorium
are suspended to the radial beam system that con-
stitute its ceiling, supported along the circular
periphery.

Algeria (1969–1979)
The importance of the projects of the Universities
of Constantine and Alger greatly surpasses the
circumstance that Brazilian engineers were responsible for the calculations and construction manage-
ment for the construction of these buildings.

With the projects of Oscar Niemeyer, Brazilian engineers built structures that were considered impossible by French consultants. In a larger economic
level, this circumstance meant a progressive opening
and recognition in the international market for
Brazilian construction companies, which are now
at work in various continents. One of the pioneers
was Marco Paulo Rabello,[4] who accepted the
Algerian challenge, in the same way that, a decade
before, he had become the main builder of Brasília.

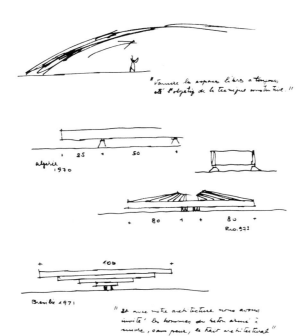

→ S. 54

→ p. 107

→ S. 107

Skizze mit den Spannweiten
diverser Projekte.

Sketch with the spans
of different projects.

– Das Parlamento Latino-Americano (São Paulo,
1992) hat einen Durchmesser von 42 Metern, wo die
vier unteren Zwischengeschosse und die Kuppel
des Auditoriums an den radialen Trägern aufgehängt
sind, die sein Dach bilden und entlang des kreis-
förmigen Umfangs aufliegen.

Algerien (1969–1979)
Die Bedeutung der Entwürfe der Universitäten von
Constantine und Algier geht bei weitem über den
Umstand hinaus, dass brasilianische Ingenieure
für die Berechnung und Bauleitung dieser Projekte
verantwortlich waren.

Mit den Entwürfen Oscar Niemeyers realisierten brasilianische Ingenieure Bauten, die bei französischen
Technikern als nicht durchführbar galten. Auf um-
fassenderer wirtschaftlicher Ebene bedeutete dieser
Umstand Öffnung und wachsende Anerkennung
auf dem internationalen Markt für unsere Bauunternehmen, die heute auf verschiedenen Kontinenten
tätig sind. Einer der Pioniere war Marco Paulo
Rabello,[4] der die algerische Herausforderung an-
nahm, so, wie er zehn Jahre zuvor zum wichtigsten
Erbauer Brasílias geworden war.

Die Universität Constantine (1969) umfasst die konstruktiv kühnsten Entwürfe. Die Kühnheit beginnt
bei dem Verwaltungsgebäude und gipfelt in zwei ein-
zigartigen Bauten, die selbst 25 Jahre nach ihrer
Fertigstellung in Staunen versetzen. Der Hörsaalblock
ist auf Pilotis aufgeständert. Seine Hauptkonstruktion
(Längskonstruktion) besteht aus 6 Meter hohen
Wandträgern aus Spannbeton in den Fassaden,
die Auskragungen von 25 Metern und Spannweiten
von 50 Metern überwinden (ihre Breite beträgt

The University of Constantine (1969) has the most
structurally audacious projects. This audacity begins
with the building of the administration building
and reaches its climax with two unique and amazing
structures, that continue to be so 25 years after
their conclusion. The lecture room block is built on
pilotis. Its main structure (longitudinal) is composed
by 6-meter-high, prestressed, wall-beams in the
façades (they are 30 centimeters thick, instead of
the 150 centimeters asked by the French) that sur-
mount 25-meter-cantilevers and 50-meter-spans. The
secondary 20-meter-spans (transversal) were surmounted by prefabricated beams in the shape of a T.

The Auditorium, in reinforced concrete, is defined
by two cylindrical and inclined half-shells (two
slopes), that are a world record in their kind. The half-
shells lean, in one extremity, on the foundation, and,
in the other, on a porch surmounting a 60-meter
free span and receiving a panel of weight of approxi-
mately 50 meters. The beam of the porch is inverted
and visible, 3,5 meters high, which results in a special plastic elegance, that fits exactly with the
structural logic. The covered area surpasses 4,000
square meters, without any internal support. As
a matter of fact, it is a structural conception in some
ways similar to that of the Library of the Memorial
da América Latina, conceived 20 years afterwards.

It is important to point out, also, that the Algerian
projects played an important role on the efficient
transference of knowledge and team work necessary
for the accomplishment of such daring projects:
Brazilian engineers and foremen and an impressive
number of Algerian workers, foremen and engineers,
apparently inexperienced in response to such a

Universität von Constantine,
Algerien. Auditorium.
Zeichnung 1970.

University of Constantine,
Algeria. Auditorium.
Sketch 1970.

30 Zentimeter im Gegensatz zu den 150 Zentimetern, die von den französischen Fachleuten als Mindestmaß gefordert wurden). Die sekundären Spannweiten von 20 Metern (in Querrichtung) wurden durch vorgefertigte T-Balken gemeistert.

Das Auditorium aus Stahlbeton ist durch zwei zylindrische Halbschalen definiert und stellt in seiner Art einen Weltrekord dar. Die Halbschalen stützen sich an einem Ende auf das Fundament und am anderen Ende auf einen Säulengang; sie überwinden eine Spannweite von 60 Metern und nehmen ein Lastfeld von praktisch 50 Metern auf. Der Träger des Säulengangs ist umgekehrt, sichtbar und ist 3,5 Meter hoch, was eine besondere plastische Eleganz bewirkt, die genau zur konstruktiven Logik passt. Die überdachte Fläche ist größer als 4000 m² und hat keinerlei innere Stütze. Im Übrigen handelt es sich um einen konstruktiven Entwurf, der in gewisser Weise demjenigen ähnelt, der zwanzig Jahre später für die Bibliothek des Memorial da América Latina entstand.

Besonders hervorzuheben bei den algerischen Projekten ist außerdem die effiziente Weitergabe von Wissen und die Zusammenarbeit bei der Ausführung solch kühner Bauwerke zwischen brasilianischen Ingenieuren und Baumeistern und einer großen Zahl algerischer Arbeiter – Baumeister und Ingenieure, denen offensichtlich die Erfahrung für eine solche Herausforderung fehlte, die jedoch – vielleicht durch diese angespornt – zu einer beachtlichen Leistung fähig waren.

→ p.55

→ p.56

Memorial da América Latina (1987)

Die Hauptkonstruktionen des Memorial da América Latina (São Paulo) stellen eines der herausragendsten Beispiele für die Interaktion zwischen Architektur und Ingenieurwissenschaft und auch einen Weltrekord dar. Wir haben hier ein und denselben konstruktiven Diskurs für die drei bedeutendsten Bauten, nämlich gerade Träger mit großer Spannweite, welche die von gekrümmten, nicht symmetrischen Schalen übertragene Last aufnehmen. Alles eigentlich recht einfach in der Konzeption und ausdrucksstark in den Dimensionen.

→ p.57

Konstruktive Merkmale: Die 90 Meter lange Spannweite der Bibliothek (größte Gebäudespannweite der Welt) wurde von einem 6,5 Meter hohen Hohlbetonträger (Festigkeit 32 MPa) mit trapezförmigem Querschnitt überwunden, dessen Hauptbewehrung aus 22 Kabeln mit 19 jeweils 15,2 Millimeter starken Drähten (Spannkraft in einer Größenordnung von 70.000 kN![5]) besteht und der an den äußeren Stützpfeilern, welche die asymmetrische Last der raumbegrenzenden gewölbten Dächer aufnehmen, einen Säulengang andeutet.

→ S.55

→ p.132

challenge, but who, perhaps stimulated by it, were capable of a surprising performance.

Memorial da América Latina (1987)

The main structures of the Memorial da América Latina (São Paulo) are one of the most remarkable examples of the interaction between architecture and engineering, which, by the way, resulted in a world record. In them, we have the same structural discourse for the three most important constructions: straight beams of large span, receiving the load transmitted by non-symmetric curved shells; everything really very simple in concept and expressively grand in scale.

Detailing, the 90-meter free span of the library (the largest free-span beam in the world inside a building) was surmounted by a hollow concrete beam (32 MPa resistance), of trapezoid section, 6,5 meters high, prestressed through 22 cables with 19 cordages of 15,2 millimeters each (prestressing force of about 70.000 kN![5]) and creating a slight porch-effect together with the extreme support pillars, that receive the load of the curved ceilings that circumscribe the space.

The celebration hall emphasizes the impressive height of the space created and reminds one of the main aisle of many cathedrals. Its ceiling is defined by a half-shell leaning, in one of the ends, on a 60-meter-span beam, and, in the other, in a vertical wall that descends to the ground. As in the library, the large beam, creating a slight porch-effect together with the extreme support pillars, is hollow, with trapezoid section and 4,5 meters high. It is prestressed through 16 cables with 19 cordages of 15,2 millimeters each. The span of this beam is extremely bold, because, besides receiving the vertical load, it has to sustain an additional loading in the horizontal level, transmitted by the asymmetric shell of the ceiling.

The auditorium completes the set, and is composed of three curved transversal shells. The first of them arises from the foundations and stretches to one wall from which the following shell then emerges, culminating in a main longitudinal girder (40-meter-span). The last shell rests on this – its other end runs right through to the foundation level.

A final oddity: just the passageway that connects the Memorial da América Latina which is divided into two spaces by an avenue, became in the end the one among so many and so daring structural pieces that demanded the most attention. At first it was built with a seemingly quite small span. However incoherent or untenable it proved itself to be, what became evident from the entire constructive design was

→ S. 56

Der Festsaal zeigt die beeindruckende Höhe des geschaffenen Raumes, der an das Hauptschiff vieler Kathedralen erinnert. Sein Dach ist durch eine Halbschale definiert, die sich an einem Ende auf einen Träger von 60 Metern Spannweite und am anderen Ende auf eine bis zum Boden hinabreichende, vertikale Wand stützt. Dem Beispiel der Bibliothek folgend, ist der große Träger, der an den äußersten Stützpfeilern einen Säulengang andeutet, hohl, von trapezförmigem Querschnitt und 4,5 Meter hoch. Seine Hauptbewehrung besteht aus sechzehn Kabeln mit neunzehn jeweils 15,2 Millimeter starken Drähten. Die Spannweite dieses Trägers erweist sich um so kühner, als er neben der Aufnahme der vertikalen Lastenaufnahme die Funktion hat, eine zusätzliche Durchbiegung in horizontaler Ebene abzufangen, die von der Last der asymmetrischen Dachschalen erzeugt wird.

→ S. 57

Vervollständigt wird das Ganze durch das Auditorium, das aus drei gewölbten Querschalen besteht. Die erste erwächst aus den Fundamenten und reicht bis zu einer Wand, aus der die folgende Schale hervorgeht, die in einem Hauptlängsträger (40 Meter Spannweite) endet. Auf diesen stützt sich auch die letzte Schale, die am anderen Ende bis zur Fundamentebene geht.

Eine Kuriosität zum Schluss: Ausgerechnet die

→ S. 132

Fußgängerbrücke, die das durch eine Allee in zwei Areale zerrissene Memorial da América Latina miteinander verbindet, ist inmitten so vieler, kühner Konstruktionen schließlich diejenige gewesen, die die meiste Aufmerksamkeit erforderte. Ursprünglich wurde sie in einer ziemlich kleinen Spannweite gebaut. Im Hinblick auf den konstruktiven Gesamtentwurf erschien die mittlere Stütze, die eine Spannweite von 20 Metern definierte, jedoch inkohärent und unhaltbar. Das veranlasste den Architekten dazu, nach einer Lösung zu suchen, die zwar polemisch war, aber die einzige, die bei der Verteidigung seines Werkes innere Kohärenz und Logik rechtfertigen würde. Daraus entstand, was zu einem der Symbole des Memorial wurde: Die mittlere Stütze wurde weggenommen und durch eine andere außerhalb der Fußgängerbrücke errichtete ersetzt, die an ihrem oberen Ende wie ein Spazierstock einen Bogen beschreibt, so dass die Last des Fußgängerstegs an ihr „hängt", wobei das vorhandene Fundament der entfernten Stütze verwendet wurde. Eine solche Maßnahme hätte die öffentliche Meinung sensibilisieren können, doch Niemeyer zögerte nicht: Er spürte ihre Notwendigkeit, kämpfte dafür, trug das Problem dem Gouverneur des Bundesstaates vor und erhielt von diesem grünes Licht.

the central support, defining a 20-meter span. This led the architect to search for a solution that was admittedly polemic but nevertheless the only solution that would justify the consistency and the internal logic in defense of his work. This was the origin of what became one of the symbols of the memorial: the central support was taken away and substituted for by another situated outside the passageway, in the shape of a cane – with its top curved in order to "suspend" the weight of the passageway – and using the foundation that had been made for the support that was removed. This operation could have been difficult from the perspective of the public opinion, but Niemeyer did not think twice. He felt that it was necessary, fought for it, presented the problem to the state governor and obtained his consent.

The co-workers

The challenge of the larger span, always present along the centuries, multiplied with the advent of the industrial revolution. It started to demand larger and larger open spaces in the factories, stadiums, auditoriums and buildings in general, forcing the engineers to understand the architectural problem and familiarize themselves with reinforced concrete.

Niemeyer, throughout the years, had a very strong interaction with his co-worker engineers listed below, who tried to help him make possible his architecture made of dream and grace, surprise and poetry, curved and straight lines, skill and courage.

Bernard Brezout, Joaquim Cardozo, Bruno Contarini, José Carlos Süssekind, Carlos Alberto Fragelli, José de Moura Villas Boas, Carlos Henrique da Cruz Lima, Marco Paulo Rabello, Elfer Albaneze, Riccardo Morandi, Emilio Baumgart, Rodrigo Coelho de Figueiredo, Fernando Rocha de Souza, Samuel Rawet, François Kozienrovski, Sebastião Brito Neto, Jacques Tricot, Waldyr Gonçalves de Amorim Jr.

1 Joaquim Maria Moreira Cardozo (1897–1978). Architect, engineer and poet who worked together with Niemeyer primarily on building Brasilia. (Note by the editor).
2 MPa = Mega-Pascal, a technical unit used to measure the crushing strength of concrete. (Note by the editor).
3 Ricardo Morandi (1902–1989). Italian civil engineer and architect. (Note by the editor).
4 Marco Paulo Rabello. The engineer responsible for the buildings in Pampulha and various buildings in Brasilia, whom Niemeyer persuaded to join him in Algeria. (Note by the editor).
5 KiloNewton = a unit that describes the forces in an edifice. (Note by the editor).

Die Mitarbeiter

Die durch die Jahrhunderte stets gegenwärtige
Herausforderung immer größerer Spannweiten ver-
vielfachte sich mit der industriellen Revolution.
Sie brachte es mit sich, dass immer größere, freiere
Räume in Fabriken, Stadien, Hörsälen und ganz
allgemein in Gebäuden gefordert wurden, was die
Ingenieure zwang, das architektonische Problem
zu verstehen und sich in wachsendem Maße mit
dem Stahlbeton vertraut zu machen.

Im Laufe der Zeit entstand eine äußerst starke Interaktion zwischen Oscar Niemeyer und den unten
aufgeführten, mit ihm arbeitenden Ingenieuren, die
danach strebten, ihn in der Durchführbarkeit seiner
Architektur, die Traum und Leichtigkeit, Überraschung
und Poesie, Krümmungen und Gerade, Technik
und Mut in sich vereint, zu unterstützen.

Bernard Brezout, Joaquim Cardozo, Bruno Contarini,
José Carlos Süssekind, Carlos Alberto, Fragelli
José de Moura Villas Boas, Carlos Henrique da Cruz
Lima, Marco Paulo Rabello, Elfer Albaneze, Riccardo
Morandi, Emilio Baumgart, Rodrigo Coelho de
Figueiredo, Fernando Rocha de Souza, Samuel
Rawet, François Kozienrovski, Sebastião Brito Neto,
Jacques Tricot, Waldyr Gonçalves de Amorim Jr.

1 Joaquim Maria Moreira Cardozo (1897–1978). Architekt,
   Ingenieur und Dichter, der mit Niemeyer v.a. bei der Konstruktion
   von Brasilia zusammengearbeitet hat (A.d.Hg.).
2 MPa = Megapascal – eine technische Größeneinheit,
   um die Widerstandsfähigkeit des Betons zu messen (A.d.Hg.).
3 Riccardo Morandi (1902–1989). Italien. Ingenieur und Architekt.
4 Marco Paulo Rabello. Ingenieur der Bauten von Pampulha
   und verschiedener Gebäude in Brasilia, den Niemeyer nach
   Algerien holte (A.d.Hg.).
5 kN = KiloNewton = Größeneinheit, um die Kräfte in der Struktur
   zu messen (A.d.Hg.).

← ←
Parlamento Latino-Americano,
São Paulo. Ansicht von den
umlaufenden Büroetagen auf
die Kuppel des Sitzungssaals.

Parliament of Latin-America,
São Paulo. View from the
surrounding office floors of
the dome of the assembly hall.

← ←
Memorial da América Latina.
São Paulo. Bibliothek. Innen-
ansicht des Lesesaals.

Memorial of Latin America,
São Paulo. Library. Interior
of the reading room.

←
Innenansicht des Festsaals.

Interior of the assembly hall.

←
Innenansicht der Bibliothek.

Interior of the library.

Oscar Niemeyer und Deutschland. Die Rezeption in der DDR
Oscar Niemeyer and Germany. Responses in East Germany

Elmar Kossel

„Brasilien ist ein aufstrebendes Land, und trotz aller gerade in Kolonialländern ängstlich gehüteten Traditionen entsteht hier mit gewaltiger Kraft Neues, von dessen Maßstab wir Europäer uns kaum Vorstellungen zu machen vermögen. [...] Mögen auch manchmal ganz gewiss europäische Einflüsse nachzuweisen sein (besonders von Le Corbusier), so beginnt sich doch durchaus nicht nur Eigenständiges zu entwickeln, sondern sogar auf Europa zurückzuwirken." [1]

So war es 1956 in einem Artikel in der Bauwelt zu lesen. Aktueller Hintergrund war die Internationale Bauausstellung (Interbau) in West-Berlin, an der sich die Rückwirkung des Neuen erstmals deutlich zeigte. Zu den eingeladenen internationalen Architekten gehörte auch der brasilianische Architekt Oscar Niemeyer.

Das achtgeschossige Wohnhochhaus, das Niemeyer im Hansaviertel errichtete, ist ein lang gestreckter Schottenbau, der von V-förmigen Stützen getragen wird. Ein durchgängiges Dachgeschoss schließt die Scheibe nach oben hin ab. Im Osten ist dem Baukörper ein dreieckiger Aufzugsturm beigestellt, der, im Unterschied zum ursprünglichen Entwurf, nicht alle Geschosse versorgt, sondern nur das Dachgeschoss und das Gemeinschaftsgeschoss im fünften Stock, in dem zahlreiche Einrichtungen für die Bewohner, wie etwa ein Kinosaal, Platz finden sollten. So sehr sich Niemeyers Gebäude im Typus unverkennbar an das Vorbild von Le Corbusiers Unité d'habitation in Marseille (1947–1953) anlehnt, unterscheidet es sich jedoch von ihm deutlich in der inneren Organisation und in den Details. Zwar weist auch Niemeyers Bau skulpturale Pilotis, Loggien und die geplanten, wenn auch nie realisierten Gemeinschaftseinrichtungen auf, jedoch werden die Wohnungen nicht über Mittelgänge erschlossen, sondern sind jeweils als Zweispänner einem zentralen Treppenhaus zugeordnet. Insgesamt sechs dieser Wohnungselemente sind hintereinander geschaltet und treten mit ihren jeweils unterschiedlich farbig gefassten Treppenhauskernen im freigestellten Erdgeschoss in Erscheinung, das der Erschließung dient. Die Lasten von jeweils zwei Schottenwänden werden im Erdgeschoss von

"Brazil is a country that aspires to great things and, despite all those traditions that colonial countries guard so very jealously, enormous energy is being dedicated to new things there, and on a scale that we Europeans can hardly begin to imagine. [...] And although European influences are certainly demonstrable (particularly that of Le Corbusier), not only is an independent style definitely beginning to emerge, but this style is even starting to feed back into architecture in Europe." [1]

Thus ran a 1956 article in "Bauwelt", a German architectural journal. The background at the time was an international building exhibition (Interbau) in West Berlin which, for the first time, clearly demonstrated the repercussions this new style was having. The international architects on the guest-list included Brazilian architect Oscar Niemeyer.

The eight-story residential building Niemeyer erected in the Hansa district is a long cross-wall structure with v-shaped supporting pillars, culminating in a top floor that runs the length of the building. To the east, a triangular elevator tower abuts to the body of the building. In contrast to the original design, this tower does not service all stories but only the top floor and the communal story on the fifth floor, intended to house numerous facilities for the residents, such as a movie theater. Admittedly, as a type, Niemeyer's building unmistakably takes its lead from Le Corbusier's Unité d'habitation in Marseille (1947–1953), but its internal layout and its details are nevertheless different. And if Niemeyer's edifice also possesses sculptural pilotis, loggias and communal facilities (whereby the latter were never actually realized), in this case the apartments were not accessed via central corridors, but were instead laid out in sets of two, opening out onto a central staircase. A total of six of these apartment units are arranged one behind the other, each with a different-colored stairwell, easily distinguishable at the open ground-floor level from which they can be accessed. On the ground floor, the load of the two sets of cross-walls is borne by v-shaped supporting pillars. Niemeyer has already used such supporting pillars as a motif before, for example in his Hospital Sul America in Rio de

Wohnhochhaus Interbau, Berlin (West). Luftansicht um 1957.

Interbau apartment block, West Berlin. Aerial view, approx. 1957.

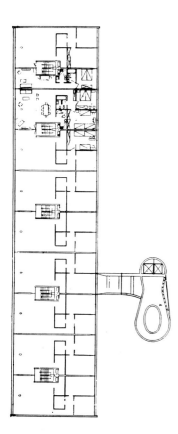

Wohnhochhaus Interbau,
Berlin (West). Grundriss.

Interbau apartment block,
West Berlin. Ground plan.

V-förmigen Stützen abgeleitet. Das Motiv dieser Stützen verwendete Niemeyer unter anderem bereits beim Hospital Sul America in Rio de Janeiro (1952–1959). Gegenüber der Berliner Variante sind die Stützen dort höher, schlanker und rundplastisch gearbeitet. Sie umschließen ein zurückgesetztes verglastes Erdgeschoss, das im Unterschied zum Wohnhaus licht und großzügig wirkt. In Berlin sind die V-Stützen mit prismatischen Kanten versehen und wirken durch den stumpfen Winkel, den sie ausbilden, wie von der Last des Gebäudes niedergedrückt. Die geringe Höhe des Erdgeschosses verstärkt diesen Eindruck zusätzlich. Eine weitere Reminiszenz an Le Corbusier bilden die unregelmäßig verteilten Schlitze des Dachgeschosses, die unverkennbar an die Lichtschlitze der Wallfahrtskapelle Notre-Dame-du-Haute in Ronchamp (1950–1955) erinnern.

Schon während der Vorbereitungen zur Interbau hatten Fachzeitschriften über die Beteiligung Niemeyers berichtet. Einen ersten Höhepunkt bildete dann 1955 der Besuch des Architekten in Berlin, der im Zuge seiner mehrmonatigen Europareise stattfand. Dieser Besuch sollte dazu dienen, seinen Beitrag zur Interbau zu konkretisieren. Die Wertschätzung, einen bedeutenden modernen Architekten gewonnen zu haben, wurde jedoch bereits im Vorfeld von scharfer Polemik begleitet, die vor allem die Abkehr Niemeyers von den strengen kubischen Prinzipien einer funktionalistischen Moderne kritisierte.

So schrieb der Schweizer Künstler Max Bill in seinem Vortragsmanuskript über die brasilianische Architektur bereits ein Jahr zuvor: „[Ich] habe […] fürchterliche Dinge gesehen. Das ist das Ende der Modernen Architektur. Es ist eine antisoziale Verschwendung, ohne Verantwortung […]."[2] Die Reihe der Kritiken in der Bundesrepublik setzte sich durch die sechziger Jahre fort und riss auch in den siebziger Jahren nicht ab. So bezeichnete der Architekt Jürgen Joedicke „eine gewisse Manieriertheit der Formensprache"[3] als ein Charakteristikum von Niemeyers Architektur, und der Kunsthistoriker Heinrich Klotz stufte sie schließlich als Modeerscheinung ein, der „die glatte Welt der Golf- und Tennisclubs […] Pate stand."[4] Die Rezeption in Westdeutschland setzt die Architektur Oscar Niemeyers mit einer manieristischen Phase der Moderne gleich.

Anders im Osten: Während seines Aufenthalts in Berlin hielt „der Meister"[5] – so die zeitgenössische Kritik auf der anderen Seite – einen Vortrag an der Technischen Universität, besuchte Ost-Berlin und traf dabei mehrfach mit Hermann Henselmann, dem damaligen Chefarchitekten Ost-Berlins zusammen, mit dem er freundschaftlich verbunden blieb. Im An-

Janeiro (1952–1959), where the supporting pillars were taller, slimmer and more rounded on all sides than in the Berlin version. They enclosed a recessed glass-plated ground floor that appeared lighter and more spacious than the residential building. In Berlin, the v-shaped supporting pillars have prism-like edges and, given their obtuse angle, appear to have been crushed by the weight of the building, an impression reinforced by the fact that the ground floor is so low. The slits located at irregular intervals along the top floor are another feature reminiscent of Le Corbusier and they invariably call to mind the slats that let in light at the pilgrims' chapel of Notre-Dame-du-Haute in Ronchamp (1950–1955).

Even during the preparations for Interbau, specialist magazines had reported on Niemeyer's involvement. The architect's visit to Berlin in 1955 as part of a several-month-long sojourn in Europe marked an initial highlight. The purpose of this visit was to flesh out the nature of his contribution to Interbau. However, from the outset, satisfaction at having recruited a major modern architect was accompanied by a sharply polemical note, with Niemeyer above all facing criticism for his rejection of the strict Cubist principles of functionalist Modernism.

For example, one year earlier, in his "Report on Brazil", Swiss artist Max Bill had written: "[I] have […] seen dreadful things. This is the end of modern architecture. It is an antisocial waste, lacking responsibility […]."[2] It continued to rain criticism throughout the 1960s and there was not even any let-up in the 1970s. Architect Jürgen Joedicke, for example, detected "a certain Manneristic quality in the formal idiom"[3] as the characteristic of Niemeyer's architecture, and art historian Heinrich Klotz even classified it as a mere fad "inspired by the glib world of golf and tennis clubs."[4] In West Germany, Oscar Niemeyer's architecture was put on a par with one of the more Mannerist phases of modern art.

In the East, things were different. During his stay in Berlin, the man contemporary critics on the other side of the Wall hailed as "the master"[5] held a lecture at the Technical University and visited East Berlin, meeting up several times with Hermann Henselmann, at the time East Berlin's chief architect, with whom he remained on friendly terms. Niemeyer subsequently described Stalinallee in glowing terms: "In East Berlin I visited Stalinallee, a street that without doubt has the air of a great European avenue."[6] Niemeyer's enthusiasm was not necessarily propagated or shared by West German newspapers. Architect Hans Schoszberger describes the situation, closing his comments with the remarks that: "The many reports of the past months really

schluss äußerte sich Niemeyer enthusiastisch über die Stalinallee: „Ich habe in Ost-Berlin die Stalinallee besucht, eine Straße, die ohne Zweifel den Aspekt großer europäischer Avenuen hat."[6] Eine Wertschätzung, die von westdeutschen Zeitungen nicht unbedingt kolportiert und geteilt wurde. Der Architekt Hans Schoszberger schildert diesen Umstand und schließt seine Ausführungen mit der Bemerkung: „Die vielen Meldungen der letzten Monate scheinen tatsächlich zu stimmen, die Sowjetarchitektur ist dabei, eine Drehung um 180 Grad zu machen vom ‚sozialistischen Realismus' zum Funktionalismus."[7]

Die Meldungen stimmten tatsächlich – und die Rezeption Niemeyers in der DDR war weitaus folgenreicher als in der Bundesrepublik, in der sie nur marginal stattfand.[8] Trotz der Tatsache, dass Niemeyer nie in der DDR gebaut hat und sein Beitrag auf der Interbau das einzige in Deutschland realisierte Projekt überhaupt darstellt, wirkte er richtungsweisend für das gesamte Baugeschehen der DDR in den sechziger Jahren.

Brasília in Berlin

Nach dem Ende der neohistoristischen Phase in der Architektur in den fünfziger Jahren und der Durchsetzung der Industrialisierung und Typisierung im Bauwesen der DDR nach Moskauer Vorbild stellte sich die Frage nach der konkreten formalen Ausgestaltung, wenn man so will, nach dem „Stil". Bereits 1954, kurz nach dem Tod Stalins, hatte dessen Nachfolger Nikita Chruschtschow auf der Moskauer „Allunionskonferenz der Bauschaffenden" erklärt, dass „Prunksucht und Manieriertheit dem Wesen der Sowjetarchitektur widersprechen."[9] Unter der Leitlinie „Besser, schneller und billiger bauen" vollzog auch die DDR ab 1955 ihre „Große Wende im Bauwesen" und schwenkte nun ihrerseits um zur Industrialisierung und Standardisierung der Architektur und, damit verbunden, letztlich zurück zur Moderne, an die man bereits 1945–1949 angeknüpft hatte. Ein Vorgang, der aufgrund der kulturpolitischen Kopplung der SBZ/DDR an die Sowjetunion und dem verordneten Neohistorismus stalinistischer Prägung unterbunden wurde.

Mit der Industrialisierung im Bauwesen gingen jedoch zunächst keine weiteren Richtlinien zu Architektur und Städtebau einher. Um stilistisch festzulegen, wie die konkrete Gestalt der sozialistischen Stadt nun auszusehen habe, und um das Eindringen von „formalistischen" Tendenzen zu verhindern, wurde 1960 die XXV. Plenartagung der Bauakademie als „Erste Theoretische Konferenz" eröffnet. Auf der Konferenz wurde vor allem von dem Architekten Hermann Henselmann und dem Architekturkritiker Bruno Flierl eine breite Rezeption internationaler Architektur unter sozialistischen Vorzeichen in

do appear to be true. Soviet architecture is in the process of effecting an about turn, from 'Socialist Realism' to functionalism."[7]

The reports really were true – and Niemeyer was to have a far greater impact in East Germany than in the Federal Republic, where his influence remained marginal.[8] Despite the fact that Niemeyer had never built anything in East Germany and that his entry for Interbau represented the only project he realized in Germany, he remained a source of inspiration for the entire East German construction industry in the 1960s.

Brasília in Berlin

At the end of the neo-historical phase of architecture in the 1950s, and after industrialization and standardization had established themselves in the East German construction industry, taking its lead from Moscow, the question of concrete formal dimensions arose, of a "style", as it were. As early as 1954, shortly after Stalin's death, the latter's successor, Nikita Chrushchev announced at Moscow's "All Union Conference of the Construction Industry", that "ostentation and affectation are foreign to the substance of Soviet architecture".[9] Taking as its motto "building better, faster and more cheaply", as of 1955, East Germany had reached a "great turning-point in the construction industry", which was now turning its hand to industrializing and standardizing architecture, and in this context once again, in the final analysis, looking to Modernism, the tradition the country had started following as early as 1945–1949. Because the cultural policies of the Soviet-occupied zone, later the GDR, were closely linked to those of the Soviet Union, and a Stalinist version of neo-historicism was the order of the day, this trend had been suppressed.

However, initially, the industrialization of the construction industry did not bring with it any further guidelines regarding architecture or urban planning. In order to define the concrete style to be adopted when designing Socialist towns and so as to prevent the spread of "formalist" tendencies, in 1960, the 25th plenary conference of the Building Academy opened as a "First Theoretical Conference". Largely under the aegis of architect Hermann Henselmann and architecture critic Bruno Flierl, this conference ushered in a wider acceptance of international architecture in East Germany, in line with Socialist ideals. "It appears to me that we have already lost too much ground," remarked Henselmann, admitting further that: "Using the simple formula that 'the architecture of the West is in the service of Capitalism and therefore bad' or 'anything that fails to adhere to simple right-angles is formalist' is not going to get us anywhere. [...] But – strange as this may seem to some

der DDR eingeleitet. „Mir scheint, dass wir bereits zu viel Terrain verloren haben", bemerkt Henselmann und räumt weiter ein: „Mit der schlichten Formel ‚Die Architektur im Westen dient dem Kapitalismus, also ist sie schlecht' oder ‚Alles, was aus dem rechten Winkel gerät, ist formalistisch' kommen wir nicht weiter. [...] Sie [die Analyse westlicher Architektur, d. Verf.] verlangt aber auch – so merkwürdig das klingen mag für manche – Anerkennung guter Leistungen, die für uns Anregungen bieten."[10]

Mit diesen Worten wird die behutsame Rezeption internationaler Architektur, sofern sie denn vordergründig hilfreich für den Sozialismus ist, eingeleitet. Der Hauptgrund ist jedoch die Sorge, dass die DDR endgültig den Anschluss an internationale Entwicklungen verlieren und ihre eigene Architekturentwicklung in einer ideologischen Sackgasse enden könnte. Weiter wurden vor allem die Bauten Oscar Niemeyers als vorbildlich und richtungsweisend in die Debatte eingebracht. Die neue brasilianische Hauptstadt Brasília, besonders die Bauten am „Platz der Drei Gewalten," würdigte Flierl, weil in ihnen „eine großzügige und einfache, überschaubare und einprägsame Gestalt der Stadt zu finden" sei. „Wir sollten unsere eigenen Städte für unser sich entwickelndes sozialistisches Leben in einer ebenso großzügigen und einfachen, überschaubaren und einprägsamen städtebaulichen Gestalt neu aufbauen und rekonstruieren [...]."[11]

Die Empfehlung der Bauten Niemeyers als Vorbild für den weiteren Aufbau des Zentrums ignoriert allerdings die Tatsache, dass Brasília eine Neugründung in einem völlig unbebauten Landstrich ist und sich seine Bauten sowie die Verkehrsplanung in keinen vorhandenen städtebaulichen Kontext einfügen mussten. Eine direkte Übernahme für Berlin schied damit eigentlich aus. Die Grundcharakteristika versuchte man jedoch in bestehende Stadtzentren – wie in Berlin, aber auch zum Beispiel in Suhl ab 1966 – mit unterschiedlichem Erfolg einzugliedern. Dieses Bemühen ist auch symbolisch zu sehen, da in ihm der Wunsch zum Ausdruck kam, die DDR als neue moderne Gesellschaft darzustellen, wofür Brasília als Hauptstadt eines modernen Landes auch ideologisch das denkbar beste Vorbild bot, schließlich bekannte sich Niemeyer selbst deutlich zum Kommunismus. Dies ist ein Bekenntnis, das zwar fragwürdig bleiben muss[12], für die DDR stellte es jedoch ein ausschlaggebendes Kriterium dar, um sich mit dem Architekten zu identifizieren. Aus diesem Grund wurde Niemeyer in der DDR auch mit keiner ähnlich negativen Kritik wie in der Bundesrepublik bedacht. Die Formulierung Henselmanns, dass nicht alles ‚formalistisch' sei, was aus dem rechten Winkel gerate, belegt dies deutlich, da ja genau diese bewegte Formensprache im Westen den Hauptkritikpunkt bildete.

people – we also need to appreciate that it [analyzing Western architecture, author's note] has served a good purpose and that it provides us with stimulus."[10] These words ushered in a tentative acceptance of international architecture, on the face of it, only to the extent to which it could be of assistance to Socialism. However, the guiding principle was the fear that East Germany might irrevocably lose touch with international trends and that its own architectural trends might end up in an ideological cul-de-sac. Furthermore, Oscar Niemeyer's buildings were brought into the debate as particularly exemplary and inspirational. Flierl praised the new Brazilian capital, Brasília, and especially the buildings on the "Square of Three Powers" remarking that the city boasted "a spacious and simple, straightforward and impressive design. For our burgeoning Socialist lifestyle we should rebuild and reconstruct our own towns in just such a spacious and simple, straightforward and impressive style [...]."[11]

Recommending Niemeyer's buildings as an example of how to expand existing town centers does, however, ignore the fact that Brasília was a new development on an expanse of land that had never been built on before and that did not need to integrate either its buildings or its transportation planning into an existing urban context. Accordingly, it really would not have been possible to adopt wholesale the same methods for Berlin. Nevertheless, attempts were made to adapt their fundamental characteristics to existing town centers – in Berlin, but also in Suhl, for example, as of 1966 – with varying success. The symbolic significance of such endeavors should also not be forgotten, since they expressed a wish to portray the GDR as a new modern society, and, as the capital of a modern state, Brasília represented the best example imaginable, ideologically speaking, too. After all, Niemeyer himself was an avowed adherent of Communism. An allegiance that must remain questionable,[12] but for the GDR a decisive criterion for identification purposes. For this reason, in East Germany Niemeyer did not receive the same kind of negative criticism his oeuvre faced in the Federal Republic. Henselmann's formulation that not everything that fails to adhere to simple right angles should be termed "formalist", clearly demonstrates this, since in the West it was exactly this turbulent formal language that was the major source of criticism.

In order to preserve East Germany's new architecture from degenerating into a mirror image of the international formal canon and thus from not remaining identifiable as "Socialist", the visual arts, or, to put it more exactly, "Socialist Realism" was entrusted with the tasks of clearly defining GDR architecture and of preserving it from monotony. "Socialist

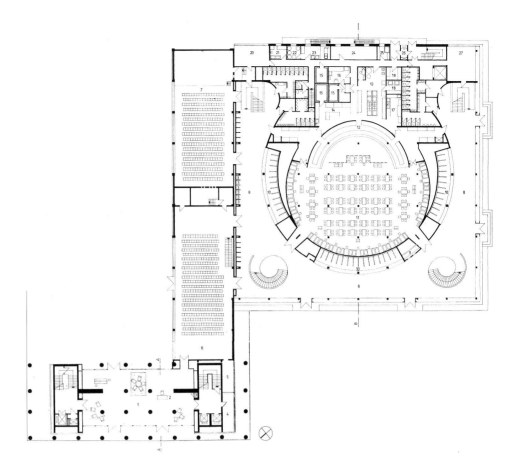

H. Henselmann,
Haus des Lehrers, Ost-Berlin.
Grundriss des Erdgeschosses.

H. Henselmann, Teacher's
House, East Berlin. Ground
plan of the ground floor.

H. Henselmann,
Haus des Lehrers,
Ost-Berlin.

H. Henselmann, Teacher's
House, East Berlin.

Um die neue DDR-Architektur davor zu bewahren, vollständig in das internationale Formenrepertoire abzugleiten und somit nicht mehr als „sozialistisch" identifizierbar zu bleiben, wird der bildenden Kunst, genauer dem „sozialistischen Realismus", die Aufgabe übertragen, die Architektur eindeutig zu kennzeichnen und sie auch vor der Eintönigkeit zu bewahren: „Die sozialistische Architektur erstrebt eine Synthese mit den neuen Schöpfungen der bildenden Kunst des sozialistischen Realismus und betrachtet diese als ein wesentliches Mittel, die Schönheit des Aufbaus des Sozialismus in künstlerischer Form widerzuspiegeln." [13]

Moderne Staatsarchitektur

Den ersten baulichen Niederschlag dieser Diskussion bildet das 1961–1964 von Hermann Henselmann (1905–1995) am Alexanderplatz in Berlin errichtete Haus des Lehrers mit der Kongresshalle, kurz HdL genannt. Das Ensemble aus zwölfgeschossiger Hochhausscheibe mit der ersten „curtain-wall" der DDR und überkuppeltem Flachbau vereinte drei Funktionen in sich: In erster Linie war das HdL bis 1989, wie die offizielle Bezeichnung verdeutlicht, das Fortbildungszentrum der Lehrer. Es erfüllte gleichzeitig durch öffentliche Cafés, Restaurants und die Nutzung der Kongresshalle für Bälle und Konzerte die Funktion eines Kulturhauses, das allen Bürgern offen stand. Als zeitweiliger Sitz der Volkskammer

architecture strives for a synthesis with the new creations of Socialist Realism's visual arts, viewing the latter as a fundamental means of reflecting the beauty of establishing Socialism in an artistic form." [13]

Modern state architecture

The first actual building to result from this discussion was Haus des Lehrers (The Teacher's House), erected by Hermann Henselmann (1905–1995) between 1961 and 1964 on Alexanderplatz in Berlin, and abbreviated to HdL. Consisting of a 12-story high-rise slab featuring East Germany's first curtain wall and a low building with a cupola roof, this ensemble fulfilled three functions at once. Until 1989, HdL was principally, as suggested by its official title, a further education center for teachers. At the same time, it housed public cafés and restaurants and used its congress hall for balls and concerts, thus fulfilling the function of a cultural center, open to all citizens. As intermittent home to the East German Volkskammer (parliament) the building was also used for state functions until the Palast der Republik (Palace of the Republic) was completed in 1976. When government was sitting, HdL's other education rooms were utilized to house the various parliamentary groups and the congress hall became a parliamentary chamber. Consequently, HdL was also East Germany's first state building with a modern look.

der DDR diente das Gebäude darüber hinaus, bis zur Fertigstellung des Palastes der Republik im Jahre 1976, auch der Staatsrepräsentation. Die Fortbildungsräume im HdL wurden während der Sitzungsperiode als Fraktionsräume genutzt und die Kongress halle als Sitzungssaal. Damit ist das HdL auch der erste Staatsbau der DDR im modernen Gewand.

Ein umlaufender Kranz mächtiger Rundstützen scheint die Hochhausscheibe emporzustemmen und → p.98 gibt den Blick frei in ein verglastes Foyer, das von weiteren Stützen dominiert wird und dadurch einen repräsentativen Charakter erhält. Die Erschließung erfolgt über zwei Treppenhäuser, die jeweils in den Stirnseiten des Gebäudes untergebracht sind. Die zweigeschossige Kongresshalle auf quadratischem Grundriss besitzt an den Schauseiten zwei vollständig verglaste Fassaden mit vorgehängtem Gestänge und wird von einer Flachkuppel bekrönt. → S.98 Die Kombination von Hochhausscheibe und überkuppeltem Flachbau lehnt sich deutlich an die Parlamentsbauten Niemeyers am „Platz der drei Gewalten" in Brasília an. Die Kombination von Hoch- und Flachbau wird von Henselmann mit der Dialektik des „Produktiven Widerspruchs"[14] charakterisiert, einem Ausspruch Goethes, mit dem Henselmann Moderne und Humanismus zu verbinden sucht.

Bezeichnenderweise orientiert sich das HdL jedoch nicht nur an Brasília, sondern vor allem auch an Lúcio Costas 1937–1943 in Zusammenarbeit mit Niemeyer und Le Corbusier entstandenem Ministerium für Erziehung und Gesundheit in der alten Hauptstadt Rio de Janeiro, dem Gründungsbau der modernen Staatsarchitektur in Brasilien. Von diesem Bau übernahm Henselmann die Eingangssituation mit den Pilotis, die auf Niemeyer zurückgehen, der sie gegenüber dem Entwurf von Le Corbusier erhöhte.

Das Ministerium ruht auf schlanken, 10 Meter hohen Pilotis und bildet damit einen durchlässigen und monumentalen Eingangsbereich aus. Weiterhin ist die Absetzung des Erdgeschosses zur Fassade durch eine massive Dachplatte relevant sowie die Disposition der Treppenhäuser zu den Stirnseiten des Baus, die Henselmann am HdL übernahm. Auch die Integration der bildenden Künste und der Gebrauch der traditionellen Keramik des Azulejo am Ministerium boten, neben den richtungsweisenden Arbeiten der mexikanischen Muralisten, vielfältige Anregungen für den Fries am HdL. Der Fries mit dem Titel „Das Leben in der DDR" wurde von dem Künstler Walter Womacka im Kollektiv mit Günter Bendel, Harald Hakenbach und Gerhard Bondzin entwickelt. Hinter ihm waren die Bücher der Lehrerbibliothek lichtgeschützt untergebracht. Das Voranschreiten der Entwicklung einer moder-

Costa/Niemeyer u. a., Ministerium für Erziehung und Gesundheit, Rio de Janeiro. Eingangssituation.

Costa/Niemeyer and others, Ministry of Education and Health, Rio de Janeiro. Entrance.

A surrounding crown of round supporting pillars appears to be lifting the high-rise slab heavenwards, allowing us an unimpeded view of a glass-plated foyer, loomed over by further supporting pillars and thus offering an imposing spectacle. Access to HdL is via two staircases, both located at the front of the building. The two-story congress hall is square in shape and, on the sides visible from the square, boasts two fully glazed façades fronted by suspended railings. It is crowned by a low dome. This combination of high-rise slab and low building with a cupola roof clearly echoes Niemeyer's parliament buildings on the "Square of Three Powers" in Brasília. Using dialectic terms, Henselmann characterized this combination of high-rise and low building as a "productive contradiction",[14] a dictum of Goethe's, by means of which Henselmann attempted to reconcile Modern Art with humanism.

Significantly, however, HdL was inspired not only by Brasília, but also, and more especially, by Lúcio Costa's Ministry of Education and Health in the former capital Rio de Janeiro, constructed between 1937 and 1943 in collaboration with Niemeyer and Le Corbusier, which marked the beginning of modern state architecture in Brazil. For his building, Henselmann used the same kind of entrance scenario, opting for similar pilotis to those used by Niemeyer, who had made them higher than in Le Corbusier's original design.

The Ministry rests on slender, 10 meter pilotis, thus creating an airy, monumental entrance area. The fact that the ground floor is separated from the façade by a solid roofing plate is also relevant, as is the location of the stairwells at the front of the building, something Henselmann also used for HdL. Alongside ground-breaking works by Mexican muralists, the idea of integrating the visual arts and using traditional Azulejo ceramics next to the Ministry provide wide-ranging inspiration for the frieze at HdL. Entitled "Life in the GDR", this frieze was designed by artist Walter Womacka collectively with Günter Bendel, Harald Hakenbach and Gerhard Bondzin. Behind it the books belonging to the teachers' library were housed.

It is possible to trace the progress made towards developing a modern kind of state architecture in East Germany in the 1960s, with one eye on Brasília, by looking at the kind of buildings going up on what used to be known as Marx-Engels-Platz in Berlin. When redesigning East Berlin, lining up individual sculptural, monumental buildings along a monumental axis as was the case in Brasília, did appear an interesting proposal, however, in view of the existing urban structure, this approach could only be implemented sporadically. Consequently,

nen Staatsarchitektur der DDR in den sechziger Jahren mit Blick nach Brasília lässt sich anhand der Bebauung des ehemaligen Marx-Engels-Platzes in Berlin verfolgen. Die Reihung von plastischen und monumentalen Solitären entlang einer Monumentalachse wie in Brasília war für die Konzeption Ost-Berlins zwar von Interesse, dieses städtebauliche Modell konnte jedoch aufgrund der vorhandenen Stadtstruktur nur ansatzweise umgesetzt werden. Das Ost-Berliner Zentrumsband ist daher keine Reihung von Gebäuden entlang einer Monumentalachse, sondern eine Folge von Platzräumen und Gebäuderiegeln, deren Erschließung durch das bestehende Straßennetz erfolgt und nicht über eine zentrale Achse.[15] Die Figur des Zentrumsbandes erschließt sich daher im Wesentlichen nur als Bild aus der Vogelschau.

Aber nicht nur die städtebaulichen Bemühungen, auch die Architektur kündet von einer Auseinandersetzung mit Niemeyer. Das von Josef Kaiser (1910–1991) erbaute Ministerium für Auswärtige Angelegenheiten der DDR (1963–1966 erbaut, 1995 abgerissen) weist in den verschiedenen Entwurfsstadien eine Rezeption von Niemeyers Standardministerien für Brasília auf. Ursprünglich plante Niemeyer, die Ministerien auf Stützen zu stellen, ein Fassadenaufriss während der ersten Entwurfsphase 1957 zeigt eine mächtige Hochhausscheibe, die von prismatischen, stark plastischen Stützen getragen wird.

Kaisers Bau in Berlin war ebenfalls ein scheibenförmiger Riegel, für dessen Fassaden- und Erdgeschossgestaltung zahlreiche Studien angefertigt wurden. Ein Entwurf Kaisers von 1965 zeigt den Baukörper auf plastischen Mittelstützen aufgeständert, mit einer ornamentalen Fassade. Finanzielle Kürzungen und Uneinigkeit der Entscheidungsträger erzwangen den Verzicht auf diese ambitionierte Lösung zugunsten einer schlichteren und blockhaften Gestaltung des Gebäudes.[16]

Monumentalität und „Bildzeichen"
Auch in den späten sechziger Jahren riss die Rezeption der Architektur Niemeyers nicht ab, sondern wurde noch einmal vor dem Hintergrund verspätet rezipierter Architekturdiskussionen und im Zusammenhang mit dem 20-jährigen Bestehen der DDR 1969 aktuell.

Ab Mitte der sechziger Jahre war der unmittelbare Wiederaufbau der Stadtzentren weitgehend abgeschlossen. Die Planungen verlagerten sich jetzt zu einer angestrebten „sozialistischen Umgestaltung" der Zentren, die oft großflächige Abrisse der historischen Substanz vorsahen, wie etwa der geplante Umbau Schwerins (Wettbewerb 1970), und eine

the central ribbon in East Berlin does not consist of a series of buildings aligned along a monumental axis, but a succession of squares and blocks of buildings which were accessed via the existing network of streets and not via a central axis.[15] Consequently, basically speaking, the line of a central ribbon could only be made out from a bird's-eye perspective.

But it was not only East Berlin's endeavors with regard to town planning, but also its architecture that demonstrated Niemeyer's influence. In its various design phases, Josef Kaiser's (1910–1991) East German Ministry of Foreign Affairs (built from 1963–1966, pulled down in 1995) manifests a familiarity with Niemeyer's standard ministries for Brasília. Niemeyer had originally planned to build these ministries on supporting pillars. A vertical section taken during the initial design phase in 1957 shows an imposing high-rise slab held in place by prism-like, highly sculptural supporting pillars.

Kaiser's building in Berlin was also a slab-like block, and numerous studies were produced for the design of its façade and ground floor. One of Kaiser's designs dating from 1965 shows the body of the building on sculptural central supporting pillars, with an ornamental façade. Budget cuts and disagreements between the decision-makers forced Kaiser to abandon this ambitious project in favor of a simpler, block-like design for the building.[16]

Monumentality and "pictorial symbols"
Nor did interest in Niemeyer's architecture subside in the late 1960s. On the contrary, the subject became topical once again as discussions on architecture were rekindled at this later date and in connection with the GDR's 20th anniversary in 1969.

As of the mid-1960s the immediate reconstruction of the city centers was largely completed. The focus of planning now shifted towards implementing a "Socialist redesigning" of these centers. This often involved demolishing large areas of their historical substance, as in the planned conversion of Schwerin (1970 competition), and subsequently using tall buildings that dominated the skyline for highlighting purposes. Contemporary critics, led especially by Bruno Flierl, described such edifices as "pictorial symbol architecture".[17]

According to Flierl's theory, the aim of all these buildings is to illustrate a Socialist iconography. For a long time, this misleading view was an impediment to an unbiased appraisal of the buildings, which in fact, on the contrary, represented the expression of a renaissance in modern architecture. On the sur-

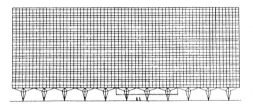

Projekt zu den Standardministerien, Brasília. Fassadenaufriss um 1957.

Project for the Standard Ministry, Brasília. Elevation around 1957.

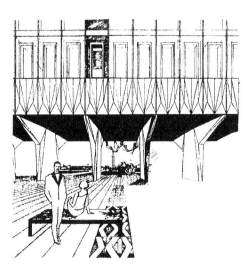

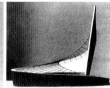

←
J. Kaiser, Projekt für das
Ministerium für auswärtige
Angelegenheiten der DDR,
Ost-Berlin. Zeichnung mit
Pilotis um 1965.

J. Kaiser, Project for
the Ministry of Foreign Affairs
of the GDR, East Berlin.
Sketch of the pilotis around
1965.

H. Henselmann, Projekt für
die Bibliothek am Leninplatz,
Ost-Berlin. Modell, um 1968.

H. Henselmann. Plan for the
library at Lenin Square, East
Berlin. Model, approx. 1968.

anschließende Markierung mit Höhendominanten.
In der zeitgenössischen Kritik, die vor allem Bruno
Flierl prägte, werden die Höhendominanten und
damit vor allem Bauten von Henselmann als „Bild-
zeichenarchitektur" gelesen.[17]

Alle diese Gebäude sollen, so Flierls These,
Elemente einer sozialistischen Ikonografie abbilden.
Diese irreführende Sicht verstellte lange Zeit einen
unvoreingenommenen Blick auf die Bauten, in denen
vielmehr eine Renaissance der Moderne unter vor-
dergründig sozialistischen Vorzeichen zum Ausdruck
kommt, als ein einfaches Abbilden sozialistisch
konnotierter Motive. Denn gerade für das HdL, einem
Schlüsselwerk der „DDR-Moderne", kann Flierl kein
„Bildzeichen" nennen. Und auch für die geplante
Bibliothek am Leninplatz (heute Platz der Vereinten
Nationen) bemüht Henselmann nicht, wie Flierl es
meinte, eine „rote Fahne", sondern lehnt sich an die
Kapelle des Alvorada-Palastes (1957–1958) in
Brasília an. Der Platz geht auf einen Entwurf Henselmanns von 1968 zurück. Geplant war ein siebenfach
abgetrepptes Hochhaus, das von zwei niedrigeren
Wohnschlangen gerahmt wird. Vor dem Hochhaus
sollte sich als Zentrum des Platzes die Leninbiblio-
thek befinden – ein spiralförmiges Gebäude, das zugleich Leninmonument sein sollte.[18]

Gegenüber der spiralförmigen Kapelle des Alvorada-
Palastes, die sich aus zwei gekrümmten Wandscheiben zusammensetzt, deren höchster, von einem
Kreuz bekrönter Punkt sich außen neben dem Portal
befindet, ist Henselmanns Entwurf der Bibliothek
durch eine einzige gekrümmte Wandscheibe gebildet,
deren höchster Punkt innen liegt. Dort befinden sich
auch Hammer und Sichel, mit denen der Monumen-
talcharakter des Gebäudes hervorgehoben wird.

Diese wenigen Beispiele zeigen, dass die endgültige
Etablierung der Moderne in der Architektur der DDR
in zentralen Punkten mit Oscar Niemeyer verbunden war. Sein Bekenntnis zum Kommunismus und
seine persönliche Beziehung zu Henselmann waren,
genau wie das Vorbild der modernen Hauptstadt
Brasília, wichtige Eckpfeiler, die eine Übernahme
der Moderne im Sozialismus möglich machten. Denn
bei der Rezeption der Moderne stand für die DDR
einmal das Bemühen im Vordergrund, an internationale Entwicklungen anzuknüpfen, um sich nicht
weiter zu isolieren, und weiter damit verbunden
die Problematik, die eigene Architektur gleichzeitig
sichtbar als „sozialistisch" charakterisieren zu
müssen, um sie vordergründig von der zuvor als
„formalistisch" diffamierten Moderne im Westen zu
unterscheiden. Niemeyers Architektur bot dafür viel-
fältigste Anregungen, gerade auch durch die Integration der bildenden Künste in seine Arbeit. Jedoch bleibt die Rezeption nicht auf ihn beschränkt,

face, they purported to be driven by Socialist aims
and were described as no more than illustrations
of motifs with Socialist connotations. However, for
HdL in particular, one of the key works by the "East
German Moderns", Flierl is unable to find a "pictorial
symbol". For the planned library on Leninplatz
(now Platz der Vereinten Nationen) Henselmann was
not, as Flierl imagined, thinking about a "red flag",
but was taking as his example the chapel in the
Alvorada Palace (1957–1958) in Brasília. The square
itself is based on a 1968 design by Henselmann.
The plans called for a high-rise with seven staircases,
framed by two lower spiraling residential units. The
idea was to locate the Lenin Library in the middle of
the square in front of the high-rise – a spiral-shaped
building that would, simultaneously, function as a
monument to Lenin.[18]

Unlike the Alvorada Palace's spiral-shaped chapel,
which consists of two curved wall sections, whose
highest point is crowned with a cross and located
on the outside next to the portal, Henselmann's
design for the library calls for a single curved wall
section whose highest point is on the inside. This
is also the location of the hammer and sickle which
accentuate the monumental quality of the building.

As these few examples demonstrate, Oscar
Niemeyer is a central figure as regards the definitive
establishment of the architecture of the Modern age
in East Germany. Along with the shining example
of Brasília, that modern capital, both the latter's
espousal of Communism and his person relationship
with Henselmann were important cornerstones,
allowing the Socialist state to embrace the Modern
age. For, in its response to the Modern age, East
Germany's prime concerns were firstly, to latch on
to international trends so as not to isolate itself any
further, and secondly, in the same connection, to
deal with the problems of simultaneously visibly
defining its own architecture as "Socialist", so as to
distinguish it ostensibly from the Modern age in
the West, which the country had already condemned
as "formalist". Niemeyer's architecture offers all
kinds of possibilities in this respect, especially, for
example, by integrating the visual arts into his work.
However, the response was not limited to him and
accordingly the vast majority of designs typical of
the 1960s are to be found in East Germany's architecture. A response to this movement was also
observable on a theoretical level. Sigfried Giedion's
work "Neun Punkte über Monumentalität – Ein menschliches Bedürfnis" (Nine Items Concerning Monumentality – A Human Need) played a central role
in this process. The text had been formulated
as early as 1943, together with José Lluis Sert and
Fernand Léger and debated at the CIAM's sixth
meeting in Bridgewater in 1947, but not discussed

und so findet sich der überwiegende Teil der zeit-typischen Formen der sechziger Jahre in der Architektur der DDR. Darüber hinaus fand in diesem Zusammenhang auch eine Rezeption auf theoretischer Ebene statt. Eine zentrale Stellung nimmt dabei Sigfried Giedions Schrift „Neun Punkte über Monumentalität – Ein menschliches Bedürfnis" ein. Der Text wurde bereits 1943 zusammen mit José Lluis Sert und Fernand Léger formuliert und bei der sechsten Zusammenkunft der CIAM in Bridgewater 1947 thematisiert, aber erst Ende der sechziger Jahre in der DDR verstärkt, wenn auch verspätet diskutiert. Die Fachzeitschrift „Deutsche Architektur" bespricht 1969 Giedions Forderungen, die erstmals die emotionalen Bedürfnisse des Individuums berücksichtigen, und sucht die Monumentalität für den Sozialismus und dabei besonders für die Höhendominanten nutzbar zu machen. [19]

Mit Hilfe der Monumentalität sollte, so Giedion, der ahistorische und „ortlose" International Style vom Funktionalismus zur emotionalen und symbolischen Verbundenheit mit dem Menschen und dem Ort überführt werden. Erste bauliche Niederschläge dieser Ideen bildete die Errichtung der neuen indischen Provinzhauptstadt Chandigarh durch Le Corbusier ab 1950 und nicht zuletzt die plastische Formensprache Niemeyers in Brasília.

Auch die DDR ist ein aufstrebendes Land, so schien es zumindest, vermittelt durch die Architektur der sechziger Jahre. Mögen auch manchmal ganz gewiss brasilianische Einflüsse nachzuweisen sein (besonders von Oscar Niemeyer), so beginnt sich doch durchaus auch Eigenständiges in dieser Zeit zu entwickeln.

in East Germany in depth until much later, at the end of the 1960s. In 1969, specialist magazine "Deutsche Architektur" examined Giedion's demands that took into account the emotional requirements of the individual for the first time and attempted to make monumentality utilizable for Socialism and particularly for those tall buildings that dominated the skyline. [19]

According to Giedion, with the aid of monumentality, the ahistorical and "dislocated" international style could be made to move on from functionalism and establish an emotional and symbolic link with mankind and its location. The first concrete examples of this style of building include the creation of Chandigarh, a new provincial capital in India, by Le Corbusier as of 1950 and, not least, Niemeyer's sculptural formal language in Brasília.

East Germany was also a country that aspired to great things, at least, this is what the architecture of the 1960s appeared to be conveying. And although, without doubt, Brazilian influences were sometimes discernable (particularly that of Oscar Niemeyer), independent ideas were also beginning to emerge in those times.

1 *Bauwelt*, Heft 14, 1956, S. 327.
2 Max Bill: „Architekt, Architektur und Gesellschaft." Vortrag vom 9. Juni 1953 an der Fakultät für Architektur und Urbanistik der Universität von São Paulo. Abgdruckt in diesem Buch S. 115 ff.
3 Jürgen Joedicke: Moderne Architektur. Strömungen und Tendenzen, Stuttgart 1969, S. 68.
4 Heinrich Klotz: Die röhrenden Hirsche der Architektur. Kitsch in der modernen Baukunst, Luzern / Frankfurt 1977, S. 42.
5 *Bauwelt*, Heft 12, 1955, S. 232f.
6 *Bauwelt*, Heft 12, 1955, S. 231.
7 Ebd.
8 So etwa im Siegerentwurf des 1957 ausgelobten Wettbewerbs „Hauptstadt Berlin" der Architekten Friedrich Spengelin, Fritz Eggeling und Gerd Pempelfort. Das scheibenförmige Parlamentsgebäude, das von V-Stützen getragen wird, zeigt eine Orientierung an Niemeyer, aber auch die Ministerien, die deutlich von den Ministerialbauten in Brasilia inspiriert sind. (Vgl. dazu: Hauptstadt Berlin, Internationaler städtebaulicher Ideenwettbewerb 1957/58, Hg. Berlinische Galerie, Helmut Geisert u.a., Berlin 1990).

1 *Bauwelt*, issue 14, 1956, p. 327.
2 Max Bill: "Architect, architecture and society." Talk on June 9, 1953 in the Faculty of Architecture and Urban Development of the University of São Paulo. Printed in this book pp. 115.
3 Jürgen Joedicke: Moderne Architektur. Strömungen und Tendenzen, Stuttgart, 1969, p. 68.
4 Heinrich Klotz: Die röhrenden Hirsche der Architektur. Kitsch in der modernen Baukunst, Lucerne / Frankfurt, 1977, p. 42.
5 *Bauwelt*, issue 12, 1955, pp. 232.
6 *Bauwelt*, issue 12, 1955, p. 231.
7 Ibid.
8 One example is the winning design in a 1957 competition, "Capital City Berlin" by architects Friedrich Spengelin, Fritz Eggeling and Gerd Pempelfort. Their slab parliament building with its v-shaped supporting pillars manifests Niemeyer's influence, as do the ministries, which are obviously inspired by the ministry buildings in Brasilia. (On this point see: Hauptstadt Berlin, Internationaler städtebaulicher Ideenwettbewerb 1957/58, ed. Berlinische Galerie, Helmut Geisert et al., Berlin, 1990.)
9 Nikita Chrushchev; quoted by Nils Gutschow, Werner Durth, Jörn Düwel: Architektur und Städtebau in der DDR, Frankfurt / Main, 1998, vol. II, p. 464.
10 *Deutsche Architektur*, issue 12, special supplement, 1961, pp. 5–7.
11 Ibid., pp. 13.
12 Niemeyer often had to put up with the reproach, both from critics and from colleagues, that although a convinced Communist he was building not for the people, but for a more elevated clientele, and that his lifestyle stood in crass contrast to his political convictions. For example, Brazilian landscape architect Roberto Burle Marx remarked: "Politically speaking, I am not as intractable as Oscar Niemeyer, who always declares himself to be a Communist. But he is a particular kind of Communist. I am not sure what I should call it. Perhaps Festival Communism. He is one of those people who talk a great deal and don't actually do anything." (Burle Marx in an interview with Alexander Fils 1981; in: Alexander Fils: Brasilia. Moderne Architektur in Brasilien, Düsseldorf, 1988, p. 143.
13 *Deutsche Architektur*, issue 10, special supplement, 1960, p.4.

9 Nikita Chruschtschow; zit. nach Nils Gutschow, Werner Durth, Jörn Düwel: Architektur und Städtebau in der DDR, Frankfurt/Main 1998, Bd. II, S. 464.

10 *Deutsche Architektur*, Heft 12, Sonderbeilage, 1961, S. 5–7.

11 Ebd., S. 13f.

12 Sowohl von der Kritik als auch von Kollegen musste sich Niemeyer oft den Vorwurf gefallen lassen, dass er, als überzeugter Kommunist, nicht für das Volk baue, sondern für eine gehobene Klientel und dass sein Lebensstil in krassem Widerspruch zu seinen politischen Überzeugungen stehe. So bemerkte etwa der brasilianische Landschaftsarchitekt Roberto Burle Marx: „Ich bin politisch nicht so festgelegt wie Oscar Niemeyer, der immer erklärt, dass er Kommunist sei. Aber er ist eine besondere Art Kommunist, ich weiss nicht, wie ich es nennen soll, vielleicht Festivalkommunismus; er gehört zu den Personen, die viel reden und nichts machen." (Burle Marx im Interview mit Alexander Fils 1981; in: Alexander Fils: Brasilia. Moderne Architektur in Brasilien, Düsseldorf 1988, S. 143).

13 *Deutsche Architektur*, Heft 10, Sonderbeilage, 1960, S. 4.

14 *Deutsche Architektur*, Heft 12, 1964, S. 714.

15 Die einstige Abfolge von Gebäuden und Platzräumen ist heute durch erfolgte Abrisse und Umbauten kaum mehr nachzuvollziehen. Von West nach Ost reihten sich am Zentrumsband als Fortsetzung der Achse Unter den Linden: das Außenministerium (1995 abgerissen), der Marx-Engels-Platz (heute Schlossplatz) mit dem Staatsratsgebäude, dem Palast der Republik (entkernt) und der anschließenden Grünanlage des Marx-Engels-Forums, die Wasserspiele und schließlich als Gipfelpunkt der Fernsehturm. Der sich anschließende Alexanderplatz bildet das Gelenk zur Überleitung in die Magistrale der ehemaligen Stalinallee, heute Karl-Marx-Allee.

16 Vgl. dazu Irma Leinauer: Das Außenministerium der DDR. Geschichte eines politischen Bauwerks, Berlin 1996.

17 Vgl. dazu: Bruno Flierl: Gebaute DDR. Über Stadtplaner, Architekten und die Macht, Berlin 1998. Darin: Ders., Hermann Henselmann – Bauen mit Bildern und Worten, S. 172ff.

18 Der Platz wurde nicht von Henselmann selbst realisiert, sondern von Heinz Mehlan und Kollektiv, 1968–1970. Dabei wurden mehrere Änderungen vorgenommen: Das Hochhaus wurde auf eine dreifache Abstufung begrenzt, und auf die Bibliothek verzichtete man zugunsten eines Lenindenkmals. Die Lenin-Skulptur von Nikolaj Tomski wurde 1992 entfernt.

19 „Bedingungen des Monumentalen in der sozialistischen Architektur"; in: *Deutsche Architektur*, Heft 4, 1969, S. 196f.

14 *Deutsche Architektur*, issue 12, 1964, p. 714.

15 Demolition and conversion work has meant that today, this one-time sequence of buildings and squares is hardly recognizable. Along a central ribbon the following elements were aligned from west to east as a continuation of the Unter den Linden axis: the Foreign Ministry (pulled down in 1995), Marx-Engels-Platz (now Schlossplatz) with the Privy Council Building, Palast der Republik (gutted) and the adjoining park belonging to the Marx-Engels Forum, the fountains and finally the TV Tower, a culminating point. Butting on to this is Alexanderplatz, forming a transition into the magisterial dignity of former Stalinallee, now Karl-Marx-Allee.

16 On this cf. Irma Leinauer: Das Außenministerium der DDR. Geschichte eines politischen Bauwerks, Berlin, 1996.

17 On this cf.: Bruno Flierl: Gebaute DDR. Über Stadtplaner, Architekten und die Macht, Berlin, 1998, in particular: Flierl: "Hermann Henselmann – Bauen mit Bildern und Worten," pp. 172.

18 The square was not realized by Henselmann himself but by Heinz Mehlan and his collective in 1968–1970. Several changes were made: the terracing of the high-rise was limited to three levels and the library itself rejected in favor of a monument to Lenin. The sculpture of Lenin by Nikolai Tomsky was removed in 1992.

19 "Bedingungen des Monumentalen in der sozialistischen Architektur," in: *Deutsche Architektur*, issue 4, 1969, pp. 196.

Zurück in die Zukunft: Oscar Niemeyer und der Retrofuturismus
Back to the future: Oscar Niemeyer and Retro-Futurism

Niklas Maak

Wenn man in den achtziger Jahren das Gelächter auf seiner Seite haben wollte, musste man nur jene Zeitschriften aus den fünfziger Jahren herausholen, in denen sich Zeichner und Techniker vorstellten, wie das Leben in der Zukunft aussehen würde. In den alten Magazinen sieht man nierentischförmige Mondhäuser mit überglasten Vorgärten und blinkende Roboter, die Nierentische abstauben. Ford plante allen Ernstes ein atomgetriebenes Auto, ein Plan, der, wie man nach drei Jahren merkte, daran scheitern musste, dass ein Reaktor schlecht auf die Größe eines Motors heruntergeschrumpft werden kann, von Sicherheitsfragen im Kollisionsfall einmal abgesehen. Nichts war komischer als die Vergangenheit der Zukunft. In den fünfziger Jahren lachte man über die Zukunftsbilder der Jahrhundertwende, in den achtziger Jahren lachte man über verquere Vorstellungen der Fünfziger; nur heute gibt es in dieser Hinsicht nicht viel zu lachen. Wenn man sich im Jahr 2001 das Design anschaute, dann sah es größtenteils so aus, wie es sich Stanley Kubrick 1967 in seinem Film „2001 – Odyssee im Weltraum" vorgestellt hatte: flache Plastikmöbel, runde, quellende Formen, eine Mischung eben aus Verner Pantons orange farbenen Zukunftsgrotten und Oscar Niemeyers überhitzter Schwungmoderne. Das Ende der Postmoderne und das Scheitern jener anämischen Kästchenarchitektur, die als „Zweite Moderne" von einer ältlichen Kritikerschar in den Rang einer kraftvollen Erneuerungsbewegung emporgejubelt wurde, sind unübersehbar; beide haben es nicht geschafft, außerhalb verschworener Fachkreise Anerkennung zu finden. Stattdessen suchen Architekten und Designer, Lifestylemagazine, Musiker und Modemacher die Formen der Zukunft in der Vergangenheit, und zwar genau an jenem historischen Punkt, an dem der Glaube an eine expansive, lustvolle Zukunft noch ungebrochen war: im experimentellen Geist der mittleren sechziger Jahre, im Pop des Plastikzeitalters, im Autodesign jener Fahrzeuge, deren Karossen noch nicht von ökologischen und sicherheitstechnischen Bedenken deformiert waren, in der Architektur der letzten Idealstädte, in Le Corbusiers Chandigarh und, vor allem, in den Formen der Idealstadt Brasília. Die südamerikanische Retortenstadt, die jahrzehntelang als Babylon einer hybriden, technokratischen und unmensch-

If you wanted to have a good laugh in the 1980s all you had to do was pull out the newspapers from the 1950s in which illustrators and technologists depict what life in the future would be like. In such magazines you see moon dwellings shaped like kidney tables, with glass-covered front gardens and blinking robots dusting those kidney tables. Ford seriously planned a nuclear-powered car, until after three years planning they realized it was doomed to failure, as a reactor could hardly be shrunk to the size of a car – not to mention the question of safety in the event of a crash. There was nothing funnier than the future in the past: in the 1950s, people laughed at the future images produced at the turn of the century, in the 1980s you laughed at weird ideas from the 1950s. Yet today there is little left to laugh about. If you paid attention to design in 2001 you would have seen that to a large extent, it looked pretty much the way Stanley Kubrick imagined it in his 1967 film "2001 – A Space Odyssey". Flat plastic furniture, round swollen forms, a mixture of Verner Panton's orange futuristic grottoes and Oscar Niemeyer's overheated, curvaceous Modernism. There is no overlooking the fact that Post-modernism has ended and that the anemic, box-style architecture (hailed by an older flock of critics as a powerful revival movement) has come to nothing; neither trend has met with recognition outside the circles of the initiate. Instead, architects and designers, lifestyle magazines, musicians and fashion-makers seek future forms in the past, indeed, they endeavor to find it exactly at that historical point when people still believed that joyful progress would continue unabated, namely in the experimental mindset of the mid-1960s, in the Pop of the plastic age, in the design of cars with chassis not yet distorted by ecological and safety considerations, in the architecture of the last ideal cities, in Le Corbusier's Chandigarh and above all in the shapes of the ideal city of Brasília. The South American test-tube city, derided for many decades as the Babel of a hybrid, technocratic and inhuman Modernism, has in the space of a few years, become a Mecca for a new movement that is having such a forceful impact on the present and quite beyond the domain of architecture. It could perhaps be called Retro-Futurism.

lichen Moderne verteufelt wurde, ist binnen weniger Jahre zum Mekka einer neuen Bewegung geworden, die weit über die Architektur hinaus die Ästhetik der Gegenwart prägt; man könnte sie den Retro-futurismus nennen.

Die Renaissance einer maßgeblich von Niemeyer geprägten Popmoderne hat inzwischen sogar Berlin erreicht. Am Askanischen Platz, auf dem Gelände des ehemaligen Anhalter Bahnhofs, haben die jungen Architekten Doris Schäffler und Stephan Schütz einen Bau errichtet, der auf den ersten Blick wie eine Wiedergeburt von Oscar Niemeyers Kathedrale in Brasília wirkt. Das neue Tempodrom sieht so aus, als sei es in der bodennahen Blockrandwelt von Berlin nur zwischengelandet: so strahlend weiß, so futuristisch und weltraumstrebend zackig, als wolle es mit seinen Spitzen den braven neuen Bürokisten die Sandsteinplatten von den dünnen Stahlbeinchen reißen. Größer könnten die Gegensätze nicht sein: hier die schmutziggelbe Ruine des Bahnhofes, dort die aseptisch weiße, himmelszackende Silhouette des neuen Tempodroms, dessen Name schon ver-spricht, was die Architektur verkörpert: Aufbruch, Beschleunigung, zukunftsfrohe Raserei. So weiß, wie dieses Dach leuchtet, strahlt kaum etwas in Berlin; es ist die gleiche Rhetorik des Hellen, mit der schon Oscar Niemeyer spielte, als er in den rötlichen Staub der Steppe die weiße Stadt Brasília stellte, deren Leuchten allein schon ein Versprechen war: Hier gab es keine Spuren von Verfall, keine Geschichte, nur Neuanfang, Reinheit und Zukunft. Das kathedralen-artige Tempodrom ist weniger ideologisch aufge-laden: Hier geht es nicht gleich um eine neue Welt, sondern erst einmal um gute Unterhaltung. Die von der Krankenschwester Irene Moesinger 1980 ge-gründete Institution, in der eine Mischung aus Klein-kunstprogramm, Konzerten und Tagungen stattfindet, zog in Berlin mehrfach um, bis sie in dem Bau am Askanischen Platz eine endgültige Unterkunft fand. Die Architekten hatten bei ihrem Entwurf zunächst eine Hommage an das alte Zirkuszelt im Hinterkopf – aber es wurde eine Hommage an den Geist einer Moderne daraus, die mit dem Verfall von Brasília erledigt schien. Schäffler und Schütz, die Architekten, die für den Entwurf verantwortlich zeichnen, sind Angestellte der Hamburger Architekturfabrik von Gerkan, Marg und Partner, einem eher konservativen, der technischen Eleganz verpflichteten Büro, in dem solche donnernden, bisweilen die Grenze von Manierismus und Retrokitsch streifenden Setzungen wie das Tempodrom selten vorkamen. Dass auch in den ehemaligen Bastionen der gediegenen Gebrauchsarchitektur mit einer jüngeren Generation die Formen der Niemeyer'schen Moderne Einzug halten, zeigt, wie unaufhaltsam der Retrofuturismus seinen Siegeszug fortsetzt. Niemeyer ist zu einem der wichtigsten Referenzpunkte der neuen Archi-

The renaissance of a Pop Modernism so strongly influenced by Niemeyer has now even reached Berlin. At Askanische Platz, on the grounds of the former Anhalt Rail Station, young architects Doris Schaeffler and Stephan Schütz have erected a building which at first glance looks like a reincarnation of Oscar Niemeyer's cathedral in Brasília. The new Tempodrom looks as if it has just temporarily touched down in the down-to-earth world of Berlin's suburban blocks-of-flats: so brilliantly white, so futuristic and jaggedly space-probing as if it wished with its peaks to rip the sandstone paneling from the thin little steel legs of the boring new office boxes. The contrast could not be greater: here, the dirty yellow ruins of the station and there, pointing skyward, the anti-septically white silhouette of the Tempodrom whose name already promises what the architecture embodies – the scent of change, acceleration, racing happily to the future. There is almost nothing in Berlin which shines as whitely as this roof; it is the same rhetorics of white light with which Oscar Niemeyer already played when he placed the white city of Brasília in the reddish dust of the pampa, whose radiance alone already bore promise – here there was no trace of decay, no history, just a new beginning, purity and future. The cathedral-like Tempodrom is not so steeped in ideology: the issue there is not a brave new world but first and fore-most good entertainment. The institution, founded in 1980 by the nurse Irene Moesinger, in which a mixed agenda of small arts, concerts and con-gresses take place, relocated any number of times in Berlin before finding its final resting place in the building on Askanische Platz. At first, the architects had the old circus tent in mind for the design – but it soon became a homage to the spirit of Mod-ernism which seemed to have been dashed with the dilapidation of Brasília. Schäffler und Schütz, the architects responsible for the design drawings are employed by Gerkan, Marg and Partners, a Hamburg-based architectural office that is some-what conservative and devoted more to technical elegance. Seldom had it faced such thundering posi-tionings as the Tempodrom, which at times verges on the Mannerist or on Retro-kitsch. The fact that along with the younger-generation's minds the forms of Niemeyer's Modernism have entered the former bastions of staidly tasteful everyday architecture proves how unstoppably Retro-Futurism has pursued its forward march. Niemeyer has become one of the most important reference points in new architec-ture; and likewise young offices such as Hamburg-based Akyol Gullotta Kamps unabashedly quote the stirring Martini Modernism of the 1960s in projects such as the Kish hotel complex in the Persian Gulf. Hadi Teherani, the brains behind the successful BRT architectural office in Hamburg, declared in an interview that Oscar Niemeyer was the figure whom

Gerkan, Marg & Partner, Tempodrom Veranstaltungs-halle, Berlin.

Gerkan, Marg & Partner, Tempodrom events hall, Berlin.

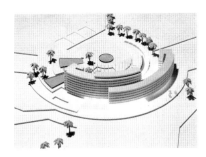

Akyol Gulotta Kamps,
Projekt Seaside Hotel Kish
am Persischen Golf.

Akyol Gulotta Kamps,
Seaside Hotel Kish project
on the Persian Gulf.

Future Systems,
Nat West Media Center,
London.

R. Lovegrove,
Chaise Lounge RL00.

tektur geworden; junge Büros wie die Hamburger Architekten Akyol Gullotta Kamps zitieren in ihren Projekten, etwa dem Hotelkomplex von Kish im Persischen Golf, unverhohlen den schwingenden Martini Modernism der Sechziger; Hadi Teherani, Kopf des erfolgreichen Architekturbüros BRT in Hamburg, erklärte in einem Interview Oscar Niemeyer zu der Figur, die er am meisten von allen Architekten bewundere, ebenso der Biomorphist Greg Lynn, dessen quellende Wohnblasen aussehen wie die Nachfahren jener aufgeweichten Moderne, für die wie kein anderes Wohngebäude Niemeyers freiförmig durch den Urwald schwingender Wohnbungalow steht.

Ein weiteres Werk der neuen Zukunftsnostalgie ist das Nat West Media Center in London, entworfen von dem englischen Büro Future Systems, dessen Mitglieder fast zwei Jahrzehnte als belächelte Plastikpropheten überwinterten und die sich mittlerweile vor Aufträgen nicht retten können. Wie ein Rasierapparat aus den sechziger Jahren steht da über dem Kricketstadion eine eigenartige Blase, in der bis zu 120 Journalisten auch bei schlechtem Wetter vom Spiel berichten können. Passend zu den schwingenden und schwebenden Bauformen einer neuen Brasília-Moderne, entwerfen Designer Objekte, die direkt aus den Zeitgrotten der Zukunftsästhetik zu kommen scheinen: Ross Lovegroves Loom-Lounger, der so flach über dem Boden schwebt wie die Sessel in Oscar Niemeyers Parlaments-Lounge in Brasília, ist eine windschnittige Verbeugung vor dem dynamischen Schwebe-Look der Sechziger; auf den Möbelmessen in Mailand und Köln dominieren seit nunmehr vier Jahren orangefarbene Möbel, in deren Design die Wohn- und Schlaflandschaften von Panton späte Triumphe feiern, und sogar Ikea popularisiert mit stapelbaren, kieselrunden Plastiksitzschalen das allgegenwärtige Retro-Revival. Die erfolgreichsten Autos der letzten Jahre waren ausnahmslos von einem Design geprägt, das Modelle aus den sechziger Jahren zitiert. Alfa Romeo erlebte mit dem Modell 156, das den Stil der Giulia paraphrasiert, eine beispiellose Renaissance, BMW hat mit dem New Mini alle Verkaufserwartungen übertroffen und statt der im Bestfall erwarteten 100.000 Minis im ersten Jahr bereits über 140.000 verkauft. Der Designer Marc Newson entwarf den 021C, der dem maroden Ford-Konzern ein neues Image verleihen sollte; ein knalloranges Auto, das aussieht, als habe man der NASA den Auftrag gegeben, einen Trabant in eine Weltraumkapsel zu verwandeln. Seltsam glänzend stehen all diese Dinge da und verbreiten die Aura von Tiefkühlprodukten, frisch und alt zugleich, als habe man sie 1967 eingefrostet. Was ist passiert?

he admired more than any other architect. The same holds true for biomorphist Greg Lynn, whose swollen, living spheres look to be, more than other residential buildings, the offspring of that softened Modernism for which Niemeyer's free form, jungle-swinging domestic bungalow stands.

Another work of future nostalgic is the Nat West Media Center in London – designed by the English office Future Systems whose members have survived being labeled the prophets of plastic for almost two decades and now are veritably swamped in contracts. Like a razor from the 1970s, it rises up above the cricket grounds, a unique sphere in which up to 120 journalists can report on the games in all weather conditions. In tune with the curvaceous and floating building forms of a new Brasília-style Modernism, designers have been busy creating objects which appear to stem straight from the time capsules of futurist aesthetics: Ross Lovegrove's Loom-Lounger seems to hover just above the ground like Oscar Niemeyer's Parliament Lounge in Brasília. It is a streamlined tribute to that dynamic floating feel of the 1960s; at the furniture fairs in Milan and Cologne orange furniture has now dominated the last four years with furniture in which the living and sleeping landscapes of Panton triumph at long last, and even Ikea is popularizing the ubiquitous retro revival with stackable plastic seating shells as round as pebbles. The most successful cars of the past few years were without exception characterized by a design which cited models of the 1960s; Alfa Romeo, with its Model 156 (paraphrasing the style of the Giulia) has enjoyed an unprecedented renaissance, BMW topped all sales forecasts with the New Mini and instead of reaching the most optimistic target of 100,000, Minis sold over 140,000 in the first year. Designer Marc Newson created the 021C, intended to revamp the Ford Group's tired image; a bright orange car which looks like NASA has been contracted to turn an East German Trabant into a space capsule. Shining strangely, all these objects stand around exuding the aura of deep-frozen goods – as fresh as can be and yet old, as if they had been shock-frozen back in 1967. What has happened?

Retro-Futurism is not your usual revival along the lines of the purely nostalgic Bonnie and Clyde trend or the Gatsby style of the early 1970s. In Retro-Futurism two things have come together for the first time which formerly did not belong together – nostalgia and the future. What is quoted here is the image of "future" per se, a notion composed before future utopias came crashing to earth with Postmodernism. The atomic-speed, streamlined, sensually physical nature of these forms was also always the promise of unlimited growth and boundless

M. Newson,
Projekt Ford 021C.

Der Retrofuturismus ist kein normales Revival, wie es etwa die rein nostalgische Bonnie-und-Clyde-Mode oder der Gatsby-Stil der frühen siebziger Jahre war. Im Retrofuturismus wird erstmals zusammengebracht, was bisher nicht zusammengehörte: Nostalgie und Zukunft. Was hier zitiert wird, ist das Bild von „Zukunft" schlechthin, das man sich zuletzt, vor dem Zerfall der Zukunftsutopie in der Postmoderne, gemacht hatte. Das Atomschnelle, Windschnittige, Sinnlich-Körperhafte dieser Formen war immer auch das Versprechen von unbegrenztem Wachstum und grenzenloser Lust, des Aufbruchs in eine neue Welt und des großen Abenteuers, für das wie kein anderer moderner Fetisch die Mondrakete stand. Der Plastikpop ist eine Raumfahrtästhetik, so wie der Bau von Brasília eine Mondbesiedelung avant la lettre war: der Neuanfang im Nichts, die Eroberung der Leere, und damit das letzte, pathetische Bild einer fortschrittsgläubigen Moderne, deren Expansionsdrang bis in unbekannte Galaxien führte. Danach begann die Postmoderne – und jetzt, nach Dekonstruktivismus, Zweiter Moderne, Neuer Einfachheit und Neoneohistorismus wird die Zukunft als Stilkategorie entdeckt. „Future Style" heißt das im Wallpaper; die Zukunft wird sich selbst historisch.

Auch in der Werbung richten sich die Träume vom besseren Leben mittlerweile in der Brasília-Moderne ein. Wenn bis vor kurzem irgendwo in der Werbung Architektur auftauchte, dann war es entweder eine paradiesnahe raffaelloweiße Luxusvilla oder aber eine Binding-Lager-Yuppie-Skyline, wie man sie von den Dekortapeten der achtziger Jahre kennt. Doch statt Villenglück und Bacardiparadies, von dem für den Konsumenten am Ende doch nur Schulden und die Flasche übrig blieb, setzt die Werbung neuerdings darauf, in der angeblichen Tristesse des Betons ästhetische Qualitäten zu erblicken. Parkdecks prägen die neue Werbeästhetik eher als die goldstrotzenden Luxusvillen der Gründerzeit, die lange den Hintergrund für Limousinen und Managershampoos abgaben.

Durch die Werbung wird die einst elitäre moderne Architektur zum Bestandteil des Mainstreams und prägt kollektive Idealbilder. Auf der Hülle der neuen A-Ha-CD sieht man einen kompromisslos modernen Flughafen, eine PaloAlto-CD ziert ein Blick auf die Fassade des in den sechziger Jahren errichteten Endloshauses an der Pariser Gare Montparnasse. Brasília schließlich wird im Werbespot zum Inbegriff visionärer Zukunftssicht: Sowohl der Werbefilm der Post als auch die Visa-Reklame wählten die brasilianische Hauptstadt als den Hintergrund, vor dem der Fortschritt von Kommunikation und Zahlungsverkehr sich am besten ausdrücken kann. Auch zeitgemäßer Luxus muss absolut modern daherkommen: Der Dessous-

pleasure, the dawning of a new world and the great adventure, as symbolized so perfectly by the lunar landing craft rather than any other modern fetish. Plastic Pop is a space-travel aesthetic – just like the building of Brasília was a lunar space station avant la lettre: the new launch out into the void, the conquest of emptiness and thus the last pathetic picture of a Modernism that believes in progress and whose urge to expand led all the way to unknown galaxies. And it was followed first by Post-modernism and now, after deconstructionism, by Second Wave Modernism, New Simplicity and Neo-Neo-Historicism: the future is the newly discovered category for a style. "Future Style" means that in wallpaper; the future itself becomes historical.

In advertising, dreams of a better life are also busy outfitting themselves in Brasília-Modernism. When architecture appeared in advertising, up until a short time ago, it was either a paradise-found bounty-white luxury villa or a yuppie skyline such as those we know from decorative wallpapers in the 1980s. But instead of the villa dreamworld and basking Bacardis (which in the end only leave you in debt and staring down an empty bottle), advertising is now relying on the aesthetic qualities of the purported poverty of concrete; parking decks characterize the new advertising aesthetic more than the gold-lamé luxury turn-of-the-century villas that for a long time supplied the backdrop for limousines and manager shampoos.

Through advertising, what was once elite modern architecture has become established mainstream and leaves its mark on collective images of the ideal. The cover of the new A-Ha CD sports an uncompromisingly modern airport, a PaloAlto CD offers a view of the facade of the Endless House erected in the 1960s at Gare Montparnasse, Paris. Brasília has finally become the embodiment of a visionary future outlook: the German postal service's TV commercial and the Visa ad both chose the Brazilian capital as the background against which to best portray the advances in communication and payment transactions. Contemporary luxury also needs to look thoroughly modern: lingerie manufacturer Hanro puts its model in front of the Kaufman House in Palm Springs, the magazine "Brigitte Young Miss" chooses Hadi Teherani's futuristic house on the slopes of the Elbe in Hamburg as the backdrop to their advertisement, and even the Bree brand (which tended to have a fresh-as-pine, Birkenstock, eco-freak end-of-the 1970s feel to it) now boasts a blond in its ad, watering cacti in a cool, modern bungalow. Aesthetic potential is still squeezed out of dismal, anonymous, functional buildings. In the video clip of German band Echt one of Berlin's pre-fabricated apartment blocks is hailed as the stage set for youthful happi-

Hersteller Hanro stellt sein Model vor das Kaufman House in Palm Springs, die Zeitschrift Brigitte Young Miss wählt als Hintergrund ihrer Werbung Hadi Teheranis futuristisches Haus am Elbhäng in Hamburg, und sogar die Marke Bree, die eher einer kiefernholzselig verbirkenstockten Öko-Ästhetik der Endsiebziger nahe steht, lässt in ihrer Werbung eine blonde Frau in einem kühl modernen Bungalow Kakteen gießen. Noch den trostlosesten anonymen Zweckbauten wird ein ästhetisches Potenzial abgerungen. Im Videoclip der deutschen Band Echt wird ein Berliner Plattenbau zur Kulisse jungen Glücks emporgesungen; das Gucci-Model schaut durch seine braunmetallicfarbenen Brillengläser auf eine betonkühne Autobahnbrücke.

In einer Zeit, die, von einigen Bauskulpturen abgesehen, kaum eine erkennbare Gegenwartsästhetik ausgeprägt hat, wird zurückgegriffen auf die Zukunftsbilder der letzten modernitätsgläubigen Epoche. „Brasília steht wie nichts anderes dafür, etwas völlig Neues zu bauen", sagt Frank Lotze von der Werbeagentur Jung von Matt, die mit der in Brasília gedrehten Kampagne für die Post architekturikonografisch an der Spitze der Bewegung steht. Man hätte im Post-Spot auch die Skyline von Dallas zeigen können – aber Brasília biete die besseren, unverbrauchteren Bilder. Die Liebe zu Brasília und den Relikten des Pop trägt Züge dessen, was Susan Sontag einmal als „Camp" bezeichnet hat: die Liebe zum Artifiziellen, Größenwahnsinnigen, zu letztendlich gescheiterten und gesellschaftlich wertlos gewordenen Ambitionen – zu goldenen Opel-Limousinen, die nie Mercedes wurden, zu rotglühenden Guzzinilampen, die es nie in neue Galaxien schafften, und zu Projekten wie Brasília, die das Land dann doch nicht in die erste Welt katapultierten. Beide retrovisionären Bewegungen, die kritische Rekonstruktion, mit der Berlin das Raumgefühl des 19. Jahrhunderts wieder finden soll, und die Retrowelle in der Werbung, versuchen gesellschaftliche Leitbilder zu schaffen – nur dass die in Stein gemeißelte deutsche Leitkultur wenig gegen die Omnipräsenz jener Leitbilder ausrichten kann, die in Werbespots und Musikvideos propagiert werden.

Der Retrofuturismus, zumindest im Produktdesign, eine Sehnsucht nach Orientierung. In den sechziger Jahren war noch klar, wie die Zukunft aussieht: Zukunft waren Atomkraftwerke und Weltraumraketen, und beide hatten erkennbare Formen; ein gutes, modernes Auto hatte also wie eine Rakete auszusehen, weswegen die Designer den amerikanischen Limousinen als Zukunftsornament stilisierte Raketenleitwerke ins Blech pressten, die später irreführenderweise als „Haifischflossen" verballhornt wurden. Mit den Haifischflossen wurde die rationale Form des stromlinienförmigen Autos zur manieriertsym-

ness; a Gucci model peers through his brown-metallic glasses at a daringly concrete autobahn bridge.

In an age which, with the exception of a few building sculptures, has barely created a discernible contemporary aesthetic, people are resorting to the future images of that last epoch which believed in Modernity. "Brasília stands, like nothing else, for building something completely new," says Frank Lotze of the Jung von Matt ad agency – which in terms of architectural iconography heads the movement with its Deutsche Post campaign shot in Brasília. The ad could have included the Dallas skyline – but Brasília offered the better, fresher images. A love of Brasília and the relics of Pop take after what Susan Sonntag once referred to as "camp": the love of the artificial, megalomania, and, essentially, failed ambitions that have become socially worthless – those golden Opel limos that would so desperately like to be a Mercedes but never will, the glowing red Guzzini luminaries which never made it to new galaxies, and projects such as Brasília which have still not catapulted the country into the first world. Both are retro-visionary movements, namely the critical reconstruction (with which Berlin is supposed to regain that spatial sense of the 19th century), and the retro-wave in advertising. And both are attempting to create social models – it is just that the German hegemonic culture written on stone tablets can do little to counter the omnipresence of the models propagated in TV commercials and music videos.

Retro-Futurism, at least in product design, is a longing for orientation. In the 1960s, it was still clear what the future looked like. The future was nuclear power plants and rockets for outer space, and both had distinguishable forms; a good, modern car was thus supposed to look like a rocket which is why the designers of American limousines pressed sheet steel into stylized rocket fins which were later misleadingly dubbed shark fins. With shark fins, the rational form of the streamlined car became an affected symbolism; the car looked faster although it was actually slower as a result of these additions. At the same time, architects grew uneasy in the face of the bloodless rationalism of building forms.

The first manifestation of this growing criticism of ideology, which Niemeyer was also to fundamentally influence, was, however, not made of plastic but concrete: The pilgrim's church in Ronchamp, built in 1955 by Le Corbusier in the Vosges mountains, related to classical Modernism like Mannerism to the High Renaissance: over-stretched, physical bulges instead of right angles, Dionysian thunder in place of Apollonian clarity. The undisguised eroti-

bolischen; das Auto sah schneller aus, obwohl es durch die Anbauten langsamer wurde. Parallel dazu äußerte sich in der Architektur ein Unbehagen am blutleeren Rationalismus der Bauformen.

Das erste Manifest dieser quellenden Ideologie-kritik, das auch Niemeyer wesentlich prägen sollte, war allerdings nicht aus Plastik, sondern aus Beton: Die Wallfahrtskirche von Ronchamp, 1955 von Le Corbusier in den Vogesen erbaut, verhielt sich zur klassischen Moderne wie der Manierismus zur Hochrenaissance: Überdehntes, körperlich Schwellendes, statt rechter Winkel, dionysisches Tosen statt apollinischer Klarheit. Die unverhohlene Erotik dieser bewusst anthropomorphen Formen war das Gegengift zur entmaterialisierten Kühle, die der scharfkantige Minimalismus ihrer Zeit allenthalben verbreitete. Autos wie der Citroen DS, der als „Déesse", als fahrbare, göttliche Frau verkauft wurde, trugen Blechhüften und Chrombrüste; das in den sechziger Jahren gegründete Architekturbüro Future Systems entwarf Hochhäuser in Form von Geschlechtsorganen, und Oscar Niemeyer betonte, dass der weibliche Körper eine wesentliche Inspirationsquelle sei. In den späten siebziger Jahren kam es dann zur ideologischen Schubumkehr; die Plastik- und Betonorgien des Pop-Jahrzehnts galten nicht mehr als Vorboten einer besseren Zukunft, sondern schlicht als umweltschädliche Emanation des allgegenwärtigen Konsumterrors. Doch der notwendige politische Protest gegen die Ressourcenverschwendung wurde in defensiver Ästhetik aufgelöst. Kiefernholz war fortan das Material ökologisch-antikapitalistischer Correctness: Die Ideologiekritik war im Design angekommen, Niemeyer verschwand mit den jetzt ebenfalls unter Ideologieverdacht stehenden Träumen von brasilianischer Musik, Stränden und Palmen auf der Müllhalde stigmatisierter Utopien. Doch es folgte keine Bewegung, die mit vergleichbarem Pathos Zukunftsperspektiven vortrug. An die Stelle Blech gewordener Göttinnen trat deprimierendes Ölkrisendesign; Autos sahen zunächst freudlos kantig, dann harmlos affirmativ aus. Im Kleinwagendesign hielt ein albern zoomorphes Kugeldesign Einzug: Der Renault Twingo stand da wie ein Blech gewordener Dackelwelpe. Mit der bewussten Infantilisierung des Autodesigns wurde die ökologische Bedenklichkeit des Fahrzeugs in einem Gemenge aus Gefühligkeit und politischer Resignation aufgelöst. Welcher Smartfahrer protestiert heute noch gegen das „Waldsterben"?

Was die gegenwärtige Architektengeneration an Niemeyer fasziniert, ist offensichtlich seine skulpturale Erfindungskraft. Vieles an Niemeyers Werk ist Decorum und Maniera; mit Brasília entfernte sich die Moderne vom strengen Rationalismus und blieb

cism of these consciously anthropomorphic forms was the antidote to the dematerialised coolness which the hard-edged Minimalism epidemic spread everywhere in its day. Cars such as the Citroen DS, which was sold as "Déesse" – a divine, drivable woman sported tin hips and chrome breasts; the architectural office Future Systems, established in the 1960s, designed phallic skyscrapers, and Oscar Niemeyer emphasized that the female body was a considerable source of inspiration. The late 1970s saw reverse thrust on the ideological front; the plastic and concrete orgies of the Pop decade no longer rated as forerunners of a better future, but simply as environmentally damaging emanations of the omnipresent consumer terror. The necessary political protest against a waste of resources unfortunately dissolved into a defensive aesthetic. From then on, pine was the material of choice for anti-capitalist correctness: Ideology critique had reached design, Niemeyer disappeared with the dreams (suddenly ideologically suspect, too) of Brazilian music, beaches and palms on the junk-piled stigmatized utopias. That said, no movement followed that presented future perspectives with the same degree of pathos. Instead of goddesses of sheet steel, we began to encounter depressing, oil-crisis design; At first cars looked joylessly sharp-edged, and then harmlessly affirmative. A bizarre zoomorphic spherical approach infused the design of compact cars: The Renault Twingo stood there like a tin dachshund. With the conscious infantilism in car design the ecological dubiousness of the car disintegrated into an ad mixture of emotionality and political resignation. How many Smart drivers still protest against dying forests today?

What the present generation of architects find fascinating about Niemeyer is apparently his sculptural inventiveness. Much in Niemeyer's work is decorum and manner; with Brasília, Modernism parted company with rigid rationalism and remained functional only to the point that the function was a suggestive dream image: the constructed promise of a better, dynamic world free of the dirt and decay of old cities. Trace elements of this "architecture parlante" can be found everywhere in contemporary architecture, in gmp's Tempodrom or in Christoph Ingenhoven's Stuttgart Station, whose tulip-like supports are reminiscent of the curvaceous lines of the Presidential Palace in Brasília. With Niemeyer, Modernism left the straitjacket of pure rationality and moved closer to entertainment and design – a rupture for which many have not forgiven him. His works are wonders of aesthetic effect; his tropical, over-hot Modernism naturally fell on fertile ground everywhere that architects had to design artificial paradises – be they the Tempodrom or a hotel complex in which a holiday life free from the

Ingenhoven, Overdiek und Partner, Unterirdischer Hauptbahnhof für Stuttgart. Modellansicht mit Stützen.

Ingenhoven, Overdiek and Partner, Central Underground Station for Stuttgart. View of the model complete with the supports.

J. Balladur, Feriensiedlung La Grande Motte. Kirche St. Augustin.

J. Balladur, La Grande Motte Holiday Colony. Church of Saint Augustine.

funktionalistisch nur insofern, als die Funktion hier ein suggestives Traumbild war: das gebaute Versprechen einer besseren, dynamischen, vom Dreck und dem Verfall der alten Städte befreiten Welt. Spurenelemente dieser „architecture parlante" finden sich überall in der zeitgenössischen Architektur, in gmp's Tempodrom ebenso wie in Christoph Ingenhovens Stuttgarter Bahnhof, dessen tulpenartige Stützen an die Schwünge des Präsidentenpalasts von Brasília erinnern. Mit Niemeyer verließ die Moderne den Schwitzkasten reiner Rationalität und näherte sich dem Entertainment und dem Design an – ein Bruch, den ihm viele nicht verziehen haben. Seine Bauten sind wirkungsästhetische Wunderwerke; seine tropisch überhitzte Moderne traf naturgemäß überall dort auf fruchtbaren Boden, wo die Architekten künstliche Paradiese zu entwerfen haben, ob Tempodrom oder Hotelanlagen, in denen ein vom maschinenhaften Alltag befreites Urlaubsleben auch ästhetisch Ausdruck finden soll. So kam es schon in den sechziger Jahren zu ersten interkulturellen Rückkoppelungen. Niemeyers tropische Gegenmoderne wurde wenige Jahre nach der Einweihung von Brasília zum Vorbild des französischen Architekten Jean Balladur. Der besuchte während der Planungsarbeiten an der Ferienstadt La Grande Motte Brasília, reimportierte die ins Schleudern geratene Moderne und baute im Languedoc Ferienappartements, die wie vom Schlingervirus befallen am Strand entlangkurven und jenen Spaß versprachen, den die flimmernden Discotheken und Bars im Keller der Bauten einlösen sollten.

Heute ist die Sache schwieriger. Mit dem Übergang vom Mondraketen- und Atomzeitalter ins gentechnische Jahrhundert zerfallen die Bilder des Zukünftigen. Ein Autohersteller wird, im Bemühen um stilprägende Zeitgenossenschaft, kaum ein DNSförmiges Auto bauen, auch wenn Volkswagen mit dem Bild einer Stammzelle wirbt, deren Kern die Silhouette eines Käfers hat. In der Architektur dominieren zwei nostalgische Tendenzen, die gleichermaßen von Ratlosigkeit und Unbehagen angesichts der Gegenwart zeugen: ein neuer Historismus, der am augenscheinlichsten im Hotel Adlon und den neogründerzeitlichen Villen von Hans Kollhoff auftritt, und eine „Zweite Moderne", deren gefällige Kisten wie der letzte kraftlose Abguss alter Bauhausaxiome wirken. Die grellen Designobjekte und Bauten des Retrofuturismus, die dazu als Gegenthese auftreten, wiederholen einen Grundkonflikt, der schon in den sechziger Jahren ausgetragen wurde. Damals trat der schwungvoll skulpturale Niemeyer-Modernismus gegen die verhärmte Tristesse an, die unbegabte Adepten der Charta von Athen in den großen Städten angerichtet hatten. Die Stoffmulden und Plastikhocker von Eero Saarinen und Verner Panton, die elegant schwingenden Pfeiler des Justizpalasts

machine-dominated everyday was also to find aesthetic expression. Thus as early as the 1960s, the first intercultural cross-fertilization emerged. A few years after the inauguration of Brasília, Niemeyer's tropical counter-Modernism became the role model for French architect, Jean Balladur. He visited Brasília while busy planning the holiday town of La Grande Motte, re-imported the Modernism that had slid out of control, and built holiday apartments Languedoc which snake along the beach as if infected by a creeping virus, promising the fun which the glimmering discos and bars in the cellars of the buildings purportedly offer.

Things are more difficult today. With the transition from lunar rockets and the atomic age to the decade of genetic engineering, images of the future disintegrate. A car manufacturer is hardly going to design a DNA-shaped car simply in order to concur with the style of the day – even if Volkswagen happens to advertise with an image of a stem cell whose nucleus is the silhouette of a beetle. There are two nostalgic trends dominating architecture which equally display the current age's restlessness and unease: a new historicism which is most discernible in Hotel Adlon and has also surfaced in the neoturn-of-the-century appearance of Hans Kolhoff's villas, and "Second-Wave Modernism" whose obliging boxes resemble the last exhausted replicas of Bauhaus axioms. The gaudy design objects and buildings of Retro-Futurism take the limelight as the antithesis to all this, repeating a basic conflict, which was fought out back in the 1960s. In those days the curvaceous, sculptural Niemeyer-Modernism challenged the woebegone days that the untalented adepts of the Charter of Athens unleashed on large cities. The textile hollows and plastic stools of Eero Saarinen and Verner Panton, the elegantly sweeping Palace of Justice in Brasília – these were the palace revolts of the poets within the monastic walls of Modernism, an attempt to leave the cold steel frames into which the great Mies had banished them. Today, curvaceous Modernism has also become the critical explosive. Retro-Futurism is a confused protest against the power of the timid who cultivate retrogression renouncement, and reduction as the only future options. Until the really innovative materials of the present, such as those developed for solar technology are formed into a new aesthetic, Retro-Futurist cars and houses will remain as melancholic statues, maintaining an awareness of our yearning for a future of our own.

von Brasília waren die Palastrevolte der Poeten in den Klostermauern der Moderne, ein Versuch, aus den kalten Stahlgestellen herauszukommen, in die der große Mies sie verbannt hatte. Auch heute wird die schwingende Moderne wieder zum kritischen Sprengsatz. Gegen die Macht der Mutlosen, die den Rückbau, den Verzicht und die Reduktion als einzige Zukunftsoptionen kultivieren, ist der Retrofuturismus ein verzweifelter Protest. Solange, bis die wirklich innovativen Materialien der Gegenwart, etwa die der Solartechnik, zu einer neuen Ästhetik verdichtet werden, halten die retrofuturistischen Autos und Häuser als melancholische Standbilder die Sehnsucht nach einer eigenen Zukunft im Bewusstsein.

Oscar Niemeyer und die Landschaft
Oscar Niemeyer and landscape

Paul Andreas

Stills aus dem Dokumentarfilm
„Oscar Niemeyer, un archi-
tecte engagé dans le siècle"
von Marc-Henri Wajnberg.

Stills from the documentary
"Oscar Niemeyer, un archi-
tecte engagé dans le siècle"
by Marc-Henri Wajnberg.

Man schreibt das Jahr 1991, als dieses ungewöhn-
liche Flugobjekt Kurs auf die Bucht von Guanabara/
Brasilien nimmt. In einem kurzen Manöver durch-
bricht es die Wolkendecke und taucht in die
charakteristische Hügellandschaft rund um Rio de
Janeiro ein. Im rasanten Sturzflug überquert es
die Anhöhe des „Corcovada", nähert sich gefährlich
nahe der monumentalen Christusstatue, sinkt und
überfliegt die Hochhausschluchten der Millionen-
stadt, kurzzeitig mit dem Gedanken spielend, in
dem Spielfeld eines Stadions zu landen. Am imposanten Felsmassiv des „Zuckerhutes" angekommen
– als hätte es sich die Sache noch einmal anders
überlegt –, dreht es ab und verfolgt die geschwungene Küstenlinie in Richtung Osten. Weiter geht es
die Copacabana entlang, bis eine Landzunge
gesichtet wird – ein schmaler Grat direkt am Meer.
Spontan setzt das Gefährt zur Landung an und
gelangt – dank seines heckgestützten Raketen-
antriebes – sicher auf den Boden. Flammen und ein
Nebel von Rauchschwaden steigen empor und, aus
ihnen gleichsam unbeschadet hervortretend, der
Kommandant. Gelassen – das Meer rauscht im
Hintergrund und es zwitschern die Vögel – schreitet
Oscar Niemeyer eine geschwungene, purpurrote
Rampe herab: Das Bodenpersonal hat sie eigens
dafür angedockt, so als sei die abrupte Landung nur
ein kurzer Zwischenhalt, der Weiterflug in andere
kosmische Sphären bereits beschlossene Sache
zu sein.

Mit so einem Raumschiff-Orion-Szenario könnte
sich wohl alles zugetragen haben, als das Museum
für zeitgenössische Kunst in der Stadt Niterói,
15 Kilometer Luftlinie von Rio entfernt, seinen besonders malerischen Landeplatz fand. Zumindest hat
es sich der belgische Filmemacher Marc-Henri
Wajnberg so vorgestellt und als Vorspann für seinen
mehrfach preisgekrönten Film über den Architekten
Oscar Niemeyer effektvoll ins Bild gesetzt. Lebhafter
Fantasie bedurfte das kaum. Denn das Szenario,
das in der Filmsequenz mit Hilfe einer Computer-
animation vorgeführt wird, liegt vor allem in der
futuristischen Formensprache des Gebäudes selbst
begründet.

It was back in 1991, when this unusual flying object
started to head straight for the Bay of Guanabara
in Brazil. In a brief maneuver it emerges through the
clouds and dips down over the characteristic hills
that surround Rio de Janeiro. Diving at breakneck
speed it crosses the heights of Corcovada, comes
dangerously near to the monumental statue of
Christ, continues to lose height, and flies across the
metropolis' maze of sky-rises, for a moment playing
with the idea of alighting on the playing field in
a stadium. On arriving at the impressive rock cliffs
of the Sugar Loaf – as if it has had second thoughts
– it simply turns around and follows the curves of the
coast line heading East. It continues up along the
Copacabana, until a peninsula is sighted – a narrow
ridge that drops into the sea. Spontaneously, the
object goes into descent mode and manages,
thanks to its rear-mounted rocket engines, to land
safely on the ground. Flames and a veritable fog
of smoke clouds rise up, from which, unscathed,
the commandant then emerges unscathed. Quite
leisurely – with the waves crashing in the background
and the birds chirping – Oscar Niemeyer strides
down a curved bright purple ramp which the ground
staff have docked onto the craft specially. And
yet this abrupt landing has the air of a brief sojourn
about it, as if the schedule had already been
decided, flying onwards to other cosmic spheres.

Perhaps it was the product of such a USS enter-
prise that led to the Museum for Contemporary Art
in the city of Niterói, 15 kilometers from Rio as the
crow flies, choosing its location in such marvelously
picturesque landing grounds. At any rate, this is
how Belgian filmmaker Marc-Henri Wajnberg imagined things to have been, and so impressively
depicted the event in the opening credits to his
award-winning film on architect Oscar Niemeyer.
It hardly required much imagination, as the scenario
presented in the film sequence by means of c
omputer animation has strong roots above all in
the Futuristic idiom of the building itself.

The two exhibition floors jut out like a flying saucer
over the low stump of the building's concrete core.
The almost sculpted volume of the building is molded

Wie bei einer fliegenden Untertasse kragen die beiden Ausstellungsetagen über dem niedrigen Stumpf eines Betonkerns hervor. Strukturiert wird das wie eine flache Hohlschale plastisch geformte Geschossvolumen aus weißem Sichtbeton durch ein eingeschnittenes, opak verspiegeltes Fensterband – das sorgt in den Innenräumen für die richtige Belichtung und ein berauschendes Panorama der Felsenküstenlandschaft, verleiht dem Volumen aber auch den Anschein von Rotation und Eigenbewegung. Verankert ist die ganze Betonkonstruktion auf einer massiven, am Rande deutlich abgeschrägten runden Sockelplatte, die so weit über das Sockelgeschoss auskragt, dass die Architektur gleichsam über dem Erdboden zu schweben scheint.

So futuristisch diese dynamische Architektur anmutet, so wenig ist sie jedoch ein extraterrestrischer Fremdkörper, der auf dem schmalen Felsvorsprung gleichsam nur notgelandet wäre. Die → p. 103 monumentale Großform, die sich aus der Ferne wie eine autonome Skulptur behauptet, losgelöst vom Felsengrund, korrespondiert in einem weiteren Radius deutlich mit der umliegenden Landschaft. → S. 103 Wenn man vor dem Gebäude steht, werden diese Gemeinsamkeiten in der Gestalt sichtbar: Im erst flach auskragenden, dann anschwellenden Profil des Geschossvolumens, aber auch in der horizontal über dem Boden schwebenden Spiralform der Rampe findet der Verlauf der Felsrücken seinen Widerhall, mit dem die Guanabara-Bucht am Horizont eingefasst ist. Ein um den Betonkern herum angelegtes flaches Wasserbassin scheint durch die Himmels- und Sonnenreflexionen das Meer noch weiter an das Gebäude heranholen zu wollen. Architektur und landschaftlicher Hintergrund – sie sind hier deutlich aufeinander bezogen, könnten einander näher kaum sein.

Die freien Formen der Natur
Immer wieder ist Oscar Niemeyer gefragt worden, worin denn die Inspirationsquelle seiner skulpturalen Formen läge, die die gekrümmte und geschwungene Linie so intensiv kultivieren und nicht – wie es die Doktrinen der funktionalistischen Moderne lange forderten – auf das orthogonale Raster zurückgreifen. Immer wieder hat Oscar Niemeyer die eine gleiche Antwort gegeben: „Le Corbusier sagte einmal, dass ich die Berge von Rio immer vor Augen hätte. Ich lachte. Ich ziehe es vor, so zu denken wie André Malraux, der einmal sagte: Ich trage in mir und meinem privaten Museum alles, was ich gesehen und geliebt habe in meinem Leben. (…) Es ist nicht der rechte Winkel, der mich anzieht / noch die harte, unflexible gerade Linie, die vom Menschen geschaffen wurde / Es ist die freie und sinnliche Kurve, die mich verführt / die Wölbungen, die ich sehen kann in den Bergen meines Landes / in

to nearly resemble a flat hollow bowl using white fair-faced concrete, and lent texture by a ribbon of opaque mirrored windows cut into the concrete – ensuring the rooms inside benefit from the right light and enjoy an intoxicating panoramic view out over the craggy coastline, while also giving the body of the building a sense of rotation and intrinsic motion. The entire concrete structure is anchored in a solid round base plate, a massive slab with edges that are clearly angled and that extend so far out over the ground floor that the architecture seems to float over the ground, as it were.

For all the futurist feel this dynamic architecture has, it is definitely not an extra-terrestrial alien body that was forced to opt for an emergency landing, as it were, on this narrow cliff. The immense monumental form that from a distance seems to be a sculpture in its own right, quite distinct from the rocks on which it stands, corresponds, across a broad radius with the surrounding countryside. If you stand in front of the building these common formal features swiftly become apparent in the shape. The course of the ridge of rocks and cliffs that on the horizon serves as a frame for the Bay of Guanabara is taken up and echoed in the jutting profile of the overall volume, initially flat and then gradually swelling, not to mention in the spiral form of the ramp which floats horizontally over the ground. A flat water basin positioned around the concrete core seems to wish to draw the sea even closer to the building by reflecting the heavens and the sun. Here, architecture and the background landscape are clearly interrelated and could hardly be closer to each other.

Nature's free forms
Oscar Niemeyer has repeatedly been asked on what source of inspiration his sculptural shapes draw when they so intensively nurture the curved and vibrant line, eschewing the orthogonal grid on which the doctrine of functionalist Modernists so insisted. Oscar Niemeyer has always given the same answer: "Le Corbusier said once that I had Rio's mountains in my eye. I laughed. I prefer to think like André Malraux, who said: 'I keep inside myself, in my private museum, everything I have seen and loved in my life.' (…) It's not the right angle that attracts me / Nor the hard, inflexible straight line / created by man / It's the free and sensual curve that seduces me / the curve that I can see in the mountains of my country / in the sinuous curves of its rivers / On the sea waves / On the body of a favorite woman / The universe is all made of curves / Einstein's curved universe." [1]

Niemeyer's architectural creed is simple and makes do without any grand theoretical superstructure. This is the creed of an artist, a drawer who finds the shapes for his art in the world of the sense that sur-

den gewundenen Biegungen seiner Flüsse/auf den Wellen des Meeres/am Körper einer Frau, die mir gefällt. Das ganze Universum ist aus Krümmungen gemacht, Einsteins gekrümmtes Universum."[1]

Niemeyers architektonisches Credo ist einfach, kommt ohne einen großen theoretischen Überbau aus. Es ist das Credo eines Künstlers, eines Zeichners, der die Formen seiner Kunst in der sinnlichen, ihn umgebenden Welt findet und in Beton gießen lässt – freilich ohne diese dabei ganz konkret abbilden zu wollen. Niemeyers Verhältnis zu den organisch geschwungenen Formen der Natur ist ein modernes anti-mimetisches – auch wenn der Architekt immer wieder Frauenakte skizzierte, um die Prinzipien der Wölbung zu demonstrieren und – auch das sicherlich – zu propagieren. Auch im Zusammenhang mit dem Museum von Niterói hat denn Niemeyer darauf hingewiesen, dass ihm bei dem Entwurf des Baukörpers der Blütenansatz einer tropischen Pflanze Pate gestanden habe.[2]

Niemeyers Formensprache orientiert sich an den freien Formen der Natur, aber sie tut es in einem allgemeinen, autonomen, abstrahierenden Sinne – die konkrete Natur, die Landschaft und der Ort stehen ihm zwar Modell, er vertraut sich ihnen aber nicht blindlings an. Kontextualismus ist nicht Oscar Niemeyers primäres Anliegen – auch wenn er vor den Bauherren seine eigenwilligen Formen oftmals damit begründen musste.[3] Wichtiger sind die Fantasie und die Erfindungskraft, mit der der Architekt die natürlichen Krümmungen zu ausgreifenden skulpturalen Formen ergänzt, die den euklidischen Gesetzen der Geometrie und der tradierten konstruktiven Logik widerstehen. Ein wenig wie bei den modernen Skulpturen Henry Moores entstehen dabei Gebilde, die sich im Zwischenraum von Abstraktion und Figuration, von Bio- und Anthropomorphismus bewegen.

Ein anderes Verhältnis zur Landschaft

So sehr Niemeyers Gebäude als autonome architektonische Gebilde verstanden werden müssen, hat der Architekt stets versucht, in Kontakt mit dem Ort und der Landschaft zu treten, beide so einzubinden, dass sie visuell erfahrbar werden. Oftmals, vor allem bei den Projekten im städtischen Kontext, als imposanten Hintergrundprospekt, der vor einer Dachterrasse oder aber einer Fensterfront ausgebreitet wird – strukturiert und rhythmisiert durch Öffnungen, Fensterprofilierungen und Brise-Soleils. Aber auch unmittelbarer, ohne Distanz und Sicherheitsabstand, wie in dem Wochenendhaus, das der Architekt sich und seiner Familie 1953 in Canoas bei Rio de Janeiro errichtete. Auch heute noch liegt es inmitten eines tropischen Waldes, am Hang einer jener Hügelketten, die das Landschaftsszenario rund um die

← pp. 13–15

← S. 13 –15

Büro des Architekten in Rio de Janeiro. Ausblick auf die Copacabana.

The architect's office at Rio de Janeiro. View on the Copacabana.

rounds him and then has them poured in concrete – without wishing to depict them quite concretely. Niemeyer's relationship to the organic curving shapes of nature is modern, and most certainly antimimetic, too – even if the architect has repeatedly sketched female nudes in order to demonstrate the principles of the curving protrusion and to propagate them. Indeed, in connection with the Niterói Art Museum Niemeyer has also pointed out that when devising the shape of the building he took as his model the blossom of a tropical plant.[2]

Niemeyer's formal idiom takes its cue from the free forms of nature, but it does so in a general, independent, abstracting sort of way – although actual nature, the landscape and a particular location function as his models, he does not blindly trust them. Contextualism is not Oscar Niemeyer's primary intention, even if he has often cited it to justify to his clients why he has chosen such idiosyncratic shapes.[3] More important are the imagination and the powers of invention with which he supplements the natural curves of such extensive sculptural shapes, forms that resist the Euclidian rules of geometry and traditional structural logic. A little like Henry Moore's modern sculptures, edifices thus arise that move in some halfway zone between abstraction and figuration, between bio- and anthropomorphism.

A different relationship to landscape

However much we must understand Niemeyer's buildings as an independent architectural construct, he has always endeavored to establish links to the place and landscape, to incorporate both in such a way that they can be visually experienced. Often, above all with his projects in an urban context, he achieves this by including them as an impressive background vista that unfolds before a roof-top patio or the front window) – structured and given a rhythm by openings, window profiles and brise-soleils. Yet again, he also does so directly, avoiding distance and any safety zone, as in the week-end residence that he built for himself and his family in 1953 in Canoas, near Rio de Janeiro. Today, it still lies in the middle of a tropical forest, on the slope of one of those ridges of hills that define the look of the landscape round the Bay of Guanabara. The layout of the two stories is fully determined by the natural relief of the ground on the site – Niemeyer almost left it in its virgin state. While the lower floor, which houses the bedrooms, fits snugly into the slope and has few openings, Niemeyer interpreted the story with the living quarters as a free-standing pavilion borne by pillars transparent on all sides, which, with its amoeba-like curved roof (it juts out significantly over the outer line of the building), is placed on a generous terraced platform set into

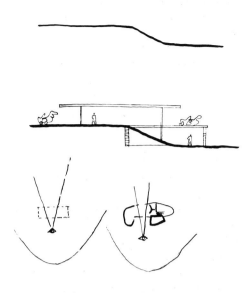

Haus in Canoas. Zeichnung mit Geländequerschnitt und verschiedenen Durchsichten.

House at Canoas. Sketch with site's cross-section and different views.

Guanabara-Bucht bestimmen. Die Disposition seiner beiden Geschosse ist ganz durch das natürliche Bodenrelief bestimmt – der Architekt beließ es nahezu in seinem ursprünglichen Zustand. Während sich das Sockelgeschoss mit den Schlafräumen deutlich an den Hang anschmiegt und nur mit wenigen Öffnungen versehen ist, interpretierte Niemeyer das Wohngeschoss als einen freistehenden, auf Stützen gelagerten, nach allen Seiten hin transparenten Pavillon, der sich mit seinem amöbenartig geschwungenen und weit auskragenden Dach auf einer großzügigen, in den Hang hineingebauten Terrassenplattform platziert. Herzstück des Entwurfes ist ein am Ort vorgefundener Granitfelsen, den der Architekt mit großem Geschick in die Komposition des Hauses einzubinden verstand: Wie ein Gelenk verschränkt der in seiner natürlichen Form und Dimension belassene, die organisch geschwungene Glaswand sanft penetrierende Findling den Pavillon mit dem kleinen Pool, der einige Meter davor in die Terrasse eingelassen wurde, und dem unteren Schlaftrakt – eine Treppe wurde in ihn hineingehauen. Innen und außen fließen hier nicht nur durch die Transparenz der vielfach gekrümmten Glasfassade, sondern auch durch die natürlichen Zwänge des Ortes meisterhaft ineinander, Schwere und Leichtigkeit bilden einen spannungsreichen Kontrast.

Die konsequente Einbindung des vorgefundenen Terrains und die Nähe zur üppigen tropischen Vegetation machen das Haus von Canoas zu einem Manifest eines besonderen Naturverhältnisses. Anders als sein Vorbild Le Corbusier, der wohl die Bedeutung der Landschaft für die moderne Architektur erkannte, sie aber doch als ein Phänomen ansah, das der bewussten Distanzierung und der Rasterung bedurfte, legte es Niemeyer hier darauf an, mit der Umgebung auf unmittelbare Tuchfühlung zu gehen. Ernesto Rogers, der 1954 anlässlich der Architekturbiennale von São Paulo einer der illustren ausländischen Besucher war, erkannte diesen Unterschied sofort: „Der Hauptteil des Hauses ist in seinem Charakter nach draußen orientiert, und zwar nicht nur, weil sich das Wohnzimmer fortsetzt, ohne durch Wände oder andere Raumteiler unterbrochen zu sein, sondern auch, weil er dazu tendiert, sich romantisch mit der Natur zu identifizieren und ein Teil von ihr zu werden." [4]

Nicht allein wegen des besonderen tropischen Klimas, um Schatten und Schutz vor Regen zu spenden, sondern auch aus ästhetischen Gründen greift denn auch das Amöben-Dach des Pavillons so weit über den Glasvorhang hinaus. Die weit jenseits des Grundstückes liegenden Anhöhen des Serra-do-Mar-Massivs rücken dadurch näher an den Betrachter heran und lassen den Felsen mit

the slope. Pride of place in the design is given to the granite rock that was found on site and which with great dexterity Niemeyer managed to incorporate into the composition of the house: the rock, left in its natural form and size, functions almost like a joint, softly penetrating the organically curving glass front wall to marry the pavilion, the small pool, dug into the terrace a few meters in front of the building, and the sleeping quarters below – a staircase was carved into the rock. Inside and outside are blended here masterfully, not only owing to the transparent quality of the multi-curved glass façade, but also owing to the natural site-specific constraints: gravity and a sense of lightness combine in an exciting contrast.

The consistent inclusion of the given terrain as found, and the proximity of the opulent tropical vegetation ensure that the Canoas House is a true manifesto on a special relationship to nature. Unlike his role model Le Corbusier, who probably recognized the importance of the countryside for modern architecture but considered it a phenomenon that required a deliberate policy of distantiation and grid zoning, here Niemeyer endeavors to forge a direct interface with the surroundings. Ernesto Rogers, who was one of the illustrious foreigner visitors in 1954 on the occasion of the São Paulo Architectural Biennial, immediately spotted the difference: "The main part of the house is outward in character, not only because the living room space continuous uninterrupted by walls or other partitions out into the open, but also because it romantically tends to identify itself with nature and become a part of it." [4]

The amoeba-like roof of the pavilion juts out so far over the glass curtain wall not only owing to the particular tropical climate, in order to provide shade and protection against rain, but also for aesthetic reasons. It likewise brings the heights of the Serra do Mar Mountains that rise up a long way in the distance far closer to the viewer, and as a consequence the rock and the swimming pool have the feel of a miniature landscape in the midst of the broader landscape.

Home and Garden: Projects with landscape architect Roberto Burle Marx

Numerous buildings created by Oscar Niemeyer are surrounded by paths and covered connecting walkways, shaped with the same curves as are so typical of the bodies of many of his buildings. Often it was Niemeyer himself who devised them, who has Le Corbusier's "promenade architecturale" actually commence outside the building proper. Anyone walking towards a Niemeyer building is immediately made aware of the visual dynamics of a succession of constantly changing views. In some of his projects,

dem Swimmingpool gleichsam wie eine Miniaturlandschaft vor der Landschaft wirken.

Haus und Garten: Projekte mit dem Landschaftsgestalter Roberto Burle Marx

Nicht wenige Bauten Oscar Niemeyers sind von Wegen und überdachten Verbindungsgängen umgeben, die mit dem gleichen Schwung geformt sind, der auch vielen seiner Volumen eigen ist. Oft lässt Niemeyer Le Corbusiers „promenade architecturale" bereits außerhalb des Gebäudes beginnen. Wer sich seinem Gebäude nähert, bekommt die Dynamik sukzessiver, sich ständig verändernder Ansichten vorgeführt. Bei einigen Projekten ist diese äußere Erschließung durch eine Gartengestaltung ergänzt, die in vielen Fällen von dem bekannten brasilianischen Landschaftsarchitekten und Künstler Roberto Burle Marx (1909–1994). Im Folgenden soll an einige Stationen dieser Projektzusammenarbeit erinnert werden, bei der Architektur, Garten und umliegende Landschaft in einen abwechslungs- und spannungsreichen Dialog eintreten. [5]

Niemeyer und Burle Marx lernten sich durch ihren gemeinsamen Lehrer, den Architekten-Urbanisten und späteren Brasília-Entwerfer Lúcio Costa, kennen. Burle Marx, der Malerei studierte, aber auch Kurse in Architektur gehört hatte und nicht zuletzt wegen seiner außergewöhnlichen botanischen Kenntnisse von Costa als Gartengestalter engagiert wurde, war Ende der dreißiger Jahre an dem international viel beachteten Projekt für das Ministerium für Erziehung und Gesundheit beteiligt, das Costa, Niemeyer und eine Reihe weiterer junger Architekten unter der Zuratnahme von Le Corbusier konzipierten und realisierten. Burle Marx assistierte hierbei nicht nur dem Mosaikkünstler Cândido Portinari, sondern lieferte auch die Pläne für die Grünanlagen, darunter den Dachgarten auf dem Flachbau der Anlage, der beim Ausblick von den oberen Etagen des 18-stöckigen Hochhauses noch heute wie ein abstraktes Gemälde wirkt. Seine biomorphen, organisch aneinander gefügten Stromlinienformen artikulierte Burle Marx zum einen durch die Wegeführung, zum anderen durch eine differenzierte Bepflanzung mit einer Vielfalt verschiedenfarbiger, zu großflächigen Pflanzgruppen zusammengefasster tropischer Gewächse – auch das übrigens eine Neuheit, denn bis dahin waren Gartenanlagen in Brasilien durch die Verwendung europäischer Arten kolonial geprägt.

Als Oscar Niemeyer 1940 den Auftrag zu einer eleganten Wohnsiedlung mit verschiedenen Freizeiteinrichtungen nahe eines künstlichen Sees in Pampulha, einem Vorort der Industriestadt Belo Horizonte, bekommt, scheint er an die einstige Zusammenarbeit anknüpfen zu wollen und greift für die Land-

these external impressions are buttressed by the garden landscaping, devised and added by the renowned Brazilian landscape designer and artist Roberto Burle Marx (1909–1994). In the following I wish to draw attention to a few of the stages of this collaboration, thanks to which architecture, gardens and the surrounding landscape enter into an exciting dialog that changes from one site to the next.[5]

It was Lúcio Costa, champion of architectural urbanism and at a later date the mind behind Brasília, who taught both Niemeyer and Burle Marx, who ensured the two first became acquainted with each other. Burle Marx, who studied painting, but also attended lectures in architecture and was employed as a garden designer by Costa, not least owing to his exceptional knowledge of botany, took part at the end of the 1930s in the Ministry of Education and Health project that so caught the international eye – Costa, Niemeyer and a series of other young architects devised and realized it, seeking the advice of Le Corbusier in the process. Burle Marx not only assisted mosaic artist Cândido Portinari, but also devised the plans for the greenery sections, (including the roof gardens on the terrace-roofed building); when viewed today from one of the upper floors of the 18-storey high-rise, the greenery still resembles an abstract painting. Burle Marx lent voice to its biomorphic, organically linked streamlined shapes both in the routes he chose for the pathways and by a differentiated choice of plants of different colors that included a broad variety of tropical flora and were brought together to form larger groups – this, too, was a novelty, as until that time gardens tended to be arranged in a colonial vein with the preference being for European plants.

When in 1940 Oscar Niemeyer was commissioned to design an elegant residential estate with various leisure-time facilities near to an artificial lake in Pampulha, a suburb of the industrial city of Belo Horizonte, he apparently re-vitalized the earlier collaboration and asked Burle Marx to plan the layout of the gardens. The park-like complex was commissioned by Belo Horizonte's mayor of the day and later President Juscelino Kubitschek, the champion of modernization and the founder of Brazil's capital city. The grounds included not only a casino and a yacht club, but also a restaurant with dancing and a chapel, that were spread around the lake's shores as isolated standalone buildings, in sight of one another – a planned hotel never materialized owing to financial problems. It is impossible today to find an unequivocal answer to the question whether it was the hilly terrain around the lake, the agenda with its emphasis mainly on leisure-time quality and relaxation, or simply the discovery of just what

R. Burle Marx, Dachgarten auf dem Flachbau des Ministeriums für Erziehung und Gesundheit, Rio de Janeiro, Foto um 1940.

R. Burle Marx. Roof garden of the low building of the Ministry of Education and Health, Rio de Janeiro. Photo around 1940.

schaftsplanung auf Burle Marx zurück. Der vom Bürgermeister von Belo Horizonte, dem späteren Modernisierungs-Präsidenten und Hauptstadtgründer Juscelino Kubitschek in Auftrag gegebene parkartige Komplex umfasst neben einem Kasino und einem Yachtclub ein Tanzrestaurant und eine Kapelle, die sich als isolierte Solitäre mit Sichtbezügen um das Seeufer herum verteilen – ein geplantes Hotel kam wegen finanzieller Probleme nicht zur Ausführung. Ob es die hügelige Landschaft rund um den See, das in erster Linie auf Unterhaltungswert und Freizeitvergnügen angelegte Programm oder aber nur die Entdeckung der ungeahnten Möglichkeiten des Spannbetons waren, die Niemeyer dazu bewegten, seine Vorstellungen von einer plastischen, von den Doktrinen des Funktionalismus entbundenen Formensprache umzusetzen, kann bis heute nicht eindeutig beantwortet werden. Eins ist jedoch sicher: Burle Marx' Form der Gartengestaltung scheint Niemeyer dabei gut ins Konzept ← p. 9 gepasst zu haben. Seine organische Formensprache, die bereits Ende der dreißiger Jahre von der Auseinandersetzung mit der abstrakten Malerei (v.a. Arp, Calder, Miro) kündet, aber dabei doch ganz auf den dreidimensionalen Freiraum zugeschnitten ist – gleichsam nur umherwandelnd, aus verschiedenen Sichtperspektiven erlebt werden kann – nimmt viel von jener Formenfreiheit voraus, nach der Niemeyer strebt und die er mit dem Pampulha-Projekt erstmals in Beton zu gießen versucht.

← S. 9 Vor allem der Bau des Tanzrestaurants Casa do Baile – 1942 auf einer schmalen künstlichen Insel im See errichtet – führt vor, wie eng Architektur und Landschaftsgestaltung in dem Projekt aufeinander bezogen sind: Die geschwungene Uferlinie der Insel wird deutlich von den Umrissen der transparenten Glasfassade aufgenommen, die hinter den Pilotis des Rundbaus mit der zentralen Tanzbühne zurückspringt. Aus ihm wächst eine Kolonnade mit einem flachen Dachschirm hervor, die sich – ebenfalls auf Pilotis gestützt – stromlinienförmig bis zu einer runden Außenbühne schlängelt, einen kleinen nierenförmigen Teich mit Seerosen hinterfangend. Die vor der Glasfront ausgebreitete, durch ein Pflanzbeet und eine Skulptur aufgelockerte Terrasse nimmt diese dynamisch geschwungenen Formen auf und führt sie in einem wellenförmigen Muster als Bodenmosaik fort. Die Vielzahl der übereinander gelagerten und ineinander gefügten Krümmungslinien von Architektur, Garten und Terrain versetzen die gesamte Insel in Schwingungen – dass sich dies auf das tanzende Publikum übertragen möge, auch das könnte einer der wirkungsästhetischen Hintergedanken beim Entwurf der Anlage gewesen sein.

undreamt-of possibilities pre-stressed concrete had to offer that prompted Niemeyer to put into practice his ideas of a sculptural idiom, freed of the trammeling doctrine of functionalism. However, one thing can be said for certain: Burle Marx's way of designing gardens jelled well with Niemeyer's approach. Burle Marx's was an organic formal vocabulary, that in the late 1930s already stands witness to his critical inquiry into the abstract paintings of Arp, Calder, Miró and others, yet it was tailored carefully to meet the three-dimensional requirements of outdoor settings – it can be experienced from various vantage points as if it were simply there for you to wander around it, as it were. This pre-empts much of that freedom of form which Niemeyer aspired to achieve in his architecture and which he first essayed to realize in the shape of molded concrete for the Pampulha project.

Above all, the building of the Casa do Baile dance restaurant – erected in 1942 on a narrow artificial islet on the lake – shows how closely architecture and landscape gardening are inter-related in the project: the curved shoreline of the island is clearly emulated by the outline of the transparent glass facade which recedes behind the pilotis of the circular building with its central dance-floor stage. From it emanates a colonnade with a flat roof top, which (likewise supported by pilotis) winds its streamlined way to a round outdoor stage, in this way backing up a small kidney-shaped pond with lilies. The terrace that spreads out before the glass front, leisurely arranged with a flowerbed and a sculpture, repeats this dynamic curved shape and takes it up in the wave-shaped pattern of the mosaic on the ground. The large number of superimposed and dovetailed curving lines of the buildings, garden and terrain set the entire island in vibrant motion – perhaps to seize hold also of those in the restaurant and get them dancing, or so we can imagine Niemeyer may have construed the effect of the aesthetics of the complex.

Niemeyer succeeded in persuading Burle Marx to work with him on a series of projects well into the mid-1950s. Opulent private residences with expansive grounds arose, such as the project for Burton Tremaine in Santa Barbara (California, 1947) – one of those in which the architect developed buildings that strongly extended out into the surrounding space, whereby a lounge landscape complete with swimming pool, bar and open-air living area arises around an organically curved, shady roof top. Burle Marx adds not only high beach palms, but also takes up the curving lines Niemeyer had defined for the architecture and driveway and paths, paraphrasing them in the organically curved contours of the expansive, staggered colors of the

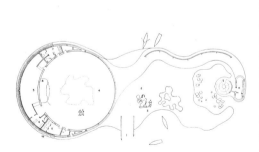

Casa do Baile, Tanzrestaurant, Pampulha. Grundriss.

Casa do Baile. Dancehall and restaurant, Pampulha. Ground plan.

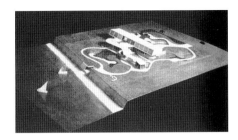

Haus Burton Tremaine,
Santa Barbara.
Modell um 1947.

Burton Tremaine Residence,
Santa Barbara.
Model around 1947.

Bis in die Mitte der fünfziger Jahre gelingt es Niemeyer, Burle Marx für eine Reihe von Projekten zu engagieren. Opulente Privathäuser mit ausladenden Gartenanlagen entstehen dabei, wie etwa das Projekt für Burton Tremaine in Santa Barbara (Kalifornien/USA 1947) – eines von jenen Projekten, in denen der Architekt mit seinen Bauten weit in den Außenraum hinausgreift und um einen organisch geschwungenen, Schatten spendenden Dachschirm herum eine Lounge-Landschaft mit Swimmingpool, Bar und Open-Air-Living-Zone entstehen lässt. Burle Marx fügt dem nicht nur hohe Strandpalmen hinzu, sondern nimmt auch die Kurvenlinien auf, die Niemeyer in der Architektur und in ihren Erschließungswegen vorgibt, und paraphrasiert sie in den organisch geschwungenen Konturen der großflächigen, farblich abgestuften Pflanzbeete, den Grün- und Teichanlagen. Niemeyers auf Pilotis aufgeständerter, orthogonaler Block mit den Privat- und Gästeräumen bildet dazu einen deutlichen Kontrapunkt.

Und doch müssen Architektur und Gartenanlage auch bei Niemeyer und Burle Marx nicht immer die selbe organische Formensprache sprechen. Das Landhaus für Edmundo Cavanelas (Pedro do Rio, 1954) ist da ein gutes Beispiel. Wie ein Zelt hat Niemeyer das Dach des eingeschossigen Pavillons an vier Eckpfeilern aus Feldstein aufgehängt. Frei gruppierte Wandscheiben und Glasvorhänge gliedern die Räume und ermöglichen partielle Durchsichten durch das Gebäude. Das flache, eine sanfte Kurve beschreibende Hängedach rahmt die karge Berglandschaft im Hintergrund.

Haus Cavanelas, Rio do Pedro.
Ansicht vom Garten.

Cavanelas Residence, Rio do
Pedro. View from the Garden.

Roberto Burle Marx fügt dem zwischen zwei Bergrücken eingestellten Haus zwei Gärten hinzu: Der Vorgarten bettet das Haus in die vorhandene Landschaft ein, indem er, wie gehabt, die Kurvenlinien der Architektur, des Daches und der Zufahrt, aber auch des Bergpanoramas in den Konturen der Rabatten, Rasenflächen, Teichanlagen etc. aufnimmt. Der rückwärtige Terrassengarten setzt dagegen deutlich auf Kontrast: Ein quadratisches, schachbrettartiges, von hellen und dunklen Bodendeckern gebildetes Parterre breitet sich vor der Terrasse flach aus, ordnet dem Haus den orthogonal geschnittenen Swimmingpool asymmetrisch zu – das Raster Mies van der Rohes oder auch das des amerikanischen Landschaftsarchitekten Dan Kiley scheinen hier bei der Landschaftsgestaltung Pate gestanden zu haben.

flowerbeds, the greenery and the ponds. This is a clear counterpoint to Niemeyer's orthogonal block with the private residence and guest rooms, which stand on pilotis.

That said, for Niemeyer and Burle Marx the architecture and garden landscaping did not always have to speak the same organic formal language. A good example of this fact is the country house for Edmundo Cavanelas (Pedro do Rio, 1954): Niemeyer suspended the roof of the single-story pavilion like a tent from former corner pillars made of rubble stone. Freely grouped window panes and glass curtain walls structure the rooms and offer partial views through the building. The flat suspended roof with its soft curve is framed by the barren mountain vista in the background.

Roberto Burle Marx added two gardens to the house, positioned between two mountain ridges: the front garden embeds the house in the existing landscape by allowing the flowerbed borders, lawns, ponds, etc. to trace the curving lines of the architecture (the roof and the driveway), not to mention those of the mountain panorama. The terrace garden at the back is a deliberate contrast here: a square, checkerboard ground level made of light and dark floor covering unfolds flat before the patio, and the orthogonal swimming pool is thus set asymmetrically to the house – it would seem that the gridding promulgated by Mies van der Rohes or US landscape designer Dan Kiley was the model for this.

In the wake of the project plans devised in the 1940s and 1950s, and incidentally they included larger public projects such as the Hospital Sul America (Rio de Janeiro, 1955) and the Ibirapuera exhibition park (São Paulo, 1953), Niemeyer and Burle Marx then met again in the course of the plans made for the new capital city Brasília. In 1960, Burle Marx was involved in the planning for the first time. One year later he handled the design of the expansive green-belt sections of the Major Axis, although he was not able to really implement his own ideas in full. The brief he was given by urbanist Lúcio Costa was quite simply too detailed.[6] Not until a few years later, when Niemeyer designed the ministry buildings, did the landscape designer get the opportunity to at least put parts of his vision of a "tropical city [...] in the midst of plants"[7] into practice.

Much has been written about the broad dry high plateau of the Planalto, which under the aegis of President Kubitschek was swiftly cleared and steamrollered in order to inscribe in it the axis coordinates of the new capital. And in his buildings for the government center, Oscar Niemeyer also

Nach den Planungen der vierziger und fünfziger Jahre, zu denen übrigens auch größere öffentliche Projekte wie das Hospital Sul America (Rio de Janeiro, 1955) und der Ibirapuera-Ausstellungspark (São Paulo, 1953) zählen, treffen Niemeyer und Burle Marx im Zuge der Planungen für die neue Hauptstadt Brasília wieder aufeinander. 1960 war Burle Marx erstmals darin miteinbezogen worden. Ein Jahr später führt er die weiträumigen Grünanlagen der Großen Achse aus, ohne dabei allerdings seinen eigenen Vorstellungen freien Lauf lassen zu können. Zu detailliert sind die Vorgaben, die der Urbanist Lúcio Costa dazu macht.[6] Erst einige Jahre später, als Niemeyer die Ministerialbauten entwirft, bekommt der Landschaftsarchitekt Gelegenheit, seine Vision einer „tropischen Stadt [...] inmitten von Pflanzen"[7] zumindest punktuell umzusetzen.

Es ist viel geschrieben worden über die weite, trockene Hochebene des Planalto, die unter Präsident Kubitschek innerhalb kürzester Zeit gerodet und planiert wurde, um ihr das Koordinatenkreuz der neuen Hauptstadt einzuschreiben. Auch Oscar Niemeyer bezieht sich in seinen Bauten für das Regierungszentrum auf diese Landschaft, indem er die monumentalen Volumen entsprechend im Außenraum platziert, die Standardministerien als Abstandsriegel einführt und an den Gebäuden selbst, auf den Außengalerien, für spektakuläre perspektivische Durchsichten sorgt – seine erfindungsreichen Stützen-Kreationen am Platz der Drei Gewalten, die die weite Steppenlandschaft mit den roten Lateritböden und den dynamischen Wolkenbewegungen rahmen, helfen ihm dabei.

Die Bauten, die Niemeyer unter der Mitarbeit von Burle Marx realisiert, verorten sich ebenfalls in dieser Landschaft, bilden dazu aber gleichsam einen Kontrast, indem sie von Wasserbassins und Grünanlagen umgeben sind. Wie Oasen in der Wüste holen sie die üppige botanische Vielfalt des Amazonas in die trockene Einöde. Das Justizministerium, das an seiner Schaufassade Wasser aus monumentalen, plastisch geformten Betonschalen in ein Bassin gießt, stammt aus dem Jahr 1970. Es stellt eine Abwandlung des Projektes dar, das Niemeyer und Burle Marx Anfang der sechziger Jahre gemeinsam in Angriff nahmen, des Itamaraty-Palastes, Sitz des brasilianischen Außenministeriums.

1962 wurde der viergeschossige Glaskubus, der von einer monumentalen Schirmdachkonstruktion aus Spannbeton überdacht wird, von Niemeyer entworfen. 1965 verpasst Burle Marx dem Solitär ein umlaufendes Wasserbassin, in dem sich der Form nach variierte Betonbeete sparsam verteilen.

→ p. 93

→ pp. 88/89

→ pp. 91/92

→ S. 93

→ S. 88/89

→ S. 91/92

draws on this countryside, placing the monumental buildings deliberately in the outer sections, introducing the standard ministries as a distance marker and ensuring that the buildings themselves, thanks to the outer galleries, afford any number of spectacular angles of vision through to the interiors – his inventive pillar structures at the Square of the Three Powers, which frame the wide steppe with the red laterite ground and the dynamic movement of the clouds help him in this connection.

The buildings which Niemeyer realized with the assistance of Burle Marx likewise embed themselves in this landscape, at the same time forming a counterpoint, for they are surrounded by water basins and green belts. Like oases in the desert, they introduce the opulent botanical diversity of the Amazon into this arid plain. The Ministry of Justice, down the front façade of which water from monumental sculpted concrete bowls runs to a basin, was made in 1970. It is a variation on a project which Niemeyer and Burle Marx jointly undertook in the early 1960s: the Itamaraty Palace, home of the Brazilian Foreign Affairs Ministry.

Niemeyer designed the four-story glass cube, which is covered by a monumental station-roof structure made of pre-stressed concrete in 1962. In 1965, Burle Marx outfitted the free-standing building with a water basin that ran right round it, and in which concrete beds of various shapes were sparsely placed. In part, they are covered by water and serve as homes for various types of water lilies. In part, they protrude from the water and form small archipelagos with densely grouped exotic bushes. They are reflected on the water's surface together with the concrete roof pillars, which Niemeyer designed to resemble arcades, and ensure that visually the building seems to float – a massive palace that apparently drifts across the water like a raft.

In a manner similar to the way Burle Marx uses the gardens to create an external frame for the architecture, Niemeyer acts as a scene-designer for the landscape design. The small roof gardens, filled with a wide variety of tropical plants, are located on the spacious upper unwalled story underneath the station roof, and their marvelous vegetation unfolds against the background of the sculpturally shaped arches of the arcades. With their slender shafts they seem as if they had grown upwards and had taken the gardens with them at once – a floating and flowing everywhere.

Zum Teil sind sie vom Wasser bedeckt und geben verschiedenen Seerosenarten eine Heimstätte. Zum Teil ragen sie aus dem Wasser heraus und bilden kleine Archipel mit dicht gruppierten exotischen Sträuchern. Zusammen mit den Dachstützen, die Niemeyer wie Arkaden aus Beton geformt hat, spiegeln sie sich auf der Wasseroberfläche und halten das Gebäude sichtlich in der Schwebe – der wuchtige Palast scheint gleichsam wie ein Floß auf dem Wasser zu treiben.

In gleicher Weise, wie Burle Marx mit den Gartenanlagen einen äußeren Rahmen für die Architektur schafft, betätigt Niemeyer sich als Kulissenbauer für den Landschaftsgestalter. Die kleinen, mit vielfältigen tropischen Gewächsen bevölkerten Dachgärten, die sich auf der weitläufigen oberen Freietage unterhalb des Schirmdaches befinden, entfalten ihre vegetalen Formen vor dem Hintergrund der plastisch ausgeformten Arkadenbögen. Mit ihren schlanken Schäften wirken sie so, als wären sie emporgewachsen und hätten dabei die Gärten gleich mitgenommen. Ein Schweben und Fließen allerorten.

Itamaraty-Palast, Brasília.
Dachgärten.

Itamaraty Palace, Brasília.
Roof Gardens.

1 O. Niemeyer: My architecture, Rio de Janeiro 2000, S. 17.

2 Auch in seiner Autobiographie beschreibt Niemeyer seine Vorliebe für tropische Gewächse: „Wir gingen oft in den Botanischen Garten, wo ich gerne die Kieselwege entlangschritt und die üppige tropische Pflanzenwelt bewunderte, oder innehielt an Pflanzen, um ihre komplizierten wissenschaftlichen Namen zu lesen oder mir einen Teich, die riesigen Wasserlilien und das allerorten unvergängliche Blühen anzuschauen. Genauso oft hielt ich an, um eine Pflanze zu zeichnen, sie mit einigen wenigen Strichen meiner Architekturperspektive einzufangen." (O.Niemeyer: The curves of time. The memoirs of Oscar Niemeyer, London 2000, S.19.)

3 „Von Pampulha bis Brasília folgte meine Arbeit dem gleichen Drang zu plastischer Freiheit und architektonischem Erfindungsreichtum [...]. Wenn ich also eine andere Form entwarf, musste ich sie mit guten Argumenten vertreten können. Wenn ich etwa einen geschwungenen, frei im Gelände stehenden Block entwarf, präsentierte ich außer den Bauplänen auch Skizzen, aus denen hervorging, dass die Geländekonturen zur Bauform angeregt hatten. [...] Wenn ich ein Auditorium entwarf, dessen Form an ein vergleichbares Objekt aus der Dingwelt erinnern konnte, führte ich die inneren Sichtverhältnisse an." (O. Niemeyer: Aus meinem architektonischen Vermächtnis (1992); abgedr. in: Der Architekt, Heft 5, 2000, S.40.)

4 Erstmals veröffentlicht in Casabella, als Auszug in engl. Sprache in: Architectural Review, Nr. 116, 1954, S. 240.

5 Inwieweit es dabei tatsächlich zu einem produktiven Austausch zwischen Architekt und Landschaftsarchitekt gekommen ist, lässt sich heute kaum mehr genau sagen – Streitigkeiten um Geld und politische Meinungsverschiedenheiten, die im Zuge der Bauarbeiten für Brasília und danach entstanden, haben das Klima zwischen den beiden offenbar so sehr vergiftet, das weder Burle Marx noch Niemeyer darüber berichten wollten. Vgl. etwa die Interviews von Alexander Fils mit Niemeyer und Burle Marx Anfang der achtziger Jahre. Abgedr. in: A. Fils: Brasília. Moderne Architektur in Brasilien, Düsseldorf 1988, S.137, 140, 143.

6 Vgl. das Burle Marx-Interview von 1981 von Alexander Fils. Abgedr. in: A. Fils: Brasília. Moderne Architektur in Brasilien, Düsseldorf 1988, S.143 f.

7 R. B. Marx: „Arquitetura e arquitetura de Jardins"; in: Habitat (SP), No.13, 1953, S. 52f. (Engl. Zusammenfassung).

1 O. Niemeyer: My architecture, transl. from the Brazilian, Rio de Janeiro, 2000, p.17.

2 In his autobiography Niemeyer likewise writes of his love of tropical plants: "We often went to the Botanical Gardens, where I loved to walk along the gravel paths and admire the lush tropical vegetation, or pause by plants to read the complicated scientific names, or look at the pond and the huge water lilies and everlastings blooming everywhere. Every so often I stopped to draw a plant, attempting to capture it with a few strokes of my architectural perspective." (O.Niemeyer: The curves of time. The memoirs of Oscar Niemeyer, London, 2000, p. 19).

3 "From Pampulha to Brasília, my work has followed the same compulsion to bring sculptural freedom and architectural invention to bear [...].In other words, when I devised a different form I had to be able to deploy good arguments in its favor. For example, if I created a curved free-standing block for a site I presented not only the construction plans but also sketches that showed that the contours of the site had encouraged me to create such a shape. [...] If I developed an auditorium, whose shape might be reminiscent of a comparable object from the world of things, then I also enumerated the view from within." (O. Niemeyer: Aus meinem architektonischen Vermächtnis (1992); reprinted in: Der Architekt, no. 5, 2000, p. 40).

4 First published in Casabella, then excerpted in English in: Architectural Review, no. 116, 1954, p. 240.

5 It is hard to gauge today to what extent there really was a productive exchange of views between the architect and the landscape designer – arguments over money and differences of political opinion that emerged during the construction work for Brasília and thereafter evidently poisoned the relationship between the two to such a degree that neither Burle Marx nor Niemeyer have wanted to talk about it. See, for example, the interviews conducted by Alexander Fils with Niemeyer and Burle Marx in the early 1980s and printed in: A. Fils: Brasília. Moderne Architektur in Brasilien, Düsseldorf, 1988, pp.137, 140, 143.

6 See the Burle Marx interview conducted in 1981 by Alexander Fils. Printed in: A. Fils: Brasília. Moderne Architektur in Brasilien, Düsseldorf, 1988, pp. 143.

7 R. B. Marx: "Arquitetura e arquitetura de Jardins"; in: Habitat (SP), no. 13, 1953, pp. 52. (English summary).

Brasilia. Luftaufnahme
der Großen Achse.

Brasilia. Aerial view
of the Grand Axis.

Justizministerium,
Brasilia. Schaufassade mit
den Wasserfällen.

Ministry of Justice,
Brasilia. Main facade with
the waterfalls.

Justizministerium, Brasilia.
Ansicht der Betonschalen
der Wasserfall-Fassade.

Ministry of Justice, Brasilia.
View of the concrete basins
of the waterfall facade.

←

Itamaraty-Palast.
Außenministerium, Brasília.
Fassadenansicht.

Itamaraty Palace. Ministry
of Foreign Affairs, Brasília.
Facade.

Alvorada-Palast, Brasília.
Fassadenansicht mit
der Kapelle.

Alvorada Palace, Brasília.
View of the facade and
the chapel.

Alvorada-Palast, Brasilia.
Aussicht von den Kolonnaden.

Alvorada Palace, Brasilia.
View from the colonnades.

→
Kathedrale, Brasilia.
Ansicht mit Glockenturm
und Baptisterium.

Cathedral, Brasilia. View with
the belfry and the baptistry.

Kathedrale, Brasilia.
Innenansicht.

Cathedral, Brasilia.
Interior.

Itamaraty-Palast. Außen-
ministerium, Brasília.
Innenansicht des Foyers.

Itamaraty Palace. Ministry
of Foreign Affairs, Brasília.
Interior of the foyer.

Nationalkongress,
Brasília.

Verteidigungsministerium,
Brasília. Versammlungshalle.

National Congress,
Brasília.

Ministry of the Army, Brasília.
Assembly hall.

Pantheon der Freiheit
und Demokratie Tancredo
Neves, Brasília.

Tancredo Neves Pantheon
of Liberty and Democracy,
Brasília.

→
Museum für zeitgenössische
Kunst, Niterói. Fernansicht.

Museum of Contemporary
Art, Niterói. View from
the distance.

Museum für zeitgenössische
Kunst, Niterói. Ansicht
des Betonrumpfes mit dem
Zuckerhut im Hintergrund.

Museum of Contemporary Art,
Niterói. View of the swung
concrete core and the Sugar
Loaf in the background.

Museum für zeitgenössische
Kunst, Niterói. Ansicht von
der Rampe

Museum of Comtemporary
Art, Niterói. View from
the ramp.

Museum für zeitgenössische
Kunst, Niterói. Ausstellungs-
raum. Innenansicht

Museum of Contemporary Art,
Niterói. Exhibition room.
Interior.

Museum für zeitgenössische
Kunst, Niterói. Aussicht
von den Ausstellungsräumen.

Museum of Contemporary
Art, Niterói. View from
the exhibition rooms.

Espace Niemeyer, Kultur-
zentrum, Le Havre.
Ansicht der Betonvolumen.

Espace Niemeyer. Cultural
Center, Le Havre. View
of the concrete volumes.

Universität Constantine,
Algerien. Auditorium und
Hörsaalblock.

University of Constantine,
Algeria. Auditorium
and lecture hall block.

in europa täglich begegnet. le corbusier verdanken wir die einführung dieser formen in der landschaftsgestaltung, und er hat sie auch in der architektur eingeführt, wo er geschwungene wände und dachgärten anwandte (in dem er diese freien formen benutzte). letztlich hat er auch, immer als erfinder, diese freien formen mit seinem projekt für die stadt algier in nordafrika im städtebau eingesetzt. er war nicht der erste, der diese idee hatte, denn bereits im achtzehnten jahrhundert wurden in der stadt bath in england zwei wichtige quartiere nach einem ähnlichen plan gebaut. die freie form kann nützlich sein, wenn es sich darum handelt, eine funktion zu verfolgen, ein gebäude nutzbarer zu machen. aber das ist die ausnahme. aber die meisten anwendungen der freien form, die wir heute antreffen, sind rein dekorativ und haben als solche nichts mit ernst zu nehmender architektur zu tun.

das zweite element ist die glasfassade, deren geschichte die folgende ist: 1910 baute walter gropius eine fabrik, 1914 ein bürogebäude und 1926 das bauhaus, mit ganzen fassaden aus glas. diese ganz verglasten fassaden sind ein bisschen in mode gekommen. besonders le corbusier begann gebäude mit solchen glasfassaden zu bauen. aber seine arbeiten wie auch die feinen schöpfungen von mies van der rohe zeigten, dass dies jedoch nicht ohne klimaanlagen und aufwendige gebäudetechnik funktioniert.

um die glasfassaden zu schützen – wenn man die brennende sonne und das stechende licht nicht aushielt –, erfand le corbusier ein drittes element: die brises-soleil. heute trifft man diese sonnenbrecher als unerlässliche begleiterscheinung der glasfassadenmanie an. man versucht schon gar nicht mehr, nach neuen lösungen für unterschiedliche bedingungen zu suchen. hier in são paulo gibt es sogar beispiele mit brises-soleil auf allen vier seiten des gebäudes.

und das vierte element der so genannten modernen architektur sind die pilotis. in den letzten jahren haben sie sich immer der „neusten mode aus paris", das heisst dem atelier von le corbusier, angepasst.

[Exkurs – A.d.Hg.] vor meiner reise nach brasilien dachte ich, wie viele architekten der europäischen avantgarde, dass die lösung von le corbusier mit häusern auf pfeilern und ohne innenhöfe das ideal einer künftigen stadt sei. als ausgezeichnet ausgeführtes beispiel haben wir immer das berühmte ministerium für bildung und gesundheit in rio de janeiro angesehen, für das le corbusier als beratender architekt tätig war und welches in seiner konzeption typisch für die von ihm propagierten ideen ist. aber schon vor meiner reise nach brasilien hatte ich bedenken betreffend dieser urbanistischen auffassung, die auch ich mit

a building more practical. but this is the exception. indeed, most examples of the free form we find today are purely decorative, and as such have nothing in common with serious architecture.

the second element is the glass facade, whose history is as follows: in 1910, walter gropius built a factory, in 1914 an office building and in 1926 the bauhaus, all with facades of glass. these floor to ceiling glass facades have acquired a certain popularity. in particular le corbusier began to design buildings with such glass facades. but both his works and the fine creations by mies van der Rohe demonstrate that they did not function without air-conditioning systems and complicated facilities technology.

to protect the glass facades – if the scorching sun and searing light was too much – le corbusier invented a third element: the brises-soleils. today, you come across brises-soleils as essential accompaniments to the glass facade mania. people no longer look to find new solutions for various conditions. for instance, here in são paulo we find buildings fitted with brises-soleils on all four sides.

and the fourth element of so-called modern architecture are the pilotis. in recent years they have always followed the "latest trend from paris", in other words the atelier of le corbusier.

[Digression – editor's note] prior to my trip to brazil like many architects of europe's avant-garde i thought le corbusier's solution to have houses on stilts and without interior courtyards would be the ideal of a future city. we have an excellent example of this in the famous ministry of education and health in rio de janeiro, for which le corbusier acted as consultant architect, and whose conception is typical of the ideas he promoted. but even prior to my trip to brazil i had my reservations about this urban development attitude, which i myself had previously supported with a certain enthusiasm. i realized that the courtyard which was replaced by the new le corbusier concept was there to fulfill certain functions that had been sacrificed to these changes. these old interior courtyards firstly direct pedestrian flows and also offer tranquility. what is more, without them you also get serious problems with air circulation, the climate, lighting and protection against the sun. i have studied this problem that hardly plays a role at all in northern countries such as switzerland, germany or sweden, but is of great significance in italy, spain and southern france. i realized that in the latter countries such a courtyard has a function that cannot be dispensed with. this makes it important to find new, contemporary solutions that exploit the advantages interior courtyards offer while eliminating their disadvantages. this is a more

einem gewissen enthusiasmus unterstützt hatte. ich stellte fest, dass der innen-hof, der durch die neue le corbusier'sche konzeption ersetzt wurde, bestimmte funktionen zu erfüllen hat, die der veränderung zum opfer fallen würden: es sind dies die konzentration der fussgängerwege und die stille dieser alten innenhöfe. zudem entstehen ernsthafte probleme mit der luftzirkulation und dem klima, der beleuchtung und dem schutz gegen die sonne. ich habe dieses problem studiert, das in nördlichen ländern wie der schweiz, deutschland oder schweden keine so grosse rolle spielt, jedoch in italien, spanien und südfrankreich be-reits eine grosse bedeutung hat. ich habe dort festgestellt, dass der innenhof eine funktion erfüllt, die man nicht abschaffen kann. es ist deshalb wichtig, neue zeitgemässe lösungen zu finden, indem wir die vorteile der innenhöfe benützen, aber ihre nachteile beseitigen. dies wird viel organischer sein, als sie durch bauten in form von „kisten auf pfeilern" zu ersetzen. diese beobachtung ist folg-lich ein angriff auf das berühmte bildungsministerium in rio de janeiro, das meines erachtens nicht nach den organischen bedingungen des landes entworfen wurde. das soll nicht heissen, dass ich nicht allen respekt vor den anstrengun-gen dieser architekten habe, aber ich bin dennoch gezwungen zu bemerken, dass sie damals gewissen irrtümern unterlegen sind, indem sie einer doktrin gefolgt sind, die in ihrem land nicht ohne erhebliche verbesserungen angewandt werden kann. ich will nicht behaupten, bereits selbst die richtige antwort zu haben; es ist die aufgabe der architekten, die ihrem land entsprechende, best-mögliche lösung zu finden. [Ende des Exkurses – A.d.Hg.]

ursprünglich waren die pilotis gerade, nun beginnen sie die barockesten formen anzunehmen. auf den ersten blick glaubt man, eine höchst einfallsreiche konstruktion zu haben, aber sie sind reine dekoration geworden.

hier ein beispiel: hier in são paulo habe ich eine baustelle gesehen. in diesem gebäude habe ich fürchterliche dinge gesehen. das ist das ende der modernen architektur. es ist eine antisoziale verschwendung, ohne verantwortung weder gegenüber dem benutzer als mieter noch gegenüber dem kunden, der dort seine einkäufe machen wird. da ich lediglich die konstruktion der beiden ersten stockwerke gesehen habe, weiss ich nicht, ob bei diesem gebäude auch noch glasfassaden und brise-soleils hinzukommen werden. aber ich habe hier die letzte verzerrung der freien form und die abstruseste anwendung von pilotis vorgefunden. das ist der urwald im bauwesen im schlimmsten sinne, das ist völlige anarchie. ich habe dieses noch nicht fertig gestellte gebäude als beispiel gewählt, weil sie es alle besuchen können. es ist kein theoretisches fallbeispiel, es ist wirklichkeit. wenn sie nicht sehr gut über die aufgaben des architekten im dienste des menschen und der gesellschaft nachdenken, könnten sie in ähn-

organic approach than replacing them with "boxes on stilts". consequently, this observation is an attack on the famous ministry of education in rio de janeiro, which to my mind does not follow this nation's organic conditions. that is not to say i do not respect the efforts these architects made but i nonetheless feel compelled to observe that they made certain errors in following a doctrine that cannot be applied in their country without considerable alterations. for all that, i do not claim to have the correct answer myself. it is the task of architects to find the best possible solution that suits their country. [End of digression – editor's note]

initially pilotis were straight, but they are now starting to take on highly baroque forms. at first sight you think you have a highly original structure but they have become pure decoration.

here is an example: i saw a building site here in são paulo. the building under construction had some awful elements. this is the end of modern architecture. it is anti-social waste without responsibility towards either the user as tenant or the customers who do their shopping there. as i only saw the first two floors i don't know whether the building was to get a glass facade and brise-soleils. but i did see here the final distortion of free form, and the most abstruse use of pilotis. it is the jungle in architecture in the worst possible sense, it is total anarchy. i selected this uncompleted building as an example because you can all see it for yourselves. it is not a theoretical example to illustrate a point, it actually exists. if you do not have a very high opinion regarding the architect's tasks in the service of mankind and society, you might succumb to similar mis-takes because at first sight this architecture might appear revolutionary, and as a result you might even see it as a work of art.

the first thing you notice on entering the site is an awful confusion of different architectural systems, thick pilotis, thin pilotis and pilotis of peculiar forms, without any structural sense, aligned in different directions, and finally entire walls of reinforced concrete. the walls and pilotis intersect for no reason at all, the forms destroy and cut into one another. it is the greatest chaos i have ever seen on a building site. i asked myself how such a misunderstanding could come about in a country whose modern architecture enjoys world renown, a country where you don't find new buildings in an old style. i wondered how such a wild construction (for which the building site i saw was a prototype), could come about in a country that has a ciam group (congrès international d'architecture moderne), a journal called "habitat" and which is host to an architecture bien-nial. buildings like this stem from a mind devoid of modesty and responsibility for

liche irrtümer fallen, denn im ersten moment könnte diese architektur revolutionär erscheinen und aus einem missverständnis heraus sogar als kunstwerk betrachtet werden.

wenn man den bauplatz betritt, bemerken sie sofort ein furchtbares durcheinander von bausystemen, dicke pilotis, dünne pilotis und pilotis mit absonderlichen formen, ohne jeglichen konstruktiven sinn, in verschiedenen richtungen angeordnet, und schliesslich ganze wände aus armiertem beton. die mauern und die pilotis kreuzen sich grundlos, die formen zerstören, zerschneiden sich. es ist die gigantischste unordnung, die ich jemals auf einer baustelle gesehen habe. ich habe mich gefragt, wie ein solches missverständnis geschehen konnte in einem land, dessen moderne architektur weltweit bekannt ist und in welchem man keine neuen bauten in altem stil sieht. ich habe mich gefragt, wie in einem lande, in dem es eine ciam-gruppe gibt (congrès international d'architecture moderne), eine zeitschrift namens „habitat" und wo es eine architektur-biennale gibt – wie man in diesem lande zu so wilden bauten kommen kann, für welche die baustelle, die ich gesehen habe, der prototyp ist. bauten dieser art entspringen einem geist, der ohne bescheidenheit ist, ohne verantwortung gegenüber den menschlichen bedürfnissen. dies ist der geist des dekorativen, etwas diametral entgegengesetztes zur architektur, der bau-kunst, dieser beispielhaften sozialen kunst.

ich fürchte, dass sich auch unter ihnen freunde dieses geistes befinden, und weil ich ihnen ja helfen will, nicht solchen fehlern zu verfallen, will ich ihnen in wenigen worten erklären, was der beruf des architekten ist. und wenn nur einer oder zwei von ihnen das begreifen werden, werde ich schon sehr glücklich sein. es werden diejenigen sein, die für eine wirklich moderne architektur kämpfen werden, für eine gesunde architektur im dienste des menschen.

die rolle des architekten in der heutigen gesellschaft ist, die umgebung des menschen bewohnbar und harmonisch zu machen. es ist der architekt, der die verschiedenen bedürfnisse und aktivitäten des menschen koordiniert. er formt die unterschiedlichsten funktionen: unterkunft, arbeit, erholung. falls es unser wunsch ist, dass der mensch nicht wie die ameisen leben soll, deren haufen gestört wurde, dann sind es wir, die architekten, die eine neue lösung auf die bedürfnisse der menschheit geben müssen.

aber wie soll diese neue form aussehen? hat sie wirklich pilotis, freie formen, brise-soleils und glasfassaden? ist sie wirklich so fotogen und spektakulär? ich glaube es nicht. die architektur ist etwas, das oft länger als nur einige jahre

man's needs. this is the spirit of the decorative, something diametrically opposed to architecture that is an art, an exemplary social art.

i suspect some members of the audience may be friends of this spirit, and because i want to help you avoid falling victim to such errors, i would like to explain briefly what the profession of an architect is. and should only one or two of you understand me that would still make me very happy. these will be the people who fight for a really modern architecture, for a healthy architecture serving human welfare.

the role of the architect in today's society is to make man's environment habitable and harmonious. the architect is the person who coordinates man's various needs and activities. he gives shape to a wide range of functions: housing, work, leisure. and if it is our desire that man should not live like the ants whose hill has been disturbed, then it is up to us, the architects, to provide a new solution to man's needs.

but what is this new form to look like? does it really have pilotis, free shapes, brise-soleils and glass facades? is it really that photogenic and spectacular? i don't believe so. architecture is something that often lasts longer than a few years; it outlives generations. you recall the architectural excesses of the past, and you laugh when you look say at the old prefecture in são paulo. but what is so funny about looking at such buildings, and why don't you laugh when you look at a simple building by the pioneers in your country? for the simple reason that in the first case neither the architect nor his client could resist the attempt to create a spectacular building whereas the pioneer produced a building that best met his own needs. perhaps you consider my viewpoint too narrow-minded, and think that architecture which is functional in the true sense of the word should be more serious. you probably think architecture is also an art that speaks for itself by expressing the artist's wishes in a building. this is not the function of architecture. architects who approach their work this way make fools of themselves. such a view stems from the illusion that architecture has a function other than that of serving a useful purpose in society, and the folly that art in general and in particular sculptural art should be something best described by the term "self-expression".

that is neither art nor architecture. what constitutes art is reproducing an idea as clearly and objectively as possible through the selection of the best means available. a work of art must have such a perfect form, have such a harmonious expression that its author cannot change it by adding or removing a brush stroke.

überdauert; sie überlebt die generationen. sie erinnern sich an architektonische exzesse der vergangenheit, und sie lachen, wenn sie zum beispiel die alte präfektur in são paulo anschauen. aber warum ist es lustig, heute solche gebäude anzuschauen, und warum lacht man nicht, wenn man sich ein einfaches gebäude der pioniere in ihrem lande ansieht? einfach deshalb, weil bei ersterem der architekt und sein kunde nicht fähig waren, dem versuch zu widerstehen, ein spektakuläres gebäude zu errichten, während der pionier ein gebäude machte, welches seinen bedürfnissen am besten entsprach. vielleicht denken sie, dass mein standpunkt zu engstirnig ist und dass architektur, die funktionell im wahrsten sinne des wortes ist, noch trockener sein wird. sie denken wahrscheinlich, dass die architektur auch eine kunst ist, die für sich selbst spricht, um die gebäude mit den wünschen von künstlern zu füllen. dies ist nicht die funktion der architektur. der architekt, der so arbeitet, macht sich lächerlich. diese ansicht entspringt dem irrtum, dass baukunst etwas anderes ist, als eine nützliche funktion in der gesellschaft zu erfüllen, und vom anderen irrtum, dass kunst im allgemeinen, und vor allem die plastischen künste, etwas sein sollten, was so schön mit „selfexpression", selbstausdruck, bezeichnet wird.

das ist weder kunst noch architektur. kunst besteht darin, eine idee so klar und so objektiv wie möglich wiederzugeben, durch die wahl der besten mittel, die zur verfügung stehen. ein kunstwerk muss eine solch perfekte form haben, von so harmonischem ausdruck sein, dass sein autor es weder ändern noch einen strich hinzufügen oder wegnehmen kann.

was die architektur betrifft, so soll sie so funktionell wie möglich sein. die schönheit der architektur basiert auf ihrer einfachheit. die architektur ist perfekt, wenn alle ihre funktionen, ihre konstruktion, ihr material und ihre form in perfekter harmonie sind. eine gute architektur ist diejenige, in der alle dinge funktionieren und in der es nichts überflüssiges gibt. um zu einer solchen architektur zu kommen, muss der architekt ein ausgezeichneter künstler sein, ein künstler, der es nicht nötig hat, durch verrücktheiten aufsehen erregen zu müssen, ein künstler mit der ganzen verantwortung für die gegenwart und die zukunft. dieser architekt wird immer, wenn er eine arbeit macht, einen plan erstellt, ein detail wählt oder die kleinste kleinigkeit für sein gebäude bestimmt, sich selbst die frage stellen: „wenn ich dieses haus in 20 jahren wiedersehe, wird es mich in verlegenheit bringen, dass ich es gebaut habe?" unaufhörlich wird er sich überlegen, wie menschen sich in seinem gebäude verhalten werden, und er wird dabei immer sehr streng gegenüber sich selbst sein.

as regards architecture it should be as functional as possible. the beauty of architecture rests on its simplicity. architecture is perfect when all its functions, its construction, materials and form are in perfect harmony. excellent architecture is one in which everything functions, and in which there is nothing superfluous. in order to produce such architecture the architect must be an excellent artist without the need to cause a stir through crazy ideas, an artist fully aware of his responsibility for the present and future. whenever he produces something, draws up a plan, selects a detail or defines the most minor of things for his building this architect will always question his work: "when i see this house again in 20 years, will it embarrass me that i designed it?" he constantly considers how people will behave in his building, and he will always be a harsh critic of himself.

he will not wonder about whether he can surprise his colleagues or the public, or how magnificent his finished creation will appear. no, above all he will remain modest in the service of mankind.

possibly you consider this a very prosaic standpoint that does not allow the architect to render man many services. for this reason, i wish to talk about several pioneers of modern architecture in the best sense of the word: henry van de velde, adolf loos and walter gropius. and then i would mention frank lloyd wright, ludwig mies van der rohe, and le corbusier. the reason i have divided them into two groups is because each group has a different approach. those in the first group are the pioneers of a general moral in architecture. those in the second group place greater emphasis on creative ability than their responsibility towards society.

that does not mean the first group were not brilliant artists, very important architects. even before 1900 van de velde elaborated a doctrine of artistic and rational architecture; amongst other things he built the famous kroeller-müller museum in otterlo in holland that houses one of the most wonderful collections of impressionist and cubist art through to mondrian. van de velde, whose 90th birthday we celebrated just two months ago, is a man who always fought for the good and healthy, and against ugliness. then there is adolf loos who designed some of the most beautiful houses in europe, of absolute simplicity and subtleness – the man who spoke out in explicit terms for excellent design, for the elegance of a perfect simplicity in articles such as "ornament and crime"; a man whose work you still encounter today, things he designed 30 years ago, that still possess an eternal, perfect quality. and then there's walter gropius, the inventor of the "glass facade", the founder of the bauhaus, the

er wird nicht darüber nachdenken, wie er seine kollegen oder die öffentlichkeit verblüffen kann oder wie prachtvoll die publikation seiner kreation sein wird. nein: er wird vor allem bescheiden im dienste des menschen bleiben.

sie denken vielleicht, dass dies ein sehr trockener standpunkt ist, mit dem man nicht viele verdienste erwerben kann. ich werde ihnen also über einige pioniere der modernen architektur im besten sinne des wortes erzählen: von henry van de velde, von adolf loos, von walter gropius. und ich nenne nachfolgend frank lloyd wright, ludwig mies van der rohe, le corbusier. wenn ich hier zwei gruppen gemacht habe, so ist dies, weil die auffassung der beiden gruppen verschieden ist. die ersten sind die pioniere einer allgemeinen moral in der architektur. die zweiten sind jene, deren kreative stärke wichtiger ist als ihre verantwortung gegenüber der gesellschaft.

dies bedeutet nicht, dass die ersten nicht sehr grosse künstler sind, sehr grosse architekten. van de velde hat schon vor 1900 eine doktrin künstlerischer und rationeller architektur aufgestellt; er hat unter anderem das berühmte kroeller-müller-museum in otterlo in holland gebaut, wo sich eine der wunderbarsten sammlungen impressionistischer und kubistischer kunst bis zu mondrian befindet. van de velde, dessen 90. geburtstag wir erst vor zwei monaten gefeiert haben, ist ein mann, der immer für das gute und gesunde und gegen die hässlichkeit gekämpft hat. dann: adolf loos, der einige der schönsten häuser in europa erbaut hat, von einer absoluten einfachheit und subtilität; der mann, der in manifesten und heftigen artikeln wie zum beispiel „ornament und verbrechen" für die gute form, für die eleganz einer perfekten einfachheit gekämpft hat; ein mann, von dem man heute noch objekte antrifft, die er vor 30 jahren gemacht hat und die immer und ewig perfekt sind. und dann walter gropius: der erfinder der „glasfassade", der begründer des „bauhauses", der lehrer einer ganzen generation von architekten; ein grosser meister mit einer künstlerischen auffassung, in der er sich keine lücken erlaubt. sie werden das werk von walter gropius an der nächsten biennale von são paulo sehen. er wird ihre stadt besuchen. ich hoffe, dass er zeit findet, ihnen – besser als ich – über seine sehr verschiedenen erfahrungen zu berichten. gropius ist der mann der zusammenarbeit, des teamwork, und die letzte form, die er für seine arbeit gefunden hat, ist die zusammenarbeit mit einer gruppe alter schüler in der „architects collaborative". sie ersehen daraus die tiefe bescheidenheit eines mannes, der so grosse verdienste in der modernen architektur hat, der ein echter künstler ist und der es sich erlauben kann, sich mehr oder weniger in die anonymität zurückzuziehen, ohne den kleinsten teil seiner persönlichkeit zu verlieren.

mentor of an entire generation of architects; a great master with an artistic attitude in which he allowed himself no voids. you will see the work of walter gropius at the next biennial of são paulo. he will visit your city. and i hope he finds the time to talk to you – better than I've done – about his various experiences. gropius is a man who favors collaboration, teamwork, and the most recent form he has found for his work is the collaboration with a group of old pupils in the "architects' collaborative". this points to the deep modesty of a man who rendered outstanding services to modern architecture, who is a true artist, and who can more or less afford to retire into anonymity without sacrificing part of his personality.

on the other hand we find the other three great artists, above all the creators of forms. frank lloyd wright who produced highly personal solutions familiar everywhere. mies van der rohe, who developed a distinct style of surfaces in space, whose work refuses to be rational or functional, yet is characterized by an unequalled aesthetic and technical perfection. and finally le corbusier, the great inspirer whose influence – since his first trip to brazil – shaped brazilian architecture, though not without his ideas sometimes being misunderstood.

all these masters are the mentors of many young architects. most of the pupils of the first group have developed an independent mode of thinking, while most of the pupils of the second group that have remained simply jumped on the band-wagon and are even imitators of their mentor. you will all see the danger inherent in an overly individualistic concept in architectural doctrine.

i ultimately believe there are enough independent forces in brazil to liberate architecture from academic principles, from superfluous principles not valid in their country. i believe in their own power to create a really modern architecture that corresponds to their excellent natural environment and economic opportunities.

finally, i would advise you to always bear in mind the true principles of modern architecture:
the architect must above all be modest and clear.
architecture is an art when all its elements – function, construction and form – are in perfect harmony with one another.
architecture is a social art; it must serve people.

auf der anderen seite befinden sich die anderen drei grossen künstler, vor allem die schöpfer von formen. frank lloyd wright, der sehr persönliche lösungen gefunden hat, die überall gut bekannt sind. mies van der rohe, der einen sehr persönlichen stil von flächen im raum geschaffen hat, dessen werk sich weigert, rationell oder funktionell zu sein, aber von einer ästhetischen und technischen perfektion ohnegleichen ist. und schliesslich le corbusier, der grosse anreger, dessen einfluss – seit seiner ersten reise nach brasilien – die brasilianische architektur nicht ohne die gefahren eines missverständnisses geprägt hat.

alle diese genannten meister sind die lehrer von vielen jungen architekten. die meisten der schüler der ersten gruppe sind unabhängig in ihrer denkensweise geworden, die meisten schüler der zweiten gruppe sind mitläufer und sogar nachahmer ihrer lehrer geblieben. sie ersehen daraus die gefahr einer zu individualistischen auffassung in der architekturdoktrin.

ich glaube schliesslich, dass es in brasilien genügend eigenständige kräfte gibt, um die architektur von akademischen prinzipien zu befreien, von überflüssigen prinzipien, die in ihrem land nicht gültig sind. ich glaube an ihre eigene kraft, eine wirklich moderne architektur zu schaffen, die ihren ausgezeichneten natürlichen umweltbedingungen und den ökonomischen möglichkeiten entspricht.

zum schluss rate ich ihnen, sich immer an die wahren prinzipien einer modernen architektur zu erinnern:
der architekt muss vor allem bescheiden und klar sein.
die architektur ist eine kunst, wenn alle ihre elemente, funktion, konstruktion und form, in perfekter harmonie zueinander stehen.
die architektur ist eine soziale kunst, sie muss dem menschen dienen.

1 Ein Wohnkomplex, der vom brasilianischen Architekten
  Affonso Eduardo Reidy in den Jahren zwischen 1950–1958 bei
  Rio de Janeiro realisiert wurde und einen Modellversuch der
  brasilianischen Regierung zum Bau von Sozialwohnungen darstellt.
  [A.d.Hg.]

1 A residential complex in Rio de Janeiro realized by Brazilian architect
  Affonso Eduardo Reidy in the period 1950–1958, and likewise
  a model used by the Brazilian government to assess the potential
  for council housing. [editor's note]

Aktuelle Probleme der brasilianischen Architektur (1955)
Current problems with Brazilian architecture (1955)

Oscar Niemeyer

Einführung

In letzter Zeit herrscht eine merkwürdige Unzufriedenheit bei einigen unserer Architekten, die, wenn auch wissend, welches Ansehen die moderne Architektur Brasiliens genießt, dieser plötzlich mit Abstand gegenüberstehen. Es lassen sich zwei Gruppen unterscheiden: Die einen, die, von den traditionalistischen Theorien beeinflusst, eine Architektur verlangen, „die sich auf die Tradition und Kultur des Volkes" stützt, und die anderen, die vom niedrigen Niveau unserer zeitgenössischen Baupraxis beunruhigt, nach einfachen und rationalen Lösungen rufen. Wir respektieren beide Auffassungen. Die erste, weil sie ehrlich ist und die nach ihrer Meinung gerechtere Lösung anstrebt, die zweite, weil ihr bedenkenswerte Gründe zugrunde liegen, auch wenn sie wichtigere und dringendere Probleme unserer Architektur in den Hintergrund verdrängt. Diesen Streit verlassend, fuhr ich nach Europa, um mich während dieser Zeit mit ausländischen Kollegen über gemeinsame berufliche Probleme auszutauschen.

Kritiken

Was mich betrifft, hegte ich keinerlei Illusionen über die kritischen Ansichten des Großteils der Architekten, die uns in den letzten Jahren besuchten. Kritische Ansichten, die unserer Auffassung nach nicht immer gerechtfertigt sind und die, nach einer ehrlichen Bilanzierung dessen, was in Europa und in Brasilien auf dem Gebiet der modernen Architektur realisiert worden ist, eigentlich nicht so unüberlegt geäußert werden sollten. Dazu bedarf es allerdings einiger Erklärungen. Zuerst seien die mangelnden Kenntnisse über unsere Arbeitsbedingungen anzuführen, die sich von denen in ihren Heimatländern unterscheiden. Dort erfordern fortschrittliche Gesellschaftsordnungen und produktionskräftige Industriezweige einfachere Lösungen, die mit normierten Fertigteilen errichtet werden.

Andererseits scheitern aber solch wohlmeinende Argumente an der Duplizität der von ihnen geäußerten Kritik, da sie diese nicht in derselben genauen und strengen Weise auf ihre eigenen Projekte anwenden. Obwohl ich der Angelegenheit keine übertriebene Bedeutung zumessen will, möchte ich mich auf das Positive und Ehrliche darin beschränken und einige kritische Anmerkungen zu der Arbeit anbringen, die in den letzten zwanzig Jahren moderner Architektur in Brasilien realisiert worden ist, ihre Schwächen und unvermeidlichen Fehler aufzeigen.

Introduction

In recent times, a degree of dissatisfaction has emerged among some of our architects who, though well aware of the standing modern Brazilian architecture enjoys, have all of a sudden begun distancing themselves from it. There are two very distinct groups: on the one hand, those who are influenced by traditionalist theories and demand architecture that is "based on the traditions and culture of the people" and, on the other, those who are alarmed at the low standard of contemporary building, and demand simple, rational solutions. We respect both points of view. The one, because it is honest and is striving for the solution that it deems most justified, and the other because it is based on facts that are worthy of consideration, even though it supercedes problems to do with our architecture that are in fact more important and indeed more urgent. Leaving this debate behind me I journeyed to Europe, to exchange views with foreign colleagues about joint professional problems during my stay there.

Critical points of view

As far as I am concerned I was under no illusion as to the critical points of view of the majority of architects who have visited us over the past few years: critical points of view, which in our opinion are not always justified and, when one takes an honest approach to what has been achieved in Europe and Brazil in the field of modern architecture, ought not to be uttered without due consideration. Some explanation is called for here however. It is worth mentioning first of all the lack of knowledge about working conditions here, which are different from those in their home countries. There, progressive societies and industrial sectors with powerful production capacities require simpler solutions that can be provided using standardized ready-made parts.

By contrast, well-meaning arguments such as these fall apart through the duplicity of the criticism leveled, since they are not applied in the same rigorous precise manner to their own products. Although I do not intend to place too much importance on the matter, I should like to restrict myself to their positive, honest aspects and apply a few critical remarks to what has been achieved in modern architecture in Brazil over the past 20 years, and address its weaknesses and unavoidable mistakes.

Inhalt

Der Mangel an Menschlichkeit ist sicherlich der Hauptgrund der Unzulänglich-keiten unserer modernen Architektur, die – wie es nicht anders hätte sein können – die sozialen Widersprüche unserer Gesellschaft, in der sie sich entwickelt hat, widerspiegelt. Wäre sie in einem sozial geordneten und fortgeschrittenen Land entstanden, in welchem sie ihr eigentliches Ziel – der Allgemeinheit zu dienen – erfüllen könnte, so würde sie in der Größe der gesellschaftlichen Pläne und in der Unterstützung der starken Industrie die Menschlichkeit und architektonische Einheit finden, an der es ihr heute fehlt. Da diese Architektur sich in erster Linie an einer Oberschicht orientiert, die kaum an Problemen der architektonischen Ökonomie, sondern vielmehr an der Darstellung von Reichtum und Luxus interes-siert ist, da es ihr an staatlichen Initiativen fehlt, die sich auf Plänen nationalen Umfanges oder den Bau von Massenunterkünften gründen, wird sie zwangs-läufig zum Objekt von Eitelkeiten, Demagogie und Opportunismus.

In diesen eingeengten Verhältnissen haben wir zwanzig Jahre lang unseren Beruf ausgeübt, der sich im Allgemeinen auf bürgerliche Häuser, Regierungs-gebäude, Mietwohnungsbau und einige Wohnkomplexe beschränkte. Es sind Arbeiten, die, wenn auch unter architektonischen Gesichtspunkten oft beach-tenswert, unweigerlich die soziale Ungleichheit des Landes wiedergeben. Sie bilden oft eine Beleidigung gegenüber dieser überwältigenden Mehrheit, die ohne die geringsten Möglichkeiten immer noch in den elenden Unterkünften wohnt, die wir alle kennen. Aus dem Mangel einer wirksamen sozialen Verankerung und dem Fehlen ergänzender umfangreicher gemeinschaftlicher Vorhaben entsteht die Unbeständigkeit unserer Architektur, ihre ökonomische Sorglosigkeit, ihre Vielfalt und ihr Formenreichtum, die durch das Ausbleiben einer starken Bauindustrie mit Fertigbauteilen noch verstärkt werden. Das, was an ihr falsch und nebensächlich ist, bedeutet für uns die zwingende Wiedergabe der gesell-schaftlichen Schichten, die sie getreu zum Ausdruck bringt. Aus diesen Gründen weigern wir uns, innerhalb der bestehenden Gesellschaft auf eine härtere und kältere – Europa-orientierte – Architektur zurückzugreifen, genauso wie wir eine „soziale Architektur" ablehnen. Damit würden wir lediglich zur Verarmung unserer Architektur beitragen, in all dem, was sie an Erneuerung und Kreativität bietet, oder sie als Täuschung, künstlich und demagogisch erscheinen lassen. Wir zogen es vor, ihre natürlichen Eigenschaften und ihre Spontaneität beizube-halten, die ihr ein intelligentes Spiel mit den benutzten konstruktiven Elementen erlaubten, und ihr ein eigenes klares Erscheinungsbild geben, welches letzt-endlich für ihre weltweite Anerkennung verantwortlich zeichnet.

Contents

A lack of human touch is without a doubt the main reason for the deficiencies inherent in our modern architecture, whereby, and this was inevitable, they reflect the social contradictions of the society in which architecture develops. Had it originated in a developed country with a proper social structure and been able to fulfill its real goal, that of serving the public in general, then it would have found that human touch and architectural unity in the greatness of plans for society and supporting strong industry, which it actually lacks today. Since this sort of architecture takes its cue for the most point from an upper strata of society that is interested less in the problems of architectural economy than in flaunting wealth and luxury, since it is lacking in any form of state initiative, which is based on plans for the whole nation or the construction of mass accommo-dation then it is condemned to becoming the object of vainness, demagogy and opportunism.

For the last twenty years we have been practicing our profession in these restrictive conditions, and in general limited our constructions to middle-class houses, government buildings, rental accommodations and one or two accom-modation blocks. These are buildings which, even though remarkable from an architectural point of view, nonetheless inevitably reflect the social inequalities of the country. They are in many cases an insult to the vast majority, who with absolutely no prospects are forced to continue living in the squalor we are all familiar with. The lack of any effective roots in society and accompanying large-scale community projects results in the inconsistency of our architecture, its carefree attitude to economy, its variety and multiplicity of shape, all of which is buttressed by the lack of a powerful construction industry with ready-made parts. All that is wrong and of minor importance about it represents for us the pressing reflection of social classes, which it expresses faithfully. For these reasons in our current society we refuse to fall back on a form of architecture that is harder, colder, more focused on Europe, just as we reject "social architecture." In doing so we would simply be making a contribution to the impoverishment of our archi-tecture, and all that it has to offer in the way of renewal and creativity, or would make it seem to be a deception, artificial and demagogic. We preferred to retain its natural characteristics and spontaneity, which allowed it to play intelligently with those constructive elements used, and gives it its own definitive appearance, which at the end of the day is what accounts for its worldwide recognition.

Tradition, Technik und plastisches Empfinden

Hierzu trugen sicherlich besondere Umstände bei, unter anderem, und das sollte man betonen, die nützliche und wohltuende Wirkung Lúcio Costas, der Repräsentant unserer Moderne, der es verstand, diese mit Sensibilität und Weitsicht zu lenken, und von Anfang an für eine Architektur kämpfte, die die funktionellen Notwendigkeiten entschieden mit der ständigen Suche nach der Schönheit und der plastischen Form verband. Ebenfalls trug die Tatsache dazu bei, dass wir – im Gegensatz zu anderen fortschrittlichen Ländern – keine großen öffentlichen Bauvorhaben zu entwerfen haben, die zu logischen, schnellen und ökonomischen Lösungen führen und die plastische Form disziplinieren und vereinfachen würden. Weiterhin ist es die dezidierte Position, die wir gegenüber der Tradition einnehmen – unsere Weigerung, sie zu kopieren – sowie unsere Absicht, die konstruktive Ehrlichkeit beizubehalten, die unsere Kolonialarchitektur immer auszeichnete. Eine Position, die wir mehr denn je als die Richtige einschätzen, zumal – wie Beispiele in einigen europäischen Ländern zeigen – es unmöglich ist, traditionelle Formen mit der Thematik und wichtiger noch mit der Vielfalt der zeitgenössischen Technik und den neuen und kreativen Lösungen, die diese bieten, in Einklang zu bringen. Dies ist die Sackgasse, in der sich bis heute diejenigen befinden, die an die „Synthese zwischen Tradition und gegenwärtiger Kunst und Technik" glauben und dabei das unüberbrückbare Hindernis des Eisenbetons außer Acht lassen, der Begriffe und Bedeutung der wichtigsten architektonischen Elemente verändert hat: Wände, die vormals Stützelemente waren, übernehmen jetzt lediglich die Funktion der Trennung und stellen somit Ballast innerhalb der Trägerstrukturen dar.

Die „Wachstumskrankheit"

Und all das trug dazu bei, dass wir innerhalb kurzer Zeit von den Lösungen Abstand nahmen, die auf Wiederholungen, kalte und geometrische Formen aus waren, und unserer Architektur eine neue Plastizität gaben, die, wenn sie denn gut angewendet wurde, Harmonie und Logik ausstrahlt und der Ausnutzung der Technik und der Funktion Ausdruck gab. Es ist richtig, und das ist Besorgnis erregend, dass die große Mehrheit unserer Bauten ein niedriges architektonisches Niveau aufweist, das durch die falsche Anwendung mancher Materialien und den Missbrauch bestimmter Formen groteske und bisweilen lächerliche Züge annimmt. Diese an sich schwerwiegende Tatsache ist leicht zu erklären. Der Erfolg der modernen Architektur in Brasilien war derart, dass sie innerhalb kurzer Zeit zur allgemeinen Volksarchitektur geworden ist. Alle, private Bauherren und Regierung, wünschten sich moderne Bauten, um hier und im Ausland Aufsehen damit zu erregen.

Tradition, technology and sculptural perception

Here special circumstances most certainly played a part, including, and this is worthy of stressing, the useful and beneficial influence of Lúcio Costa, the representative of our Modernism. He managed to guide this with sensitivity and far-sightedness and from the very beginning struggled for a form of architecture that very definitely combined functional necessities with the continuous search for beauty and sculptural effect. What likewise played a role was the fact that we, as opposed to other developed countries, are not involved in the development of large-scale public building projects, which result in logical, fast and economic solutions and would also discipline and simplify the sculptural form. The stance taken, flying in the face of tradition continues to be our refusal to copy it, as well as our intention to retain the constructive honesty that always distinguished our colonial architecture. This is a position which more than ever we consider to be the correct one since, as has been demonstrated in several European countries, it is impossible to bring into harmony traditional forms with modern technology and more importantly its various guises, and the new, creative solutions that these offer. This is the cul-de-sac in which those who today still believe in the "synthesis between tradition and contemporary art and technology" find themselves. In doing so they neglect the insurmountable hurdle of reinforced concrete, which has altered the interpretation and the importance of the most important architectural elements: Walls which were previously supporting elements now serve simply as dividing walls and as such just represent ballast within the supporting structure.

"Growth" as an illness

In a short space of time all this has resulted in us distancing ourselves from solutions entailing the repeated use of architectural forms, cold, geometric shapes and instilled in our architecture a new plasticity, which when used sensibly exudes harmony and logic and lends expression to the use of technology and function. It is correct to say, and this is the alarming thing, that the vast majority of our buildings display a low standard of architecture, which, through the incorrect use of many materials and the abuse of certain forms has produced grotesque and at times ridiculous features. There is a simple explanation for this quite serious state of affairs. The success of modern architecture in Brazil was such that it rapidly became the architecture of the people. Everybody, whether private developers or the government, desired modern buildings, so as to cause a sensation both here and abroad.

Es ist natürlich und auch verständlich, dass die Masse der Bauten im ganzen Land nicht das gleiche technische Niveau beibehalten konnte, besonders wenn man den Erfolg der qualitätsvolleren Bauten bedenkt, ihren innovativen Charakter, den sie alle – ob sie es konnten oder nicht – erreichen wollten. So lässt sich die Vielfalt und die Wiederholung bestimmter Formen erklären, die durch die Veränderung von Maßstab und Proportionen vollkommen ihren Charakter verloren haben. Und dasselbe gilt für die Übertragung einiger Bauten mit vollendeten Formen, die für weite und freie Standorte bestimmt waren und die dann, weil man sie in Baulücken ohne entsprechende Freiflächen einzwängte, zu beklagenswerten Bauten degradiert wurden, die die urbane Unausgeglichenheit und Chaos mitverursachen.

Es handelt sich bei alledem um eine Art „Wachstumskrankheit", die wir mit Nachsicht und Verständnis betrachten müssen und unter Zuhilfenahme einer hartnäckigen Aufklärungskampagne bekämpfen und beenden sollten.

Städtebau

Schlimmer ist indessen – weil fast nicht mehr rückgängig zu machen – der beklagenswerte Zustand unserer Städte, die den divergierenden Interessen der öffentlichen Hand und der zerstörerischen Tätigkeit der Immobilienhändler ausgesetzt sind, die sie mit unglaublichen Hochhausfronten erdrücken, die ihre Hügel verdecken, ihre Strände besetzen, ihnen das Licht, die Luft und die Bäume vorenthalten – essenzielle Elemente, mit denen uns die Natur großzügig beschenkt hat. Und dieses wiederholt sich in erschreckender Weise, trotz schlechter Beispiele wie der Copacabana – heute ein gedemütigter Stadtteil, ohne Wasser, öffentliche Verkehrsmittel und hemmungslose Beute der Bauunternehmen.

Insbesondere gegen diesen Unsinn müssen wir uns auflehnen, indem wir nach verantwortlichen, logischen und sachgemäßen Flächennutzungsplänen verlangen, die als Ziel die Ausnutzung der natürlichen Schönheit unserer Städte haben. Parallel dazu sollen realistische Maßnahmen gefordert werden, die den bestehenden sozialen Bedingungen mit ihren so starken individuellen Interessen Rechnung tragen und es möglich machen, die unwiderrufbaren Missstände durch eine objektive und effiziente Gesetzgebung zu lindern.

In diesem Umfeld bewegt sich die brasilianische Architektur, unter Bedingungen, die in allen noch vom Kapital beherrschten Ländern mehr oder weniger die gleichen sind. Sie berauben sie der ihr zukommenden höheren Ziele, um ihr einen

It is quite natural and indeed understandable that most buildings in the country cannot be of the same technical standard, especially when one considers the success of buildings with a higher degree of quality, and the innovative character they all strived to achieve, whether they had it in them or not. This explains the multitude and repeated use of certain forms, which through the alteration of scale and proportion have completely lost their character. The same applies for the transformation of some quite accomplished buildings, which had been intended to be free-standing in vast open spaces, but as a result of being hemmed into pockets of building space without the corresponding free space around them were degraded to lamentable edifices and help cause urban imbalance and chaos.

All these aspects can be put down to "teething problems", which we should consider with a degree of lenience and understanding and which we ought to counter and conquer with the help of a rigorous educational campaign.

Urban construction

What is worse however, because it is almost irreversible, is the wretched state of our cities, subject as they are to the diverging interests of the public sector and destructive activities on the part of real estate agents, which oppress them with unbelievable high-rise facades, concealing their hills, occupying their beaches, depriving them of light, air and trees, the natural elements that nature generously provided us with. And it is alarming how often this state of affairs repeats itself, despite bad examples such as Copacabana, nowadays a humiliated neighborhood with no water, no public transportation, the unrestrained spoils of construction companies.

We must stand up against this madness in particular by demanding the responsible, logical and proper use of land, which aims to exploit the natural beauty of our cities. Parallel to this we should demand realistic measures that take into account existing social conditions with their strictly individual interests and make it possible to relieve the irreversible deplorable state of affairs by means of objective, efficient laws.

This is the scenario in which Brazilian architecture exists, under conditions that are more or less the same in all capitalist countries and which rob it of the higher goals it deserves, giving it a discriminating and superficial character where all that counts is sculptural effect.

diskriminierenden und oberflächlichen Charakter zu verleihen, bei dem lediglich der plastische Aspekt zählt.

Hier beobachten wir untätig die zunehmende Zerstörung unserer Städte und die bedauerlichen Ungleichheiten, die das Leben in ihnen bedeutet, und beschränken uns auf eine Klassenarchitektur, der die notwendige soziale Grundlage fehlt, was zu all ihren Mängeln führt.

Die sowjetische Architektur

Erregend und zurecht interessant an der sowjetischen Architektur – die wir als kontrastierendes Beispiel nehmen – ist ihr menschlicher Charakter, der erstmalig in der Geschichte es dem Architekten ermöglichte, seine wirkliche Rolle innerhalb der Gesellschaft einzunehmen. Sie befreite ihn von den bisherigen individualistischen Aufgaben, damit er seinen gewünschten Beitrag zur Lösung kollektiver Probleme leisten kann. Während in den übrigen Ländern der Architekt fast ausschließlich den Aufforderungen einer herrschenden Minderheit zur Verfügung steht, orientiert sich in der Sowjetunion seine Arbeit an der Realisierung großer städtebaulicher Vorhaben, der Erfüllung des Glücks und dem Allgemeinwohl. Außerdem wird er nicht mit den Hindernissen konfrontiert, die bei uns fortbestehen – Hindernisse, die innig mit den sozialen Problemen verbunden sind, die unsere Kollegen beharrlich ignorieren, und die das Scheitern unserer städtebaulichen Projekte zur Folge haben, weil sie stets auf dem Papier bleiben oder auf Architekturkongressen landen, mehr oder minder akademisch und harmlos.

Dieses ist das erneuernde und menschliche Beispiel, dem zu folgen ist, indem wir von der Position des Unbeteiligten gegenüber der Politik und der Probleme der Gesellschaft abrücken und uns endlich an die Seite derjenigen stellen, die dafür kämpfen und leiden. Und wenn in jedem Land auf jedem Platz dieser Kampf auch seine Eigenart hat, so besteht doch der gemeinsame Nenner aller unterdrückten Völker in der Sehnsucht nach Freiheit und den universellen Ansprüchen nach Frieden und Gerechtigkeit.

Here we sit back and simply watch the increasing destruction of our cities and the regrettable imbalances which living in them entails and limit ourselves to class architecture which is lacking in any form of social structure, and is the cause of all the faults.

Soviet architecture

If we now take as a contrast Soviet architecture, what is exciting and quite rightly interesting about it is its humane character, which for the first time enabled architects to assume their proper role within society. It freed them of the individual tasks they had been subject to until then, in order for them to make their desired contribution to the solution of collective problems. Whereas in other countries architects are almost entirely at the disposal of a ruling minority, in the Soviet Union their work is focused on the completion of large-scale urban development projects, creating happiness and general well-being. Furthermore, nor are they confronted with the obstacles they still encounter here, obstacles that stem directly from social problems that our colleagues steadfastly ignore, meaning that our urban projects fail, because they never make it past the drawing board or architects' congresses, are purely academic and harmless.

This is the humane example of renewal that we ought to follow, abandoning our position on the sidelines of politics and society's problems and finally join forces with those who are struggling and suffering. And even if in every country, on every town square this struggle has its own characteristics, the common denominator of all oppressed peoples is the longing for freedom and a universal claim to peace and justice.

National Congress, Brasília.

Meine Architektur
My architecture

Oscar Niemeyer

Ich teile meine Architektur in fünf Zeitbereiche ein: zuerst Pampulha; dann von Pampulha bis Brasília; danach Brasília; dann noch meine Arbeiten im Ausland und abschließend die letzten Entwürfe.

Ich habe nie den Einfluss dessen, was in der Welt der Architektur vorging, auf diese Zeiträume und auf mein Denken als Architekt kommentiert. Heute, wenn ich meine Arbeiten Revue passieren lasse, verstehe ich besser, warum sie in all diesen Phasen unweigerlich ein Element der Auflehnung beinhalten.

Pampulha

Alles begann, als ich die ersten Überlegungen für Pampulha machte und bewusst den so gelobten rechten Winkel und die rationale Architektur von Reißschiene und Dreieck ignorierte, um beherzt in die Welt der Kurven und der neuen Formen einzudringen, die uns der Betonbau ermöglicht.

Und auf dem Papier, beim Zeichnen dieser Entwürfe, habe ich dann gegen diese langweilige und monotone Architektur protestiert, die so leicht zu bewerkstelligen war und sich schnell von den Vereinigten Staaten bis nach Japan ausgedehnt hatte.

Von Pampulha bis Brasília

Von Pampulha bis Brasília folgte meine Architektur immer demselben Weg der plastischen Freiheit und der architektonischen Erfindung, und ich versuchte sie immer vor den Einschränkungen der technischen Logik zu verteidigen. Wenn ich aber eine andere Form entwarf, musste ich Argumente haben, um sie zu erklären. So fanden sich die neuen Formen, die ich schuf, nach und nach in das plastische Vokabular unserer Architektur ein. Und so habe ich, im Laufe vieler Jahre, immer die neue Form gesucht und sie, bei Bedarf, immer wieder erläutert.

Brasília

Ich muss zugeben, schon beim Beginn meiner Arbeit an Brasília war ich die vielen Erläuterungen leid. Ich dachte, dass die Erfindung vorrangig sein sollte. Und ich erinnerte mich, wie bei manchem fertig gestellten Rohbau nichts von der eigentlichen Architektur erkennbar war und sie sich erst danach in einem weiteren Schritt als sekundäres Merkmal zeigte.

Meiner Ansicht nach müsste die Architektur, die strukturellen Probleme vorwegnehmend, diese Aufgabe erfüllen, um – mit der Fantasie des Architekten und der Verfeinerung der Technik – das architektonische Schauspiel möglich zu machen, wie es die heutigen Aufgaben erfordern.

I divide my architecture up into five different periods: first Pampulha, then from Pampulha until Brasília, after that Brasília, followed by my work overseas, and, last but not least, my most recent plans.

I have never commented on the influence of events in the world of architecture on these periods or on my thinking as an architect. Today, looking back at my work, I have a better understanding of why, in all five phases, it undeniably contains an element of rebellion.

Pampulha

It all began with my first thoughts on Pampulha. I consciously ignored the highly praised right angle and the rational architecture of T-squares and triangles in order to wholeheartedly enter the world of curves and new shapes made possible by the introduction of concrete into the building process.

And, on paper, as I drew these plans, I protested against that boring and monotonous architecture which it was so easy to create and which had rapidly spread from the United States as far afield as Japan.

From Pampulha to Brasília

In the period from Pampulha to Brasília, my architecture always took the same route, involving sculptural freedom and architectural invention. I always endeavoured to protect it against the limitations of technical logic. However, whenever I designed a different shape, I had to have arguments to justify it. For these newly created forms slowly but surely made there way into the sculptural idiom of our architecture. And thus, in the course of many years, I always sought to find new forms and when it became necessary, I explained them.

Brasília

I must admit that even at the beginning of my work on Brasília, I was already tired of always giving the explanations. I thought that invention should be the highest priority. And I thought about how as good as nothing of the actual architecture is to be discerned in many finished building shells and only at a second step does it become recognizable as a secondary characteristic.

It is my opinion that in anticipation of structural problems, architecture must meet this challenge in order (thanks to the architect's imagination and advances in technology) to enable the architectural showcase to arise such as today's projects require.

Ich entschied also, dass dies meine Vorgehensweise bei der Planung der Regierungspaläste Brasílias sein werde. Sie sollten durch ihre eigenen Strukturen innerhalb der vorgesehenen Formen gekennzeichnet sein. Damit würden sich kleinere Details der rationalistischen Architektur gegenüber den übermächtigen Formen der neuen Strukturen auflösen. Wenn man den Nationalkongress Brasílias oder die Regierungsgebäude betrachtet, kann man feststellen, dass mit der Fertigstellung des Rohbaus die Architektur bereits vorhanden war.

Ich suchte die Möglichkeiten des Betons herauszufordern, hauptsächlich bei den Auflagepunkten, die ich möglichst fein, extrem fein gestalten wollte, so dass die Paläste scheinbar kaum den Boden berührten.

Bei der Kathedrale beispielsweise mied ich die gängigen Lösungen der traditionellen und dunklen Kathedralen, die an Sünde erinnern. Im Gegenteil, der Zugang zur Halle wurde dunkel gehalten, der Innenraum hell leuchtend, farbig, mit bunten Glasfenstern, sich dem Unendlichen zuwendend.

Mit demselben architektonischen Erfindungsgeist entwarf ich die weiteren Gebäude.

Zwanzig Jahre herrschte eine Militärdiktatur in unserem Land. Niemand hat Brasília entwürdigt, aber andauerndes Desinteresse und Lieblosigkeit erlaubten, dass vieles entstellt werden konnte.

Arbeiten im Ausland
Einige meiner besten Bauten befinden sich außerhalb Brasiliens: Der Hauptsitz der Kommunistischen Partei Frankreichs (PCF), das Gewerkschaftshaus in Bobigny, das Kulturzentrum in Le Havre, der Hauptsitz der FATA in Turin, der Mondadori Verlag in Mailand, die Universitäten von Constantine und Algier in Algerien.

In dieser Phase meines architektonischen Schaffens überwog in mir die Absicht, nicht nur die plastische Freiheit meiner Architektur, sondern auch den Fortschritt des Ingenieurwesens meines Landes zu verbreiten. Ich suchte mit Sorgfalt die erforderlichen Lösungen eines jeden Projektes in der Absicht, meine Arbeit als Architekt klar definieren zu können.

Beim Hauptsitz der PCF zeigte ich, wie wichtig es ist, ein harmonisches Spiel zwischen Volumina und freier Fläche beizubehalten; am Gewerkschaftsgebäude in Bobigny, wie es möglich ist, preiswert zu bauen und dennoch das Haupt-

Therefore, I decided that this should be my modus operandi when planning government buildings for Brasília. They should be characterized by their own structures within the prescribed shapes. In this way, the smaller details of rationalist architecture would vanish in the face of the overpowering shapes of the new edifices. If you look at the National Congress or the government buildings in Brasília, it soon becomes clear that the architecture was already fully manifest when the buildings were still only shells.

I tried to push the potential of concrete to its limits, especially at the load-bearing points which I wanted to be as delicate as possible so that it would seem as if the palaces barely touched the ground.

For example, in the cathedral I avoided the usual solution of traditional and dark cathedrals that are reminiscent of sin. On the contrary, I kept the entrance dark and rendered the interior light and bright: it contains colourful stained glass windows which look to eternity.

It was with the same spirit of invention that I designed various other buildings.

A military dictatorship ruled our country for twenty years. Nobody dishonoured Brasília, but continued disinterest in it and a lack of affection permitted much disfigurement.

Work overseas
Some of my best buildings are outside Brazil: the French Communist Party (PCF) Headquarters, the Worker's Union Building in Bobigny, the Cultural Center in Le Havre, the headquarters of the FATA in Turin, the Mondadori Publishing House in Milan, the Constantine and Algiers Universities in Algeria.

During this phase in my architectural career, it was my overriding intention not only to create a platform for the sculptural freedom of my architecture, but also to spread the word about the progress of engineering in my country. I carefully sought out the requisite solutions for each and every project with the intention of clearly defining my work as an architect.

With the headquarters of the French Communist Party (PCF), I showed how important it is to maintain a harmonious relationship between volume and open space. The "bourse de travail" in Bobigny demonstrates how it is possible to build inexpensively and still enrich the main building through contrast with free forms. In Le Havre, I opted for a sunken main square to protect it from the

gebäude durch den Kontrast mit den freien Formen zu bereichern; in Le Havre, wie durch die Tieferlegung des Hauptplatzes dieser vor der Kälte und den dort anhaltenden Winden geschützt wird, indem die Gebäude weiche, fast fensterlose, abstrakt wirkende runde Flächen erhielten; beim Hauptsitz der FATA, wie die Geschosse an den Unterzügen der Dachkonstruktion aufgehängt wurden; beim Hauptsitz des Mondadori Verlags, wie mit einer Arkade unterschiedlicher Breiten ein neuer, fast musikalisch anmutender, charakteristischer Rhythmus entsteht; in Algerien, wie mit großzügigen freien Räumen, Spannweiten von 50 Metern und Auskragungen von 25 Metern eine imponierende Architektur entstand, die sogar die Unzulänglichkeiten der lokalen Bautechnik verschwinden ließ.

Neuere Bauten

In meinen neuen Bauten am Memorial da América Latina in São Paulo folgt meine Architektur radikal dem technischen Fortschritt am Bau. Keine kleinlichen Details, lediglich Unterzüge von 60 bis 90 Metern Ausmaß und gekrümmte Schalen.

Ich habe schon immer die mittelmäßige Idee derer, die auf einer „einfachen, volksnahen Architektur" bestehen, abgelehnt. Als wir die CIEPs[1] bauten, konnten wir mit Freuden feststellen, wie die Kinder armer Schichten sie gerne besuchten, als ob ihnen damit die Hoffnung gegeben würde, eines Tages das nutzen zu können, was bis heute nur den Reichen erlaubt ist.

Andererseits hat mich die Monumentalität nie geschreckt, wenn sie durch ein entsprechendes Thema gerechtfertigt ist. Was letzten Endes von der Architektur geblieben ist, waren die Monumentalwerke, die die Zeit und deren technische Entwicklung kennzeichnen und die – sozial gerechtfertigt oder nicht – uns doch bewegen. Es ist die Schönheit, die die Sensibilität des Menschen bestimmt.

Ah! Wie groß waren die alten Meister, die die riesigen Kuppeln, die außergewöhnlichen „voutes"[2] in den alten Kathedralen schufen!

Das ist es, was ich Ihnen sagen sollte über meine Architektur, die ich mit Mut und Idealismus anging, wohl wissend, wie wichtig das Leben, die Freunde und diese ungerechte Welt, die wir bessern müssen, sind.

---

1 CIEP – Centro Integrado de Educação Pública.
  Eine Einrichtung, die den hiesigen Volkshochschulen ähnelt. (A.d.Ü.)
2 „voutes" = Gewölbe, französisch im Original. (A.d.Ü.)

cold and constant wind while the buildings consist of gentle, almost windowless and seemingly abstract round spaces. In the case of the headquarters of FATA, I demonstrated that the floors can be suspended from the roof structure and in the headquarters of Mondadori, an arcade of varying widths results in a new, almost musically graceful and characteristic rhythm. In Algeria, an impressive edifice, which even overcame the inadequacies of local building methods, was created by large-scale open spaces, adopting 50-meter-long spans, and using vaulting which is 25 meters across.

New buildings

With my new buildings for the Latin American Monument in São Paolo, my architecture radically follows technological advances in construction. No petty details; only joists of 60–90 meters in length and curved shells.

I have always rejected the mediocre ideas of those who insist on a "simple architecture of the people". When we built the CIEP[1] we had the pleasure of seeing how children from the lower classes enjoyed attending them; as though they were somehow given the hope that they would some day be able to use that which is normally reserved for the wealthy.

By the same token, I have never been afraid of monumentality when a corresponding theme justifies it. In the end, it is the monuments which endure and which characterize the epoch and technological advances and, be this socially justified of not, move us. It is beauty which determines the sensibility of man.

Ah! How great were the old masters who created the gigantic domes, the extraordinary "voutes"[2] of the ancient cathedrals!

This is what I wanted to tell you about my architecture. I approached it with courage and idealism, fully aware of the importance of life, friends and this unjust world, which we must quite simply improve.

---

1 CIEP – Centro Integrado de Educação Pública – an institution
  for continuing education.
2 "voutes" = vaulting (in French in the original)

Memorial da América Latina, São Paulo.

Oscar Niemeyer – eine biografische Übersicht
Oscar Niemeyer – A biographical overview

1907	geboren am 15. Dezember als Oscar Ribeiro de Almeida de Niemeyer Soares in Rio de Janeiro.
1924–1929	Studium der Architektur an der Nationalen Kunstschule Rio de Janeiro, u.a. bei Lúcio Costa, in dessen Büro Niemeyer bis Ende der dreißiger Jahre arbeitet.
1936	Teilnahme am Projekt des Ministeriums für Gesundheit und Erziehung in Rio de Janeiro; erstmaliges Zusammentreffen mit Le Corbusier, der einer Einladung Lúcio Costas folgend als Berater an dem Projekt mitwirkt.
1937	Realisierung der Entbindungsstation Obra do Berco in Rio de Janeiro, Niemeyers erstes Projekt.
1940	Bekanntschaft mit Juscelino Kubitschek, dem späteren Gründungspräsidenten von Brasília, zu dieser Zeit noch Gouverneur des Bundesstaates Minas Gerais. Niemeyer erhält den Auftrag zum Pampulha-Komplex in Belo Horizonte.
1945	Eintritt in die Kommunistische Partei Brasiliens.
1947	Mehrmonatiger Aufenthalt in New York als Mitglied des Planungskomitees zum Bau des UN-Hauptsitzes. Der zusammen mit Le Corbusier erarbeitete Doppelentwurf 23–31 wird zur Ausführung empfohlen, wenn auch verändert realisiert.
1952	Beginn der Entwurfsarbeiten zu Niemeyers Privathaus in Canoas / Rio de Janeiro, das am Rande der II. São Paulo Biennale für Aufsehen sorgt.
1954	Mehrmonatige Reise nach Europa, u.a. auch nach Polen, in die UDSSR und Tschechoslowakei. Realisierung eines Wohnblockes auf der Interbau/Berlin.
1955	Gründung der Zeitschrift Moduló.
1956	Erhält von dem neu gewählten brasilianischen Präsidenten Juscelino Kubitschek den Auftrag zur Planung der neuen Hauptstadt Brasília. Niemeyer lehnt dies jedoch ab und spricht sich für einen städtebaulichen Wettbewerb aus, den Lúcio Costas plano piloto gewinnt. Niemeyer wird als Direktor der Architekturabteilung der Planungsgesellschaft NOVACAP mit dem Entwurf der Regierungsgebäude beauftragt.
1957/1958	Entwurf der ersten Repräsentationsbauten für Brasília, u.a. Alvoradapalast, Planalto, Nationalkongress, Kathedrale.
1962/1964	Mehrmonatige Reisen in den Libanon, nach Portugal, Frankreich und Israel auf Einladung verschiedener Auftraggeber zu Großprojekten.
1963	Internationaler Leninpreis (UDSSR); Ehrenmitglied des American Institute of Architects.
1967	Zunehmende Arbeitsschwierigkeiten unter der brasilianischen Militärregierung, aber auch weitere Großprojekte in Frankreich, Italien, Portugal und Algerien zwingen Niemeyer zur Verlegung des Hauptsitzes seines Büros nach Paris.
1979	Ernennung zum Offizier der französischen Ehrenlegion.
1982	Schließung des Pariser Büros. Ab 1985 entwirft Niemeyer in seinem Büro an der Copacabana/Rio de Janeiro neue Projekte für Brasília.
1988	Verleihung des Pritzker-Preises in Chicago.
1991	Mit seinem Entwurf für das Museum für Zeitgenössische Kunst in Niterói sorgt Niemeyer für erneutes internationales Aufsehen.
1998	Verleihung der Gold-Medaille des RIBA in Rio de Janeiro.
2002	Eröffnung des Novo Museum in Curitiba/Paraná im November 2002.

1907	Born December 15th in Rio de Janeiro as Oscar Ribeiro de Almeida de Niemeyer Soares.
1924–1929	Studies architecture at the National Art Academy in Rio de Janeiro, among others under Lúcio Costa, in whose office Niemeyer works until the end of the 1930s.
1936	Takes part in the project for the Ministry of Health and Education in Rio de Janeiro; first encounter with Le Corbusier, who, at the invitation of Lúcio Costa, is consultant to the project.
1937	Plans the maternity ward at Obra do Berco in Rio de Janeiro, his first project.
1940	Meets Juscelino Kubitschek, later the founding President of Brasília, at the time Governor of the State of Minas Gerais. Niemeyer is commissioned to plan the Pampulha project in Belo Horizonte.
1945	Joins the Brazilian Communist Party.
1947	Travels for several months to New York as a member of the Planning Commission for the UN headquarters. Meets Le Corbusier again.
1952	Begins planning his private residence in Canoas in Rio de Janeiro, in 1954 one of the most controversial buildings at the II. São Paulo Biennial.
1954	Spends several months in Europe, incl. Poland, the USSR and the CSSR. Designs an apartment block for the Interbau in Berlin.
1955	Founds the Moduló journal.
1956	Newly elected Brazilian President Juscelino Kubitschek commissions him to plan the new capital Brasília. Niemeyer is made Director of the Architecture Dept. of the NOVACAP planning company and organizes the competition for town planning tenders, won by Lúcio Costa's plano piloto.
1957/1958	Designs the first representative buildings for Brasília, incl. the Alvorada Palace, Planalto, the National Congress, and the cathedral.
1962	Spends several months in Lebanon and Israel.
1963	International Lenin Prize (USSR); honorary member of the American Institute of Architects.
1967	Having been forbidden by the military junta from practising his profession, Niemeyer goes into exile in Paris. In the years that follow he handles numerous large projects in France, Italy, Portugal and Algeria.
1979	Made an officer of the French Legion D'Honneur.
1982	Returns from exile to Rio de Janeiro. Starts work again, as of 1985 designs new projects for Brasília.
1988	Wins the Pritzker Prize in Chicago.
1991	Causes an international sensation with his design for the Museum of Contemporary Art in Niterói.
1998	Awarded the RIBA Gold Medal at Rio de Janeiro.
2002	Opening of the Museu Nova in Curitiba (Paraná) in November 2002.

Obra do Berco. Maternity Ward, Rio de Janeiro.

Oscar Niemeyer: Projekt- und Werkverzeichnis
Projects and buildings

1935

Sports-Club *
Rio de Janeiro, RJ, Brazil

Residence *
Rio de Janeiro, RJ, Brazil

1936

Ministry of Education and Health
(currently the Palace of Culture)
Coordination: Le Corbusier, Lúcio Costa.
Collaboration: Jorge Moreira,
Ernani Vasconcellos, Affonso Eduardo
Reidy, Carlos Leão
Rio de Janeiro, RJ, Brazil

Residence Henrique Xavier *
Rio de Janeiro, RJ, Brazil

1937

Maternity Ward *
Rio de Janeiro, RJ, Brazil

Obra do Berço / Maternity ward
and Infant's Hospital
Rio de Janeiro, RJ, Brazil

1938

Grand Hotel
Ouro Preto, MG, Brazil

Residence Oswald de Andrade *
São Paulo, SP, Brazil

1939

Pavilion of Brazil for the New York
World's Fair
Participation / Partners: Lúcio Costa,
Paul Leister
New York, USA

M. Passos Residence *
Miguel Pereira, RJ, Brazil

1940

The Pampuha Complex
– Dancehall Restaurant Casa do Baile
– Casino (currently the Museum
   of Modern Art)
– Yacht-Club
– Church of Saint Francis of Assisi
Belo Horizonte, MG, Brazil

1941

National Center of Athletics *
Rio de Janeiro, RJ, Brazil

Francisco Peixoto Residence
Cataguazes, MG, Brazil

Municipal Theatre *
Belo Horizonte, MG, Brazil

Water Tower *
Ribeirão das Lages, RJ, Brazil

1942

Residence of the Architect at Lagoa
Rio de Janeiro, RJ, Brazil

Herbert Johnson Residence
Fortaleza, CE, Brazil

Municipal Theatre
Belo Horizonte, MG, Brazil

1943

Hotel at Pampulha *
Belo Horizonte, MG, Brazil

Charles Ofair Residence *
Rio de Janeiro, RJ, Brazil

Juscelino Kubitschek Residence
Belo Horizonte, MG, Brazil

Prudente de Moraes Neto Residence
Rio de Janeiro, RJ, Brazil

1944

Yacht Club / Recreation Center at Lagoa *
Rio de Janeiro, RJ, Brazil

1945

Hotel *
Nova Friburgo, RJ, Brazil

Fluminense Yacht Club *
Rio de Janeiro, RJ, Brazil

Tribuna Popular Newspaper
Headquarters *
Rio de Janeiro, RJ, Brazil

1946

Boavista Bank Headquarters
Rio de Janeiro, RJ, Brazil

College
Cataguases, MG, Brazil

1947

Aircraft Technical Center
São José dos Campos, SP, Brasil

United Nations (UN) Headquarters
Contribution to the Project
of Le Corbusier
New York, USA

Burton Tremaine Residence *
Santa Barbara, California, USA

Gustavo Capanema Residence *
Rio de Janeiro, RJ, Brazil

1948

Auditorium for the Ministry of Education
and Health *
Rio de Janeiro, RJ, Brazil

1949

O Cruzeiro Edition Group Headquarters
Rio de Janeiro, RJ, Brazil

Regent's Hotel *
Rio de Janeiro, RJ, Brazil

Residence of the Architect
Mendes, RJ, Brazil

Residence at Gávea
Rio de Janeiro, RJ, Brazil

1950

Club of 500
Guaratingueta, SP, Brazil

Club
Diamantina, MG, Brazil

Montreal Office Building
São Paulo, SP, Brazil

Factory hall for Duchen
São Paulo, SP, Brasil

Hotel Quitandinha – First Project *
Petrópolis, RJ, Brazil

1951

Copan Apartment Building
São Paulo, SP, Brazil

Ibirapuera Park
Collaboration: Eduardo Kneese de Mello,
Eduardo Corona, Carlos Lemos
– Canopy
– Palace of Agriculture / currently the
   Detran Headquarters
– Palace of Arts / currently the Pavilion
   Manoel da Nobrega
– Palace of Industries / currently the
   Pavilion of the São Paulo Biennal
– Palace of Nations / currently the OCA
– Palace of States / currently the Prodam
   Headquarters
São Paulo, SP, Brazil

Juscelino Kubitschek Buildings
Belo Horizonte, MG, Brazil

California Building
São Paulo, SP, Brazil

Julia Kubitschek School
Diamantina, BH, Brazil

Hotel Tijuco
Diamantina, MG, Brazil

1952

Diarios Assoc. TV Station *
Rio de Janeiro, RJ, Brazil

Sul-América Hospital
Rio de Janeiro, RJ, Brazil

Gas station
São Paulo, SP, Brazil

Residence of the Architect at Canoas
Rio de Janeiro, RJ, Brazil

Leonel Miranda Residence
Rio de Janeiro, RJ, Brazil

1953

BEMGE Bank Office Building
Belo Horizonte, MG, Brazil

Colleges
Campo Grande and Corumbá, MS, Brazil

Hotel Quitandinha – Second Project *
Petrópolis, RJ, Brazil

Ermiro de Lima Residence *
Rio de Janeiro, RJ, Brazil

Francisco Pignatary Residence *
São Paulo, SP, Brazil

Sergio Buarque de Holanda Residence *
São Paulo, SP, Brazil

1954

Niemeyer Apartment Building
Belo Horizonte, MG, Brazil

Milton Campos College
Belo Horizonte, BH, Brazil

TV-Station Complex *
Rio de Janeiro, RJ, Brazil

Airport *
Diamantina, MG, Brazil

Factory Hall for Ericsson
São José dos Campos, SP, Brazil

Museum of Modern Art *
Caracas, Venezuela

Alberto Dalva Simão Residence
Belo Horizonte, MG, Brazil

Edmundo Cavanelas Residence
Pedro do Rio, RJ, Brazil

Triangulo Office Building
São Paulo, SP, Brazil

1955

Public Library
Belo Horizonte, MG, Brazil

Libanese Club *
Belo Horizonte, MG, Brazil

Eiffel Office Building
São Paulo, SP, Brazil

Interbau Apartment Building
Berlin, Germany

Getúlio Vargas Foundation
Rio de Janeiro, RJ, Brazil

Intermak Headquarters
Niterói, RJ, Brazil

1956

Marina City *
Vale do Rio Urucuia, MG, Brazil

Botafogo Football and Regates Club
Headquarters
Rio de Janeiro, RJ, Brazil

Taba-Tupi Apartment Building *
Rio de Janeiro, RJ, Brazil

Catetinho/First Residence
of the President
Brasília, DF, Brazil

1957

Commercial and Cultural Center
Havanna, Cuba

Brasília Palace Hotel
Brasília, DF, Brazil

Social Housing
Brasília, DF, Brazil

Alvorada Palace/Residence
of the President
Brasília, DF, Brazil

Chapel of the Alvorada Palace
Brasília, DF, Brazil

Financial District
Brasília, DF, Brazil

1958

Public Library *
Florianópolis, SC, Brazil

Chapel Senhora de Fátima
Brasília, DF, Brazil

Cathedral
Brasília, DF, Brazil

National Congress
Brasília, DF, Brazil

Standard Ministries
Brasília, DF, Brazil

Museum of the Foundation of Brasilia
Brasília, DF, Brazil

Planalto Palace
Brasília, DF, Brazil

Supreme Court of Justice
Brasília, DF, Brazil

National Theatre
Brasília, DF, Brazil

1959

Building for the Guard of the President
Brasília, DF, Brazil

Super Quadra 108 Sul/SQS-108
Brasília, DF, Brazil

Waterworks
Brasília, DF, Brazil

Cinema Brasilia
Brasília, DF, Brazil

1960

Barão de Mauá Building
Rio de Janeiro, RJ, Brazil

Residence of the Architect
Brasília, DF, Brazil

University of Brasília
– CEPLAN Planning Center
– Central Institute of Sciences (ICC)
– Institute of Theology
– Central Place *
Brasília, DF, Brazil

Itamaraty Palace/Ministry of Foreign
Office – First Project *
Brasília, DF, Brazil

National Steel Company Headquarters
Brasília, DF, Brazil

Teahouse at the Praça dos Três Poderes
Brasília, DF, Brazil

1961

Gymnasium and Stadium *
Brasília, DF, Brazil

Pigeon Loft
Brasília, DF, Brazil

1962

Sports Center *
Libya

International Fair Buildings
Tripoli, Libya

Prefabricated Apartment Building *
Brasília, DF, Brazil

Ministry of Justice
Brasília, DF, Brazil

Itamaraty Palace/Ministry of Foreign
Office – Second Project
Brasília, DF, Brazil

Pampulha Yacht Club/Annex
Belo Horizonte, MG, Brazil

Touring Club Headquarters
and Exhibition Hall
Brasília, DF, Brazil

1963

Center of Beauty *
Los Angeles, California, USA

Gymnasium for Young People *
Brasília, DF, Brazil

Elementary School *
Brasília, DF, Brazil

1964

Nórdia Complex *
Tel-Aviv, Israel

Panorama Complex *
Haifa, Israel

Hotel Scandinavia *
Tel-Aviv, Israel

Urban Plan for Negev *
Negev, Israel

Federmann Residence *
Herzlia, Israel

University of Haifa
Haifa, Israel

University of Ghana *
Accra, Ghana

1965

City Administration's District *
Abidjan, Ivory Coast

Airport of Brasília *
Brasília, DF, Brazil

Assembly Hall for the Legislature
of Minas Gerais *
Belo Horizonte, MG, Brazil

Tourist Complex *
Caesarea, Israel

Urban Plan Pena Furada *
Algarve, Portugal

Palace of the Government *
Brazzaville, Congo

PCF French Communist Party
Headquarters
Paris, France

Rothschild Residence *
Caesarea, Israel

National Congress/Chamber
of Deputies – Annex II/Chapel
Chamber of Deputies – Annex II
Brasília, DF, Brazil

1966

La Madeleine Club *
Préssagny l'Orgueilleux, Eure, France

Hotel and Casino
Collaboration: Vianna de Lima
Funchal, Madeira, Portugal

Manchete Publishing Company
Headquarters
Rio de Janeiro, RJ, Brazil

Dubonnet Residence *
Côte d'Azur, France

Hospital at Copacabana *
Rio de Janeiro, RJ, Brazil

City of the Future Project *
location unknown

1967

Dominican Monastery *
*Sainte-Baume, Bouches du Rhône,
France*

International Tourism Center *
Florianópolis, SC, Brazil

Urban Plan/ZUP of Grasse *
Grasse, Alpes Maritimes, France

Institute of Education of Paraná
Curitiba, PR, Brazil

Costa and Silva Bridge/Bridge of the
Lago Sul
Brasília, DF, Brazil

Vice President's Residence –
First Project *
Brasília, DF, Brazil

Apartment Buildings at Botafogo
Rio de Janeiro, RJ, Brazil

Urban Plan *
Guarujá, SP, Brazil

1968

Music Hall *
Rio de Janeiro, RJ, Brazil

Mondadori Publishing Company Headquarters First Project *
Segrate (Milan), Italy

Mondadori Publishing Company
Headquarters – Second Project
Segrate (Milan), Italy

School of Architecture
Algiers, Algeria

Satellite Station *
Itaboraí, RJ, Brazil

Agricultural Fair Building *
Brasília, DF, Brazil

National Hotel
Rio de Janeiro, RJ, Brazil

Mosque *
Algiers, Algeria

General Army Quarters
Brasília, DF, Brazil

Nara Mondadori Residence
Cap Ferrat, France

Gameleira Park
Belo Horizonte, MG, Brazil

University of Algiers
– Faculty of Human Sciences (USHA)
– Faculty of Technology (USTA)
Algiers, Algeria

University of Cuiabá *
Cuiabá, MT, Brazil

City Plan for Algiers *
– Civic Center, Business District,
Cultural Center, Commercial Center,
Living quarters
Algiers, Algeria

1969

Center of Barra/Athaydeville
Rio de Janeiro, RJ, Brazil

Exhibition Museum Barra 72 *
Rio de Janeiro, RJ, Brazil

Ecotec – Olympic Complex *
location unknown

Renault Headquarters *
Boulogne-Billancourt, France

Frederico Gomes Residence
Rio de Janeiro, RJ, Brazil

University of Constantine – First Stage
Constantine, Algeria

Embassy of Algeria *
Brasília, DF, Brazil

1970

Airport *
Manzanillo, Mexico

National Stadium *
Brasília, DF, Brazil

The Brazilian Institute of Architecture*
Brasília, DF, Brazil

1971

National Congress – Chamber
of Deputies – Annex III
Brasília, DF, Brazil

Ipanema Hotel*
location unknown

Supreme Court of Justice – Annex I
Brasília, DF, Brazil

1972

Worker's Union
Bobigny, Seine Saint Denis, France

Commercial Center
and Office Building*
Miami, Florida, USA

Oscar Niemeyer Cultural Center
Le Havre, Seine-Maritime, France

Urban Plan/ZAC of Dieppe*
Dieppe, France

Denasa Office Building
Brasília, DF, Brazil

Oscar Niemeyer Building
Brasília, DF, Brazil

Panorama Palace Hotel*
Salvador, BA, Brazil

Manchete TV Networks Headquarters
Maceió, AL, Brazil

Moura Lacerda University*
Ribeirão Preto, SP, Brazil

Urban Plan
Santo André, SP, Brazil

1973

St. Anthony's Student's Housing
College/University of Oxford*
Oxford, UK

Convention Center Medical
Association RS
Porto Alegre, RS, Brazil

Jaburu Palace/Vice President's
Residence – Second Project
Brasília, DF, Brazil

Telebras Headquarters
Brasília, DF, Brazil

Train and Coach Station
Brasília, DF, Brazil

Tower PB-17 for La Défense*
Paris, France

Club*
Brasília, DF, Brazil

1974

SAFRA Bank*
São Paulo, SP, Brazil

Ministry of Foreign Office*
Algiers, Algeria

Ministry of Foreign Office – Annex II*
Brasília, DF, Brazil

Museum of Earth, Sea and Air*
Brasília, DF, Brazil

Flávio Marcilio Residence
Brasília, DF, Brazil

World Trade Center*
Milan, Italy

Rio Office Towers*
Rio de Janeiro, RJ, Brazil

1975

Office Building*
Jeddah, Saudi-Arabia

FATA Engineering Headquarters
Pianezza (Turin), Piemont, Italy

King's Council Residence
Saudi Arabia

Josefine Jordan Residence*
Rio de Janeiro, RJ, Brazil

Toyota Branch Headquarters*
Saudi-Arabia

1976

ABC Football Club*
Natal, RN, Brazil

Army College
Brasília, DF, Brazil

Jockey Club*
Rio de Janeiro, RJ, Brazil

Marco Paulo Rabello Residence*
Rio de Janeiro, RJ, Brazil

Wilson Mirza Residence*
Rio de Janeiro, RJ, Brazil

Municipal Theatre Annex –
First Project*
Rio de Janeiro, RJ, Brazil

University of Constantine –
Second Stage*
Constantine, Algeria

Mausoleum of Juscelino Kubitschek
Brasília, DF, Brazil

Lambert Residence*
Brussels, Belgium

1977

Prefabricated Apartment Buildings*
Algeria

Museum of Mankind*
Belo Horizonte, MG, Brazil

Adolfo Bloch Residence*
Cabo Frio, RJ, Brazil

1978

Convention Center*
Foz do Iguaçu, PR, Brazil

Architectural Ensemble
(Theatre and Hotel)*
Venice, Italy

Curicica Complex at Barra da Tijuca*
Rio de Janeiro, RJ, Brazil

Ilha Pura Complex at Barra da Tijuca*
Rio de Janeiro, RJ, Brazil

Urban Plan/ZAC*
Villejuif, France

Nutritional Technology Institute
Headquarters*
Constantine, Algeria

Standard Ministries Annex
Brasília, DF, Brazil

Road Terminal
Londrina, PR, Brazil

French School
Brasília, DF, Brazil

Residence Petrônio Portella*
location unknown

Manchete Building Headquarters
Brasília, DF, Brazil

National Congress/Chamber
of Deputies – Annex IV*
Brasília, DF, Brazil

1979

Cartiere Burgo Headquarters
San Mauro, Turin, Italy

CESP Energy Company of São Paulo
Headquarters – First Project*
São Paulo, SP, Brazil

EMBRATUR Headquarters*
Brasília, DF, Brazil

Zoological Garden of Algiers*
Algiers, Algeria

City of Tomorrow Project*
location unknown

1980

Alcalis RN Headquarters*
Natal, RN, Brazil

Assembly Hall of the Legislature
of Espírito Santo*
Vitória, ES, Brazil

Pernambuco Administration Center*
Recife, PE, Brazil

Hotel and Leisure Center*
Brasília, DF, Brazil

Tiradentes Museum*
Brasília, DF, Brazil

Municipal Theatre Annex –
Second Project*
Rio de Janeiro, RJ, Brazil

Square on Avenue Atlántica
Rio de Janeiro, RJ, Brazil

1981

Commercial Center and Monument
of the Libyans*
Benghazi, Libya

CESP Energy Company of São Paulo
Headquarters – Second Project*
São Paulo, SP, Brazil

Center of Leisure*
Abu Dhabi, United Emirates of Arabia

TV Manchete – Second Headquarters*
Rio de Janeiro, RJ, Brazil

Civic Center*
La Paz, Bolivia

Residential Building*
location unknown

1982

Convention Center*
Abu Dhabi, United Emirates of Arabia

Niemeyer Apartment Buildings
Fonteney-Sous-Bois, France

Museum of the Indian
(currently Museum of Contemporary Art)
Brasília, DF, Brazil

SESC Building at Copacabana
Rio de Janeiro, RJ, Brazil

1983

Urban Plan for the Salinas Perynas
Company*
Cabo Frio, RJ, Brazil

Costeira Palace Hotel*
Natal, RN, Brazil

Hotel*
Cabo Frio, RJ, Brazil

Sambodrome/Passerella of Samba
Rio de Janeiro, RJ, Brazil

Exhibition Pavillion*
Brasília, DF, Brazil

Residence Carlos Miranda
Rio de Janeiro, RJ, Brazil

Residence Darcy Ribeiro
Maricá, RJ, Brazil

Multi-functional Saloon
Vacaria, RS, Brazil

Residential Quarters at Algies*
Algies, Portugal

1984

Academy of Literature MG*
Belo Horizonte, MG, Brazil

Camelódromo Restaurant*
Rio de Janeiro, RJ, Brazil

Center of Public Education/CIEPs
Rio de Janeiro, RJ, Brazil

CESP Energy Company of São Paulo
Headquarters – 3rd Project*
São Paulo, SP, Brazil

Ricardo Medeiros Residence*
São Pedro da Aldeia, RJ, Brazil

Theatre and Convention Center*
Padua, Emilia-Romagna, Italy

1985

Cangulo Residential Quarters*
Duque de Caxias, RJ, Brazil

Guignard School*
Belo Horizonte, MG, Brazil

Tancredo Neves Pantheon of Liberty
and Democracy
Brasília, DF, Brazil

Bridge of the Academy*
Venice, Italy

Townhall*
Macaé, RJ, Brazil

Castelinho Residence*
Brasília, DF, Brazil

Marcos Antõnio Rezende Residence*
Ilha Bela, SP, Brazil

Greek Theatre*
Ceilândia, DF, Brazil

Tribunal of Justice*
Rio de Janeiro, RJ, Brazil

1986

Cantador's House
Ceilândia, DF, Brazil

Cultural Center*
Brasília, DF, Brazil

School*
Brasília, DF, Brazil

Stadium*
Turin, Italy

Art Gallery*
São Paulo, SP, Brazil

Church*
Petrópolis, RJ, Brazil

Orthodox Church
Brasília, DF, Brazil

Flowers Market
Brasília, DF, Brazil

Bridge of the Northern Wing*
Brasília, DF, Brazil

José Aparecido de Oliveira Residence
Conceição do Mato Dentro, MG, Brazil

Pontão 45 Restaurant
Brasília, DF, Brazil

Theatre*
Rio Verde, GO, Brazil

Urban Plan of Park Tieté*
– Civic Center, Residential Quarter,
Leasure Center
São Paulo, SP, Brazil

Training Center Bank of Brazil
Brasília, DF, Brazil

1987

Cultural Center*
Cabo Verde, Brazil

Crematorium*
Brasília, DF, Brazil

Embassy of Brazil*
Havana, Cuba

Miguel Torga Institute*
Paris, France

L'Humanité Headquarters
Saint-Denis, France

Memorial da America Latina
– Library, Restaurant, Pavilion of Popular
Creativity, Lecture Hall, Annex
of Members of Congress, Annex of
Artists, Celebration Hall (Salão de Atos),
Administration Building,
Center of Latin American Studies
São Paulo, SP, Brazil

PMDB Party of the Brazilian Democratic
Movement Headquarters
Brasília, DF, Brazil

Agora Urban Plan*
Maringa, PR, Brazil

Sundial / City Park of Brasilia
Brasília, DF, Brazil

3rd Bridge over the Lago Sul*
Brasília, DF, Brazil

Sebastião Camargo Correira Residence
Brasília, DF, Brazil

UNE National Union of Students RJ
Headquarters*
Rio de Janeiro, RJ, Brazil

1988

Chamber of the Legislature
at the Federal District*
Brasília, DF, Brazil

Amateur Theatre
Brasília, DF, Brazil

Administration Center*
Este, Venetia, Italy

Center of Indian Studies
(University of Brasília)*
Brasília, DF, Brazil

Marco Sul Building*
Angra dos Reis, RJ, Brazil

Mondadori Publishing Company
Second Headquarters*
Milan, Italy

Espaço Oscar Niemeyer
Brasília, DF, Brazil

Sambrasília / Passarella of Samba*
Brasília, DF, Brazil

Urban Plan for the Park of Agua Branca*
São Paulo, SP, Brazil

1989

Chapel of Santa Cecilia
Miguel Pereira, RJ, Brazil

Cultural Center*
Uberlândia, MG, Brazil

Espaço Lúcio Costa
Brasília, DF, Brazil

Multi-functional Stadium
Barretos, SP, Brazil

Praça Oxum / Oxum's Place*
Salvador, BA, Brazil

Supreme Court of Justice Headquarters
Brasília, DF, Brazil

Theatre at Ibirapuera Park*
São Paulo, SP, Brazil

Trianon Theatre*
Campos, RJ, Brazil

1990

CEF Bank*
Belo Horizonte, MG, Brazil

Cultural Center*
Osasco, SP, Brazil

I.D.E.A Headquarters*
Turin, Italy

Culture and Popular Art Complex /
Sambodrome
São Paulo, SP, Brazil

Ana Elisa Niemeyer Residence*
Rio de Janeiro, RJ, Brazil

Orestes Quércia Residence
Pedregulho, SP, Brazil

Wilson Mirza Residence – First Project*
Petrópolis, RJ, Brazil

Theatre
Araras, SP, Brazil

Supreme Court of Justice – Annex II
Brasília, DF, Brazil

1991

Altar for the Pope's Mass
Brasília, DF, Brazil

Chapel of the Ile de la Gigoia*
Rio de Janeiro, RJ, Brazil

Luso-Brazilian Foundation*
Lisbon, Portugal

Getúlio Vargas Foundation – Annex*
Rio de Janeiro, RJ, Brazil

Museum of Contemporary Art
Niterói, RJ, Brazil

Parlamento Latino-Américano
São Paulo, SP, Brazil

Urban Plan for the Praça XV*
Rio de Janeiro, RJ, Brazil

Scene for the play Cristo Redentor
Rio de Janeiro, RJ, Brazil

1992

Cândido Portinari Foundation*
Rio de Janeiro, RJ, Brazil

Army's Cathedral
Brasília, DF, Brazil

UENF State University of
North Fluminense
Campos, RJ, Brazil

Olympic Villa*
Brasília, DF, Brazil

Floating Scene at Lagoa Rodrigo
de Freitas
Rio de Janeiro, RJ, Brazil

1993

Culture and Sports Center
João Saldanha*
Maricá, RJ, Brazil

Oscar Niemeyer Foundation – Annex*
Brasília, DF, Brazil

Espaçodata / National Museum of Infor-
matics and Telecommunications*
Brasília, DF, Brazil

Biennial Pavilion – Annex*
São Paulo, SP, Brazil, 1993

Federal Audit Court – Annex
Collaboration: Filgueiras Lima
Brasília, DF, Brazil

1994

Sports Center of North Fluminense*
Campos, RJ, Brazil

Museum of Man and his Universe*
Brasília, DF, Brazil

Embratel Tower*
Rio de Janeiro, RJ, Brazil

Supreme Industrial Tribunal
Brasília, DF, Brazil

1995

Auditorium at Ibirapuera Park*
São Paulo, SP, Brazil, 1995

Cultural Center
Souza, PB, Brazil

Museum of Life*
Rio de Janeiro, RJ, Brazil

Fábio Fonseca Residence*
Brasília, DF, Brazil

1996

Walter Arantes Residence*
Angra dos Reis, RJ, Brazil

1997

Caminho Niemeyer / Urban Complex*
– Cathedral of Niterói – First Project*
Niterói, RJ, Brazil

Museum of Modern Art – First Project*
Brasília, DF, Brazil

Municipal Square*
Américana, SP, Brazil

Convention Center*
Rio de Janeiro, RJ, Brazil

TECNET Headquarters*
Alphaville, SP, Brazil

1998

Urban Complex *
– Memorial, Palace of the Legislative
Ulysses Guimarães
Rio Claro, SP, Brazil

Tower *
– Restaurant, Hotel, Observatory
Brighton, UK

1999

PGR – Procurator General
of the Republic's Office Building
Brasília, DF, Brazil

OAB Association of Brazilian Advocates
Headquarters *
Brasília, DF, Brazil

2000

Ravello Auditorium *
Ravello, (Amalfi), Italy

Cultural District *
– Library, National Archive, Planetary,
Museum of Arts, Leisure Area
Brasília, DF, Brazil

Kaare Bertsen Residence *
Oslo, Norway

Caminho Niemeyer / Urban Complex *
– Theatre *
Niterói, RJ, Brazil

2001

Caminho Niemeyer / Urban Complex *
– Oscar Niemeyer Foundation *
– Cathedral – Second Project *
Niterói, RJ, Brazil

Cândido Mendes Cultural Center *
Rio de Janeiro, RJ, Brazil

Novo Museu Cultural Center
Curitiba, PR, Brazil

Oswaldo Cruz Foundation *
Rio de Janeiro, RJ, Brazil

2003

Serpentine Gallery Pavilion at Hyde Park
London, UK

Rui Barbosa Monument *
Rio de Janeiro, RJ, Brazil, 1949

Duke of Caxias Monument
Brasília, DF, Brazil, 1968

Monument of the Revolution *
Algiers, Algeria, 1968

President Juscelino Kubitschek
Memorial – First Project *
Brasília, DF, Brazil

President Juscelino Kubitschek
Monument *
Belo Horizonte, MG, Brazil, 1977

President Juscelino Kubitschek Memorial
– Second Project
Brasília, DF, Brazil, 1980

Carlos Fonseca Amador Monument *
Managua, Nicaragua, 1982

Getúlio Vargas Monument –
First Project *
Rio de Janeiro, RJ, Brazil, 1984

Monument of Cabanagem
Belém, PA, Brazil, 1984

Teotônio Vilela Memorial *
Maceió, AL, Brazil, 1984

Tancredo Neves Monument
Juiz de Fora, MG, Brazil, 1985

Zumbi dos Palmares Memorial *
Palmeira dos Indios, AL, Brazil, 1986

Bleeding Hand Monument *
Rio de Janeiro, RJ, Brazil, 1986

Amilcar Cabral Monument *
Cape Verde, Brazil, 1987

Memorial of the Bible *
Brasília, DF, Brazil, 1987

Bleeding Hand of the Memorial
da América Latina
São Paulo, SP, Brazil, 1988

Zumbi dos Palmares Memorial *
São Paulo, SP, Brazil, 1988

IX. November Monument
Volta Redonda, RJ, Brazil, 1989

President Juscelino Kubitschek
Monument
Belo Horizonte, MG, Brazil, 1989

Luiz Carlos Prestes Memorial *
Porto Alegre, RS, Brazil, 1990

Jánio Quadros Memorial
São Paulo, SP, Brazil, 1991

Monument of Negro Slavery *
Dakar, Senegal, 1991

Israel Pinheiro Monument
Brasília, DF, Brazil, 1991

Hymn of Nature Monument *
Rio de Janeiro, RJ, Brazil, 1991

Luiz Carlos Prestes Memorial
Palmas, TO, Brazil, 1992

Ulysses Guimarães Monument *
Brasília, DF, Brazil, 1992

Leonel Brizola Monument
Campos, RJ, Brazil, 1994

Roberto Silveira Memorial *
Niterói, RJ, Brazil, 1994

Getúlio Vargas Monument –
Second Project *
Rio de Janeiro, RJ, Brazil, 1994

Luiz Carlos Prestes' Column *
Santo Angelo,RS, Brazil, 1995

Zumbi Dos Palmares Memorial *
Salvador, BA, Brazil, 1995

Centenary of Belo Horizonte Monument
Belo Horizonte, MG, Brazil, 1995

Monument in memory of Eldorado
Marabá, PA, Brazil, 1996

Zumbi dos Palmares Memorial *
São Paulo, SP, Brazil, 1988

Carlos Drummond de Andrade Memorial
Itabira, MG, Brazil, 1998

Luiz Carlos Prestes' Column *
Santa Helena, PR, Brazil, 1998

Monument
São Vicente, SP, Brazil, 1999

(Dieses Verzeichnis basiert im Wesentlichen auf
den Forschungen der Fundação Oscar Niemeyer,
Rio de Janeiro / This index is primarily based on
current research conducted by the Fundação Oscar
Niemeyer, Rio de Janeiro)

* | Projekte / projects
__ | bestehende Bauten / buildings still standing
today

Über die Autoren
On the authors

Paul Andreas, *1973. Studierte Kunstgeschichte und Kulturwissenschaft in Lüneburg, Berlin, Paris und Kyoto. Magisterarbeit über die Raumerfahrung im Landschaftsgarten am Ende des 18. Jahrhunderts in Frankreich. Seit 2002 als freier Kurator am Deutschen Architektur Museum Frankfurt / Main tätig.

Max Bill (1908–1994). Architekt, Maler, Plastiker, Produktgestalter. 1927–1929 Studium bei W. Gropius, H. Meyer, L. Moholy-Nagy, P. Klee, W. Kandinsky am Bauhaus Dessau. 1932–1934 Mitglied der Künstlergruppe Abstraction-Création in Paris und der Züricher Konkreten Künstler. 1938 Mitglied der CIAM. Aufbau der Hochschule für Gestaltung in Ulm, deren Gebäude (1950–1955) und pädagogischen Ziele von Bill in der Nachfolge des Bauhauses gestaltet und formuliert wurden.

Lauro Cavalcanti, *1954. Studium der Architektur. Promotion in Sozialanthropologie. Professor an der Universität Rio de Janeiro / Fakultät für Industriedesign. Direktor des Paço Imperial, Zentrum für Kulturerbe und Zeitgenössische Kunst in Rio de Janeiro. Diverse Publikationen zu Kunst, Gesellschaft und Architektur.

Elmar Kossel, *1974. Studierte Kunstgeschichte, Klassische Archäologie und Europäische Ethnologie in Marburg und Berlin. Seit 2002 Promotion über Hermann Henselmann und die Rezeption der Moderne in der Architektur der DDR.

Carsten Krohn, *1966. Studierte Architektur, Kunstgeschichte und Stadtplanung in Hamburg und New York. Promotion über die Rezeption Buckminster Fullers in der Architektur.

Niklas Maak, *1972. Studierte Kunstgeschichte in Hamburg und Paris. 1998 Promotion. 1999 Redakteur für Architektur im Feuilleton der Süddeutschen Zeitung. Seit 2001 Redakteur für Kunst im Feuilleton der Frankfurter Allgemeinen Zeitung.

José Carlos Süssekind, *1947. Studierte Bauingenieurwesen mit den Schwerpunkten Struktur und Fundamente an der Katholischen Universität Rio de Janeiro. 1970 Master in Sciences. Diverse Lehrbücher zur Analyse der Struktur und zum Einsatz von Beton. Seit 1970 als Ingenieur für Oscar Niemeyer tätig. Vizepräsident der Fundação Oscar Niemeyer.

Paul Andreas, born 1973. Studied art history and cultural sciences in Lüneburg, Berlin, Paris and Kyoto. M.A. on the notion of space in late 18th century French landscape gardening. Since 2002, freelance curator at Deutsches Architektur Museum Frankfurt / Main.

Max Bill (1908–1994). Architect, painter, sculptor, product designer. 1927–1929 studied under W. Gropius, H. Meyer, L. Moholy-Nagy, P. Klee, W. Kandinsky at the Bauhaus Dessau. 1932–1934 member of the Abstraction-Création artists' group in Paris and of the Zurich group of Concrete artists. 1938 member of CIAM. Set up the Ulm College of Design, whose buildings (1950–1955) exhibit Bill's teaching aims, which he saw as continuing the tradition of the Bauhaus.

Lauro Cavalcanti, born 1954. Studied architecture. Ph.D. in Social Anthropology. Professor at the University of Rio de Janeiro / Faculty of Industrial Design. Director of Paço Imperial – Center for Cultural Heritage and Contemporary Art – in Rio de Janeiro. Numerous publications on art, society, and architecture.

Elmar Kossel, born 1974. Studied art history, classical archaeology and European ethnology in Marburg and Berlin. Since 2002, preparing a thesis on Hermann Henselmann and the impact of Modernism in East German architecture.

Carsten Krohn, born 1966. Studied architecture, art history and town planning in Hamburg and New York. Awarded a Ph.D. for a thesis on the impact of Buckminster Fuller on architecture.

Niklas Maak, born 1972. Studied art history in Hamburg and Paris. Awarded a Ph.D. in 1998. 1999 editor for architecture on the art desk of Süddeutsche Zeitung. Since 2001 art editor on the art desk of "Frankfurter Allgemeine Zeitung".

José Carlos Süssekind, born 1947. Studied construction engineering with a focus on structures and foundations at the Catholic University of Rio de Janeiro. 1970 Master in Sciences. Numerous textbooks on the analysis of structure and the use of concrete. Engineer of Oscar Niemeyer since 1970. Vice-President of Fundação Oscar Niemeyer.

Bildnachweis
Picture credits

Abdruckverzeichnis
List of reproductions

Die Urheber sind bei den Abbildungen im Regelfall angegeben. Bei den Abbildungen, wo nur die Quelle angegeben ist, konnte trotz intensiver Recherche von Seiten der Herausgeber der Urheber nicht ausfindig gemacht werden.

As a rule, the copyright holders have been stated along with the reproductions. Where no source is given for the reproductions, despite intensive research we were not able to establish who held the copyright.

Josep Ma Botey: 14, 19, 110/111, 128, 132
Peter Cook: 71 Mitte/middle
Ary Diesendruck: 86/87
Fondation Le Corbusier: 30 oben + Mitte/
top + middle, 38
Ford-Werke AG: 72
Foto Jerry, Rio de Janeiro, aus/from: Stamo Papadaki, The work of O. Niemeyer, N.Y.: Reinhold Publishing Corp., 1950, p. 188: 83 oben/top
Foto Wimmer, Berlin, aus/from: Stamo Papadaki, Oscar Niemeyer, Ravensburg: O. Maier Verlag, 1962, hintere Klappe/back cover: 59
Fundação Oscar Niemeyer: 30 unten/bottom, 33–35, 40, 41, 43, 47, 49, 50–51, 60, 65 oben/top, 80, 82, hintere Klappe/back cover
Christian Gahl: 63 unten/bottom, 70
Marcel Gautherot, mit freundlicher Unterstützung von/Courtesy of Instituto Moreira Salles: 32, 48, 81, 83 unten/bottom, 85
Henselmann-Archiv, Berlin: 63 oben/top, 66
Josef Kaiser, aus/from: Deutsche Architektur, Heft/issue no 11, 1965, S. 658: 65 unten/bottom
Holger Knauf: 75 oben/top
Heiner Leiska: 71 oben/top
Loom GmbH (www.loomtm.com): 71 unten/bottom
Michel Moch: Umschlag/cover, 1–2, 9–11, 13, 15–17, 54–57, 64, 79, 88–109, 112, 134, 144
Oscar Niemeyer, aus/from: Fotos & Fotos, März/March 1966: 42
Oscar Niemeyer, mit freundlicher Unterstützung von/Courtesy of Niklas Maak: 22
Office Municipal du Tourisme La Grande Motte: 75 unten/bottom
Anna-Julia Schmied: 21
Shussev-Museum, Moskow: 39
Wajnbrosse Productions, Bruxelles: 77

„Die Kurven des Lebens – ein Interview mit Oscar Niemeyer", von Niklas Maak.
"The curves of Life – an interview with Oscar Niemeyer," by Niklas Maak.
Erstmals abgedruckt in/First printed in: Süddeutsche Zeitung, Ausgabe vom/issue of 18. Mai 2000.

„architekt, architektur und gesellschaft."
Vortrag, gehalten am 9. Juni 1953 an der Fakultät für Architektur und Urbanistik der Universität São Paulo, von Max Bill.
"architect, architecture and society," talk on June 9, 1953 in the Faculty of Architecture and Urban Development of the University of São Paulo, by Max Bill.
Neuübersetzung des französischen Originalmanuskriptes./Retranslation of the original French manuscript. Alle Rechte beim/All rights held by archiv max bill, c/o max, binia und jacob bill stiftung, ch-adligenswill.

„Aktuelle Probleme der brasilianischen Architektur", von Oscar Niemeyer.
"Current Problems in Brazilian Architecture," by Oscar Niemeyer.
Neuübersetzung des brasilianischen Originaltextes, erstmals abgedruckt in/Retranslation of the original text in Brazilian, first printed in: Moduló No. 3, 1955. Alle Rechte bei der/All rights held by Fundação Oscar Niemeyer, Rio de Janeiro.

„Meine Architektur", von Oscar Niemeyer.
"My Architecture," by Oscar Niemeyer.
Gekürzter Auszug in deutscher Übersetzung aus/Short extract in German translation from: Oscar Niemeyer, *Meu sósia e eu,* Rio de Janeiro, Revan, 1992.

Sambodrome, Rio de Janeiro.